WITHDRAWN

HARVARD LIBRARY

WITHDRAWN

THE CHRISTIAN FUTURE

University
of
Queensland
Press

The Christian Future

A STRATEGY FOR CATHOLIC RENEWAL

by
Denis Kenny

© University of Queensland Press, St. Lucia, Queensland, 1971

This book is copyright. Apart from any fair dealing for the purposes of private study, research, criticism or review, as permitted under the Copyright Act, no part may be reproduced by any process without written permission. Enquiries should be made to the publishers.

Registered in Australia for transmission by post as a book

National Library of Australia card number and ISBN 0 7022 0580 X

Set in 10/11 pt. Times New Roman and printed on 100 lb. Woodfree

Printed and bound by Watson Ferguson and Co., Brisbane

Production: Norman Birrell and Cyrelle

Distributed by International Scholarly Book Services, Inc. Great Britain—Europe—North America

INTRODUCTION

Throughout the whole world there is a mounting increase in the sense of autonomy as well as of responsibility. This is of paramount importance for the spiritual and moral maturity of the human race.
Vatican II

It is not enough to portray what exists, what is necessary is to think about the desirable and possible.
Maxim Gorki

Christ was regarded by his religious and political superiors as a dangerous man precisely because he questioned and even flouted some of the most precious axioms of his culture. The Roman emperors regarded the early church as a subversive influence because it embodied an outlook and attitudes which threatened the very fabric of Roman society. The church in the age after the fall of the Roman empire was a creative force in Europe. Popes, bishops and monks were at the dynamic centre or in the vanguard of the cultural development of Christendom. But today the Christian church is almost never regarded as dangerous. It often appears ridiculous, more often appears a bore, but is seldom a threat, as Christ and the early church were, to the structural and functional elements of contemporary culture.

Somehow the Christian church has allowed itself to be relegated to the periphery of life. From this periphery it frequently bewails and condemns a variety of superficial contemporary trends and this response ensures its identity as a church. But for the most part it appears to be a refuge for the spiritually and psychologically retarded, for those who are inadequate in a technological and secular age. It appears to be one of the few remaining relics of the past, for which it seems to yearn with scarcely disguised affection.

In the eighteenth century Diderot taunted:

> Men have banished the Deity; they have relegated it to a sanctuary; the walls of a temple limit its view; it does not exist outside. Madmen that you are, destroy these circles; set God free; see him everywhere he is, or say that he does not exist at all.

The Christian church has begun to set God free from the sanctuary. The Vatican Council, the assemblies of the World Council of Churches and many contemporary theologians have attempted to bring Christianity from the periphery of life to the creative centre, to put it in contact with and make it vitally relevant to the mainstream of twentieth century life. But this attempt, initially, has had a disintegrating effect. Christianity enjoyed relative uniformity and traditional consistency in its isolated sanctuary. The mainstream of twentieth century life is an ever-accelerating vortex of social and cultural change. The transition from the cool, calm sanctuary to this historical vortex has precipitated severe crises in the traditional Christian structures, conceptions, and attitudes. Initially, especially before the Vatican Council, it was thought that a few procedural and pedagogical adjustments in the Christian approach could remedy the gap between the church and the modern world. But as Christianity moves from its security of traditional absolutes it becomes increasingly caught up in the social and cultural acceleration.

The increased tempo of change in Christian thought and practice has evoked warning cries from some theologians and commentators. The ambition of making Christianity more relevant to the world of the twentieth century has been described as a loss of nerve and a capitulation to the world. Professor Eric Mascall, writing of the Bishop of Woolwich in *The Secularization of*

Christianity, says: "One might be pardoned for supposing that Robinson had despaired of trying to convert the world to Christianity and had decided instead to convert Christianity to the world."[1] He claims that the secularized versions of Christianity promoted by many theologians today are based not on rigid scientific scholarship, nor upon a serious intuitive appreciation of the gospels, but upon a radical distaste for the supernatural. Harry Blamires, writing in *The Christian Mind,* claims that "the contemporary Christian mind has succumbed to the secular drift with a degree of weakness and nervelessness unmatched in Christian history".[2]

But what alternatives do Mascall and Blamires have to offer? The cast of mind which they represent seems to demand of the world a Canossa-style return and submission to the culture of the church generated in another age. It seems to demand a return to an obsolete, static, absolutist, and sacred view or outlook as a condition of salvation, for it is in these terms and on these conditions that the Christian church, for the most part, even today, continues to state its message and live its life.

This demand, however, implies and is based on a twofold assumption which is, both in human and Christian terms, untenable. It is a form of idolatry to invest a particular theological system, a specific code of morality or a mode of worship with the character of an absolute. Every expression of the Christian message, every embodiment of the Christian life-style, and every liturgical form is culturally conditioned. To make them incorrigibly sacred is to divinize them as if the very forms themselves contained the divinity. In the second place there is the tendency to presume that the church is God's world and that the secular world is enemy territory to be recaptured by the church for God. This presumption arises from the belief that since the world has become emancipated from ecclesiastical control and influence it has moved beyond God's control and is no longer capable of manifesting his will, his wisdom and his majesty. This is a common, though peculiar, form of Christian atheism which can blind one to the presence of God in his world and lead one to forget that the leitmotiv of the New Testament is precisely the love of God for the world.

This cultural isolation on the part of Christianity leads to a fundamental loss of cosmic direction. The Christian vision tends to become introverted and concerned with its own institutional health. The Christian focus tends to settle on the past, which is canonized and neurotically adhered to. Certainly in St. Peter's epistle we are reminded that we live as strangers in this age and in this world. But we as Christians are strangers not because we feel at home in a past age but because we belong to the future.

A tragic consequence of this cultural isolation, introversion, and preoccupation with the past has been that Christians have long since lost the initiative as the champions of human freedom and compassion. Since the middle of the nineteenth century the amelioration of human bondage and misery has taken on distinctly non-Christian if not anti-Christian significance. Today in the Hippie cult of love and freedom there is a haunting echo of the style of Christ's life in Palestine. And yet the most authentic and genuine Hippie would regard himself as at the opposite end of the cultural spectrum from most Christians.

However, there is a very real sense in which the accusation that many contemporary Christian apologists have suffered a loss of nerve is valid. While some Christians tend to invest the traditional Christian forms with absolute value, other Christians, intent on rapprochement with the contemporary world, accept as absolute the dictates of the secular culture as it confronts us today. These theologians, while courageously subjecting the traditional assertions, attitudes, and values to a harsh and honest scrutiny, tend to do so from a fixed point, the secular culture of the Western world. Often they fail to subject this culture to an equally rigorous scrutiny.

The task of the theologian today is to be radical not only in relation to his specifically Christian heritage and thought and behaviour patterns but also in relation to the general cultural situation in which he finds himself and which moulds his attitudes and values. It is too easy to stand firmly on the side of the Christian culture and criticize the secular culture, or to stand on the side of the secular culture and criticize the Christian culture. The more difficult, the more important, and the more specifically Christian task is to renounce both as explicit or implicit absolutes and maintain a dynamic, creative, and evolving interacting balance between the two. A theologian today must be a radical human being as well as a radical theologian. Far too often, and this is especially true of the death-of-God theology, theological discussion is conducted on agreed terms provided by the secular culture, which is not itself subjected to analysis and evaluation. The contemporary theologian must be equally ready to criticize the way in which the Christian church expresses its consciousness of itself and to criticize the culture from which he inherits his critical tools and values. The loss of nerve among some radical theologians manifests itself in a failure to question the socio-economic assumptions and the cultural context which seem to demand the absence of God in our age.

It is often assumed rather too facilely in the Western world that the process of secularization must inevitably take the course it has taken in Europe and America, that economic, technological, social and cultural progress could not, with the same ingredients, take radically different forms and courses. This results in a species of historical determinism and generates a kind of unacknowledged pessimism about what can be done in the future to alter the shape and the quality of our culture. Perhaps a Christianity which is authentically a cultural or social salt with a strong savour is destined to effect just this kind of social criticism and radical change.

In the document on the Church in the Modern World the Vatican Council said:

Within the individual person there develops rather frequently an imbalance between an intellect which is modern in practical matters, and a theoretical system of thought which can neither master the sum total of its ideas, nor arrange them adequately into a synthesis.[3]

It is precisely this imbalance which continues to afflict Christianity as it becomes more deeply involved in and influenced by contemporary experience. The imbalance for the Christian can be accentuated by his adherence to dogmatic, moral, and philosophical formulae which are the vestiges of an archaic cultural context. But here is the central problem. How can the Christian and the church be concerned with, influenced by and involved in the world without being *of* the world? How can the church be the symbol and the proclaimer of God's presence in the world without becoming submerged in and identified with the world? In the recent past the church maintained its separate identity by adherence to a synthesis, to a theoretical system of thought which was internally consistent and amazingly comprehensive. But this synthesis was statically structured and consequently, because of the rapidly widening gulf between its tenets and contemporary experience, increasingly incredible. It seems unlikely that any compelling modern Christian synthesis will arise in the near future capable of fusing modern experience and sensibility with a specifically Christian perspective, and yet Christians can no longer adhere to the obsolete formulations and postures which have been the identifying features of Christianity in the past.

If the church (and the Christian) is to maintain a bivalent openness to a changing cultural context on the one hand and a constantly changing appreciation of the significance and ramifications of Christianity on the other hand, three fundamental readjustments are called for in the Christian life. The first is a change in perspective so that the Christian vision is dominated not by the achievements of the past, nor by the satisfactions of the present, but by the possibilities of the future. It is this vision of the horizon of the future, the eschatological perspective, which today ensures that the Christian will be in this world, but not of this world. The second readjustment is in the way the church speaks about God, Christ, morality, and itself. Christian theology has to be structured dynamically so that its fundamental assertions are not mere units in a baroque synthesis demanding a stagnant assent of faith, but propositions challenging human beings to new depths and complexities of life and experience.

The third readjustment is in what Christians and the church *do* in the world. Perhaps the fundamental fault with the Christian church in the past century has been that it has been talking too much and talking in a language and an idiom which the rest of the world and Christians themselves find increasingly incomprehensible. It cannot but strike Christians as significant that the western world, the traditionally Christian part of the world, representing only about 20 per cent of the total population, commands 80 per cent of the world's income. The Christian part of the world is becoming richer, the non-Christian part of the world poorer each year. The basic challenge to Christianity in the twentieth century is not theoretical but eminently practical. The Vatican Council called the church "the light of the world". Light can illuminate and it can warm. Perhaps the failure of Christianity today is that it has not discerned its task; it has tried too hard and rather futilely to enlighten the world intellectually and morally when it should have been generating and applying the warmth of compassion; it has been defending dogmatic and moral refinements when it should have been attacking the grossest inequality and injustice in the distribution of livelihood in the history of the human race.

Introduction

However, before the Christian church can become a credible symbol and instrument of compassion in the world today it has to extricate itself from the speculative, theoretical, and dogmatic structure it has built up over the centuries. In commenting on I John 4: 2-12, and especially on the sentence "The loving know God; the unloving know nothing of God", Dom Sebastian Moore has said:

> The striking thing about this text is that love for God is not only not referred to but is formally said to be not here the point. To shift any emphasis on to our love for God would be to upset the balance of the thought, the whole point of which is that "the unloving know nothing of God". Is there not a profound weakness in our tradition that consists in having been voluble just where the New Testament is reticent, in having formalized as an attitude to God (and indeed a very "formal" attitude) what was originally the Christian attitude that is "of God" and that commits us to the whole world of his making and predilection? ... There's something awfully peculiar about this "Catholic God". Just in so far as he is a being whose cultivation makes us less interested in the world we live in, he is not God but an idol of our own making, the personification of our desire to keep ourselves to ourselves.[4]

Dom Sebastian's suggestion is provocative. The very conceptions we entertain and enshrine of God, of Christ, of the Christian message and of Christian morality can and evidently do conspire to alienate us from God, distort the personality and significance of Christ, and turn us in on ourselves away from the blind, the halt, the lame, and the hungry.

This book is an attempt to contribute to the mobilization of the tremendous potential of Christian compassion. It is an attempt to begin to talk about God, Christ, Christian morality, and the church in a way that will help take Christians and the church out of themselves and relate them to the modern world so that this world becomes the focus of their lives and energies but in such a way as not to submerge them in or identify them with it. Yet it will try to satisfy the contemporary demand for an economy of entities. It will presume only four unquestionable bases: the sociological fact of the church; the historical fact of the man Christ; the complexity of the world and human life in it; and the possibilities of the future.

The first part of the book, "The Cultural Context", will attempt to analyse the present cultural situation and the role of the church in this situation. The second part of the book, "Theological Probes", a title suggested, of course, by a favourite phrase of

Marshall McLuhan, will explore ways of talking about God, Christ, Christian morality, and the church which can mediate a deeper, more authentic Christian involvement in the present cultural context, and response to the triple contemporary challenges of war, racism, and poverty. Part I will inevitably appear theoretical, analytical, and somewhat pedantic. However, it is necessary first of all to attempt to make explicit many of the cultural and epistemological factors which have frightened Christians into huddling in their sanctuaries or clinging desperately to their "principles". It is necessary, secondly, to examine in detail the range of possible conceptions of the function of the church today. The Christian church is a sociological fact. It is an organization which can be grappled with and mobilized. It is more palpable than "the Word" or "grace" or "salvation". The pressing question is: what is, or what could be, its use or its function? Only then, it seems, is it possible to probe the significance of the traditional Christian vocabulary.

This book will concern itself primarily with the Catholic church, its doctrines and its attitudes. This is not a symptom of exclusiveness but a concession to the demands of succinctness and precision. A great deal of what follows, however, does apply, sometimes directly, sometimes by analogy, to the rest of the Christian churches. In the past the Christian churches have been conscious of their differences. The challenge of the secular age has made them more conscious of their similarities. In all probability the differences amongst the churches will be settled not by a laborious piecemeal removal of the barriers which at present exist, but by a common Christian exodus to a new ground where the old barriers will be ridiculous. It would be true to say that most of the Christian churches continue to maintain a rather static and absolutist world view, and rely on conceptual models within the pre-Darwinian framework. While most of the churches retain a static view of the world, ecumenical discussions will be futile. When the churches move to a new ground more compatible with contemporary experience, or rather, when all the churches become humble pilgrims of the future, ecumenical discussions will not be necessary.

On the night before he died Christ performed a simple ceremony. He intended this ceremony to be the symbol of love and reconciliation among men. It was to be the central ritual of his followers to commemorate him and to symbolize as well as generate the community of all men. At this ceremony he washed the feet of

Introduction

Peter to indicate to Peter the nature of his office. It is surely tragic that the Eucharist and the office of Peter have become two of the greatest stumbling blocks to unity among Christians. Because Christians could not agree on the precise philosophical modality of what happens at this ceremony, it has become a symbol and an agent, not of reconciliation and peace, but of division and resentment. Because many Christians see Peter as a threat of spiritual and moral coercion and domination rather than as an office of service, this too has become a source of division.

At the Fourth Assembly of the World Council of Churches at Uppsala in Sweden the official Catholic delegates received communion at a Lutheran high mass. Perhaps before long this spirit will extend to the whole of the Catholic church so that the need to celebrate the gift which is Christ will prevail over theological and ecclesiastical refinements. Only in this kind of unity can Christians begin to become effectively the salt of the earth and begin to work towards the supranational and supraracial unity of all men.

Cambridge, Mass.
July 1968

ACKNOWLEDGMENTS

The author wishes to acknowledge with gratitude permission to quote from *A Burnt-Out Case*, by Graham Greene (William Heinemann Ltd., London); *Letters and Papers from Prison*, by Dietrich Bonhoeffer (S.C.M. Press Ltd., London); *Radical Theology and the Death of God*, copyright (c) 1966, by Thomas J. J. Altizer and William Hamilton (The Bobbs-Merrill Co., Inc., Indianapolis); *The Waning of the Middle Ages*, by Johan Huizinga (Edward Arnold (Publishers) Ltd., London); *Science and Christian Belief*, by C. A. Coulson (Oxford University Press, London); *A History of Science*, by W. C. Dampier (Cambridge University Press, London); *Soundings*, edited by A. Vidler (Cambridge University Press, London); *Religion, Culture, and Society*, edited by Louis Schneider (John Wiley and Sons Inc., Publishers, New York); the Introduction by Harvey Cox in *The Grass Roots Church* by Stephen C. Rose (Holt, Rinehart and Winston, Inc., New York); the article by Donald MacKinnon in *The Listener*, 10 November 1966 (Donald MacKinnon, Corpus Christi College, Cambridge; *The Listener*, London); *The Documents of Vatican II*, edited by Walter M. Abbot and J. Gallagher (Geoffrey Chapman Ltd., London); *Sin, Liberty and Law*, by Louis Monden (Geoffrey Chapman Ltd., Publishers, London); *The Gospel of Christian Atheism*, by Thomas J. J. Altizer (Collins Publishers, London); *The Phenomenon of Man*, by Teilhard

Acknowledgments

de Chardin (Collins Publishers, London); *God Is a New Language*, by Dom Sebastian Moore (Darton Longman and Todd Ltd., London); *The Church Against Itself*, by Rosemary Ruether (Sheed and Ward Ltd., London); *The Bible on the Living God*, by Baastian van Iersel (Sheed and Ward Ltd., London); *Religion in Philosophical and Cultural Perspective*, edited by J. C. Feaver and W. Horosz (D. Van Nostrand Co. Inc., Princeton); "The Crisis of Contemporary Religious Consciousness" by Thomas F. O'Dea, in *Daedalus*, Winter 1967 (American Academy of Arts and Sciences, Boston); "Catholic Philosophy and the Death of God" by T. J. J. Altizer, in *Cross Currents*, Summer 1967 (Cross Currents Corp., West Nyack); "Theology after 'The Death of God'" by W. Richard Comstock, in *Cross Currents*, Summer 1966 (Cross Currents Corp., West Nyack); *God and Philosophy*, by Anthony Flew (Hutchinson Publishing Group Ltd., London); *Nietzsche: An Anthology*, edited by Otto Manthey-Zorn (Washington Square Press, New York); *Dostoevsky*, by N. Berdyaev (World Publishing Co., Cleveland); "The Conservatism of Situation Ethics" by J. T. Burtchaell, in *New Blackfriars*, September 1966 (*New Blackfriars*, London); *Christians in a New World*, edited by David L. Edwards (S.C.M. Press Ltd., London); *Theology of Hope*, by Jürgen Moltmann (S.C.M. Press Ltd., London; Harper and Row, Publishers, Inc., New York); *New Essays in Philosophical Theology*, edited by A. Flew and A. MacIntyre (S.C.M. Press Ltd., London; The Macmillan Co., New York); *The New Testament in Current Study*, by R. H. Fuller (S.C.M. Press Ltd., London; Charles Scribner's Sons, New York); *The New Reformation*, by John A. Robinson (S.C.M. Press Ltd., London; Westminster Press, Philadelphia); *Honest to God*, by John A. Robinson (S.C.M. Press Ltd., London; Westminster Press, Philadelphia); *Science and the Modern World*, by A. N. Whitehead (The Macmillan Co., New York; Cambridge University Press, London; copyright, 1925, by The Macmillan Co.); *Truth and Revelation*, by Nicholas Berdyaev (Harper and Row, Publishers, Inc., New York; Y.M.C.A. Press, Paris); "Religious Evolution" by Robert Bellah, in *Reader in Comparative Religion*, edited by W. A. Lessa and E. Z. Vogt (*The American Sociological Review*, Vol. 29, No. 3, June 1964; Harper and Row Publishers, Inc., New York); *The Existence of God*, edited by John Hick (Macmillan and Co. Ltd., Basingstoke; St. Martin's Press Inc., New York); *Structural*

Acknowledgments

Anthropology, by Claude Lévi-Strauss (Basic Books Inc., New York); *The Future of an Illusion,* by Sigmund Freud (Liveright Publishing Corp., New York); "New Styles in 'Leftism' " by Irving Howe, in *The New Radicals,* edited by Paul Jacobs and Saul Landau (Irving Howe, 90 Riverside Drive, New York; Random House Inc., New York); *The Politics of the Vatican,* by Peter Nichols (Praeger Publishers, Inc., New York; Pall Mall Press, London).

CONTENTS

Part I ·	**The Cultural Context**	1
1 ·	The Post-secular Age	3
2 ·	Contemporary Conceptions of Church	61
Part II ·	**Theological Probes**	111
3 ·	The Too Subtle God	113
4 ·	Christ the Man of the Future	153
5 ·	The Morality of the Noosphere	176
6 ·	The Secular Function of the Church	216
	Epilogue	251
	Notes to Text	265

"I want to be on the side of change", the doctor said. "If I had been born an amoeba who could think, I would have dreamed of the day of the primates. I would have wanted anything I did to contribute to that day. Evolution, as far as we can tell, has lodged itself finally in the brains of man. The ant, the fish, even the ape has gone as far as it can go, but in our brain evolution is moving—my God—at what a speed! I forget how many hundreds of millions of years passed between the dinosaurs and the primates, but in our own lifetime we have seen the change from diesel to jet, the splitting of the atom, the cure of leprosy."

Graham Greene
A Burnt-Out Case[1]

Part One

THE CULTURAL CONTEXT

The Post-secular Age

Our new environment compels commitment and participation. We have become irrevocably involved with, and responsible for, each other.
Marshall McLuhan

The question of bread for me is a material question. The question of bread for my neighbour is a spiritual matter.
M. Richard Shaull

The Concept of Secularization—Definitions

The twentieth century is constantly described as the secular age and the process which has led to this state of affairs is called the process of secularization. The aim of this chapter is to examine a number of definitions of secularization in order to uncover the implications for the Christian church. Christians tend to feel, instinctively, that as Christians they are threatened by this process, and the advocates of the process of secularization often indicate that they have good reason to be.

Hence a number of questions immediately suggest themselves: What is the likely end result of the process of secularization? Will it be the elimination of religion in all its forms as a category of thought and a community of persons? Will it entail and demand the persistence of sacred-secular tensions? Will it result in the coincidence of sacred and secular values in such a way as to realize and vindicate the authentic Judaeo-Christian tradition? Will the achievement of some Christian ideals and values in the process of secularization reveal new implications and higher ideals for both Christianity and the secular world, thus leading to new tensions? Will the process of secularization itself be proved to be a myth and require that a more accurate and comprehensive way of describing contemporary cultural processes be developed?

The *aim* of this chapter will be to suggest that:

a) the concept of secularization has been a useful device for drawing attention to important cultural developments

b) the concept of secularization has exercised a profound purifying and reorienting effect on Christianity

c) the concept of secularization is now inadequate for describing contemporary cultural processes.

Secularization can be defined in a weak sense or in a strong sense. Harvey Cox in *The Secular City* uses the definition of C. A. Peursen and describes it as the deliverance of man "first from religious and then from metaphysical control over his reason and his language".

It is the loosing of the world from religious and quasi-religious understandings of itself, the dispelling of all closed-world views, the breaking of all supernatural myths and sacred symbols . . . the discovery by man that he has been left with the world on his hands, that he can no longer blame fortune or the furies for what he does with it. Secularization is man turning his attention away from worlds beyond and toward this world and this time (saeculum = this present age).[1]

This is a weak or modified definition of secularization, for it leaves a number of issues and elements implicit. This is due in part to the explicit claim made by Cox to view the complex of processes resulting in the secular city, in an age of "no religion at all", from a "theological perspective". The result is, as Ruel Tyson points out, a set of "tacit and often contradictory categorical commitments Cox employs, particularly with regard to methods of explanation and assessment of thought, value and symbol".[2] Tyson is indicating that

Cox does not successfully resolve the tensions between his theological perspective and the perspective of the sociologist or cultural anthropologist. He does, however, distinguish between secularization and secularism. The former "implies a historical process, almost entirely irreversible, in which society and culture are delivered from tutelage to religious control and closed metaphysical world-views". Secularism, on the other hand, "is the name for an ideology, a new closed world-view which functions very much like a new religion . . . it menaces the openness and freedom secularization has produced."[3]

Because Cox does not pursue a process of exact linguistic analysis of his basic terms he does allow, by default, for a number of ways in which the biblical God can be allowed to persist. Man can be released from the tutelage of ecclesiastical, religious, metaphysical, mythical, and magical domination, and continue to preserve all of these categories. Man can be related to each of these categories, systems, or processes in at least three ways: he can be dominated by them, he can eliminate them, or he can use them. It is not made clear whether secularization entails merely the release of man from the domination of these categories so that he can *use* them, or whether it entails the complete elimination of them as a condition of man's freedom.

A second element in the definition given by Cox is its role in relation to the conceptions of space and time. The word "secular" derives from the Latin word *saeculum* meaning "this age" and is used in contrast to another similar Latin word denoting world, *mundus*. The process of secularization is claimed to be a shift from a Greek spatial view of reality to a typically Hebrew temporal view:

> For the Greeks, the world was a place, a location. Happenings of interest could occur *within* the world, but nothing significant ever happened *to* the world . . . For the Hebrews, on the other hand, the world was essentially history, a series of events beginning with Creation and heading toward a Consummation . . . The whole history of Christian theology . . . can be understood in part as a continuing attempt to resist and dilute the radical Hebrew impulse, to absorb historical into spatial categories.[4]

A number of difficulties arise from this dichotomy between space and time which could be crucial to the validity of conceiving contemporary cultural change in terms of secularization. To these difficulties it will be necessary to return later, for they will take more definite shape in the process of analysis of secularization.

A strong definition of secularization advocated by Freud, Marx, and positivists generally demands the abolition of church, religion, metaphysics, myth, and religious ritual as essential to the emancipation of man. They see the end product of the process of secularization as a simply and exclusively mundane-oriented and conscious society.

Their charge against religion is that even under the best possible conditions the relation between religion and culture must be terminated if mankind would achieve the stage of mature humanity, that unless the relationship is terminated, man's tendency of myth making, wish believing, and life denying and his susceptibility to superstition, credulity, and social inadequacy will assert themselves afresh and man will be hopelessly lost in secondary solutions to the problems of existence.[5]

This attitude is probably best exemplified in the outlook and life-style of Bertrand Russell, who believed that all human problems and tasks should be dealt with by impeccably rational procedures and scientific techniques in the context of the bald facts of personal birth and death:

I believe that when I die I shall rot, and nothing of my ego will survive. I am not young, and I love life. But I should scorn to shiver with terror at the thought of annihilation. Happiness is none the less true happiness because it must come to an end, nor do thought and love lose their value because they are not everlasting.[6]

Though there is the danger of erecting a definition of secularization which will prove to be a "straw-man" in the interests of validating the aim of the chapter, O'Dea's definition can provide the working basis for analysis. His claim is that secularizaiton may be said to consist in two related but fundamental transformations in human thinking:

a) The *desacralization* or the demystification of attitudes to institutions, persons, and things.

b) The *rationalization* of all areas of human activity which involves the withholding of emotional participation in thinking about the world. This process of rationalization means the use of logic and science rather than an emotional symbolism to organize thought.[7]

This division into two components, the negative and the positive, in the process of secularization can provide the framework for examining the process, or talking about it, in detail.

A. The Negative Component of Secularization: The Desacralization and Demystification of Culture

Under this heading it is necessary to examine magic, myth, metaphysics, and religion, for all of these, in one way or another, cannot be reduced to dimensions which will satisfy without residue the demands of logico-scientific criteria. Historically, each of these phenomena has been in some way related to and interdependent on the other. Nevertheless it is possible to distinguish between them, even though the chances of completely separating them from one another may be limited.

THE ELIMINATION OF MAGIC

A working definition of magic could be that it is the positing of causes in any energy system which are disproportionate to the expected effects and when the claimed nexus between the cause posited and the claimed effect cannot be tested empirically. In the first phase of cultural anthropology it was thought that magic was primitive man's substitute for science and that primitive man confused what we would call empirical and technical procedures with procedures based on faith and deriving from tradition which we would call magical. Bronislaw Malinowski showed, however, that the Trobriand Islanders made a clear-cut distinction between the two sets of procedures.

> They know quite well what effects can be produced by careful tilling of the soil and these effects they try to produce by competent and industrious labour. They equally know that certain evils, such as pests, blights, bushfires, drought or rain, cannot be overcome by human work however hard or consistent.[8]

The function of magic was to compensate for the inadequacies of man's control over his environment and provide an antidote for the inevitable frustrations arising from his environment. Man's control over his environment has expanded and he now has medical and narcotic means for dealing with the frustrations. However, the elimination of magic has not necessarily eliminated the problems with which magic was supposed to deal, for man, at both the personal and social level, is still faced with the imponderable and the unpredictable, even though these are more in the sphere of second nature than in the sphere of first nature. It is not surprising, therefore, that as Milton J. Yinger points out[9] vestiges of the magical persist in modern society and science itself can be invested with an intellectual and emotional commitment which is out of proportion to its actual capacity to achieve desired effects at any given moment.

The important question here is the relationship between magic and religion. Are they inextricably related? For Emile Durkheim the distinction between the two is that magic is essentially an individualistic and somewhat maverick phenomenon, whereas religion is essentially social and ecclesial.[10] Joachim Wach analyses the distinction as follows:

> It is possible to discern a double consequence of man's apprehension of numinous power at all times and everywhere: he either bows down to it in submission, or he reaches out in an attempt to manipulate and control the mysterious forces of which he has become aware. The first, the religious way, leads up to the highest religious act, that of adoration; the second, the way of magic, sets him on the road to conquer and to appropriate as much of the power as will yield to his command.[11]

Though this may serve as an adequate distinction it does not help in separating religion from magic because intrinsic to most religions is the establishment of some positive relationship with the numinous which is not exhausted by adoration. Yet even when the means of relating to the numinous are restricted to ritualistic adoration, this inevitably takes on an ingratiating complexion and thus assumes a tendency to be used as a means for manipulating the numinous. This leads to the conclusion drawn by Talcott Parsons: "Whatever the distinction made, magic is always continuous with religion; it always involves some relation to the strains occasioned by uncertainty, and to human emotional adjustment to such situations."[12] The basic reason for the continued association of religion and magic is the continuation of the ultimate imponderable and the ultimate uncertainty. Magic may no longer be invoked to deal with, either subjectively or objectively, penultimate or intramundane imponderables and uncertainties. This is no guarantee, however, that it will not continue to have currency in dealing with what can be called, for the time being, the ultimate problem.

Hence what is beginning to emerge and what will take on central significance in this chapter is that the whole of the modern debate which is implicit in the process of secularization revolves around whether there is an ultimate problem for man or the human race. Moreover men seem to be inevitably committed to either of two deeply unsatisfactory responses to this question:

a) The view that there is really no problem, only intramundane problems, and that the problem arises from a variety of mental, linguistic or psychological aberrations.

b) The view that there is a problem, though it is extremely difficult to articulate for it must be articulated in intramundane terms. Moreover, this view seems chronically incapable of proposing any but inadequate ways of explaining and coping with the problem.

THE FUNCTION OF MYTH

In the chapter entitled "The Structural Study of Myth" in his *Structural Anthropology,* Claude Lévi-Strauss points out that in spite of all the analysis and examination of myths in various cultures, no field of research in anthropology has made such small progress. From a theoretical point of view the situation today is much the same as it was fifty years ago, "a picture of chaos". Myths are interpreted in a wide variety of ways, most of them conflicting and in the last analysis mythology tends to be reduced "to an idle play or to a coarse kind of speculation".[13]

The main reason for the state of chaos in the theory of mythology lies in the failure to develop the appropriate technique for understanding the structure and significance of myths. Lévi-Strauss claims to have developed this technique and thus to have discovered their significance. Far from being crude and essentially pre-logical attempts at developing world-views in a tribal context, he sees them as very subtle and sophisticated ways of coming to terms with some of the basic problems of human existence.

Prevalent attempts to explain alleged differences between the so-called "primitive" mind and scientific thought have resorted to qualitative differences between the working processes of the mind in both cases while assuming that the objects to which they were applying themselves remained very much the same. If our interpretation is correct, we are led to a completely different view, namely that the kind of logic which is used by mythical thought is as rigorous as that of modern science, and that the difference lies not in the quality of the intellectual process, but in the nature of the things to which it is applied.[14]

One of the basic functions of myth is to work from the awareness of basic oppositions, such as life and death, towards their progressive mediation. This is illustrated in Lévi-Strauss's structural analysis of the Zuni emergence myth. However, the very structure and the psychological implications of this structure are of equal importance, especially in the light of the claims of Marshall McLuhan. The myth is the logical form of an oral literature. What is initially mystifying in myths is the duplication, triplication, and quadruplication of the same sequence of stories. The effect of this is analogous to the effect of the correct reading of an orchestral score. The melodic line is arranged horizontally, but the harmonic line is arranged vertically. If a myth like an orchestral score is "read" merely horizontally, i.e. diachronically, it will be repetitive and meaningless. It must be "read" horizontally, i.e. diachronically, and vertically, i.e. synchronically, simultaneously, for the melodic line and the harmony to emerge. As a consequence the myth exhibits a "slated" structure which seeps to the surface and allows the significance of the myth to seep to the surface, through the repetition process.

However, the slates are not absolutely identical to each other. And since the purpose of myth is to provide a logical model capable of overcoming a contradiction (an impossible achievement if, as it happens, the contradiction is real), a theoretically infinite number of slates will be generated, each one slightly different from the others. Thus, myth grows spiral-wise until the intellectual impulse which has originated it is exhausted. Its growth is a continuous process whereas its structure remains discontinuous.[15]

Lévi-Strauss's analysis of myth does not demand that we reinstate myths as a mode either of enlightenment or of communication. What it does is make us less ready to reject the myth as a vestige of the primitive mind. This is especially so in the light of the affinity between the function attributed to myth by Lévi-Strauss and the kind of mythology which McLuhan claims is emerging in the post-linear electronic age. There is also a haunting affinity between the conical or spiral shape of the myth of oral literature and the shape of space-time emerging from contemporary mathematical-physics as described by A. Minkowski.

The claim of McLuhan is that every culture has a dominant communications matrix that imparts a perceptual bias that in turn validates the point of view of its members. He calls media "macro-myths" since they make believable the contents they transmit. Thus the macro-myth of print, with its stress on lineal thought processes and especially the increasingly dominant macro-myth of mathematical equations help generate exclusive belief in time as a horizontal line to the exclusion of the possibility of any plane or dimension not a part of that line.[16] It is hoped that the significance of this insight into the epistemological consequences of media will emerge more clearly in the consideration of certain developments in modern philosophy and science.

Richard Rubenstein drew attention to the "important analytic insight about the function of myth and ritual in religion, their capacity to objectify and dramatize the unconscious strivings of the individual in a significant social structure."[17] However, while it is one thing to refuse to leave unacknowledged the value and the logic of myths in the past, it is another thing, in an age of highly critical self-consciousness, to be able to accept or advocate myths today. The important thing is not to eliminate the problem or the set of specifically human contradictions, real or apparent, which myths attempted to resolve. These still have to be faced even though the phrasing and the attempted resolutions of them may take different forms.

THE FUTURE OF METAPHYSICS

The structuralism of Lévi-Strauss and his advocacy of a theory of natural law, even though rather overtly deterministic, represents a rather surprising reversal of the anti-metaphysical trend of contemporary thinking. He would claim, of course, that this method is not metaphysical but a successful attempt to invest the social sciences, and especially anthropology, with the same method, vigour and clarity that the physical sciences enjoy. However, his whole enterprise is based on the assumption that there are underlying laws of human nature which manifest themselves in a variety of phenomena. His assumption and partial vindication of strata of human significance and behaviour is a challenge to the prevailing assumption that the "structure" of reality is explicit, horizontal, unilateral, and evolutionary.

The fundamental problem is a very old one in the history of philosophy. Man is faced with the particularity and the persistent flow of reality on the one hand and with his apparently incurable propensity to universalize and halt this flow in conceptual frameworks on the other. The modern antipathy to metaphysics has four sources:

a) In the past, metaphysics often reached conclusions about the nature of reality by using deductive and speculative procedures when the appropriate procedures were scientific.

b) Comprehensive metaphysical systems based on or derived from a particular cultural context came to dominate and constrict human behaviour in different or changing cultural contexts.

c) Men today seem to manage quite well without metaphysics. As Daniel Callahan says:

> Can secular man, after all, afford to ignore metaphysics? Can he really get away with a purely pragmatic solution to his sociohistorical problems? Up to a point, I think the answer is yes to both questions. It has to be yes because many men patently manage to live antimetaphysical, pragmatic lives and seem to be none the worse for it. The Christian may look at such a man with skepticism and incredulity, but there are many secular men who can confound his pessimistic expectations.[18]

d) In the case of the Catholic church, the preoccupation with ultimate answers has been an important obstacle to dealing with answers to pressing social and political problems. As a consequence of the domination of metaphysics, human problems have tended to be regarded as of merely derivative importance and man's temporal salvation has suffered by contrast with the "eternal perspective" afforded by the grand metaphysical structure.

At first sight, therefore, man seems to be faced with the inevitable choice of being incarcerated in a metaphysical system or exposed to the formless chaos and flux of the particularity of history. And yet in spite of the explicit repudiation of metaphysics, it often lurks implicitly in the mental background of the most secular man. An essential element in metaphysics, as traditionally understood, is a theory of knowledge, an implicit or explicit belief in or account of the range of human reason. Another essential element is its capacity, as Cox calls it, to bring "unity and meaning to human life and thought".[19] The means whereby unity and meaning are brought to human life and thought can be an explicit, logically coherent and complete overarching intellectual framework, or it can be an implicit, unacknowledged and even unrecognized underpinning which provides the source for a basic consistency or even inconsistency of outlook and behaviour. An explicit metaphysics may dominate behaviour and life, but it at least exercises its influence at a conscious level and is thus more amenable to critical scrutiny. In a later section we can examine this further, especially in relation to the unacknowledged epistemological assumptions of the many forms of secularism.

Before considering the positive possibilities of metaphysics, however, it could be illuminating to see how a metaphysics can be implicit even in the overtly horizontal and historical perspective taken by Cox in *The Secular City*. Claude Welch points out

> Cox's unfortunate tendency to make a systematic argument out of a historical sketch; viz. the account of development from "tribal" to "town" to "technolpolitan" culture. However interesting this analysis may be as an attempt at periodization, it becomes treacherous and finally unfair as an argument — treacherous because for this to bear weight as an argument, the development must be shown to have the character of historical necessity (thus the argumentative force is loaded into the description at the outset); unfair because substantive disagreements tend to be countered by relegating the opponent to a prior stage in historical development.[20]

The device of periodization, therefore, can take on a function analogous to, if not identical with, that of metaphysics. It might even be possible to go further to claim and justify the claim that this type of periodization terminating in the typical American secular city embodies a social, anthropological, and economic ideology.

What then is the future of metaphysics? Strictly speaking this entails a discussion of the scope and function of philosophy. However, in the terms of the discussion of secularization and the tendency to define it in anti-metaphysical terms, this analysis must be limited to what it is generally thought metaphysics consists of. It is possible to attribute three functions to metaphysics in relation to three problems which persist even in a secular age. It has been pointed out that there is a tendency in eliminating myths as an unsatisfactory literary form or means of communication, to eliminate also, and unjustifiably, the problems with which myths attempted to come to grips. The same propensity to eliminate persisting problems prevails with the tendency to eliminate metaphysics as a solution to them. There are three problem areas and hence three possible areas for metaphysical activity.

a) There is what could be called the problem of *the edge of reality* in relation to its structure. If a person's gaze is dogmatically fixed on and preoccupied with the intramundane, then the problem arising at the edge of the mundane—why reality or being at all?—can be ignored. Of course, the difficulty is not as simple as this, for the secularist stance is not merely a refusal to face the problem, but entails an answer that there is really no problem. But the argument as to whether there is a problem or not, once engaged, is metaphysics. The traditional philosophical problems of being and becoming, of the one and the many, of individuals and universals, remain, and answers to them embodied in one way or another in more practical outlooks and policies are exerting an influence for good or for evil on the real world. What is evil is that they exert their influence in an unacknowledged way, and the failure of past metaphysical endeavours to resolve these perennial problems does not justify the refusal to acknowledge them.

b) There is the problem of knowledge. It concerns the range and the possibilities of human cognition. This problem is unique among human problems. Scientific problems implicitly depend for their solutions on the functioning of the human cognitive apparatus in a way that is not self-conscious. Metaphysics, as distinct from science, arises precisely in the self-conscious reflective and critical analysis by the mind of its own acts. The results of this analysis or lack of analysis have their ramifications especially at the level of the human or social sciences. Yet when metaphysics in general or this species of metaphysical enterprise are repudiated the result is invariably a failure to make inevitable epistomological assumptions explicit. Thus when both Cox and van Buren, in different ways, speak of the impossibility of speaking of God in our age, they make this pronouncement from the standpoint of a specific answer to the epistemological problem. The difference is that while van Buren quite explicitly advocates the viewpoint of logical positivism, Cox's epistemological stance remains implicit and undifferentiated.

c) There is the problem of a synthetic "world-view". As Brian Wicker has pointed out: "This is the first priority—not the imposition of Christianity or any other '-ity' or '-ism', but the discovery of a new kind of intelligibility."[21] The scientific revolution has made possible the more accurate differentiation of human consciousness. The branches of the tree of knowledge multiply at an increasing rate every day, the volume of scientific knowledge doubles every ten years and, as a consequence, man's control of his environment is greatly increased. But it has resulted also in an "information overload". Consequently, as the Vatican Council pointed out, "Within the individual person there develops rather frequently an imbalance between an intellect which is modern in practical matters, and a theoretical system of thought which can neither master the sum total of its ideas, nor arrange them adequately into a synthesis."[22] Whether it will ever be possible to achieve such an integrating synthesis which will win any kind of consensus is difficult to say. What can be said is that the possibility and the validity of the attempt should not be excluded a priori. Nevertheless, two important procedural rules would have to govern any future metaphysical synthesis:

i) Such a synthesis must be developed, not deductively nor in isolation from all the data of experience, but inductively.

ii) It would, as a consequence, be held provisionally, so that it could be modified, or even radically reassessed, as new data became available.

Teilhard de Chardin in *The Phenomenon of Man* set a new style for metaphysics. His synthesis is certainly metaphysical, and because it is such it was rejected out of hand by many. But though it could be too cosmic and too imaginative, it is, nevertheless, a new kind of metaphysics. The fundamental fault with most of the great metaphysical systems of the past was that they began with a limited set of propositions more or less closely related to or based on reality and by a process of deductive reasoning elaborated a whole logical construct which was thought to parallel or represent the structure of the real.[23] This is not the case with Teilhard. There is a revolutionary fusion of synthetic imagination and empirical data. His metaphysics is more like a game played by small children of linking a number of dots which are numbered to reveal a pattern, where the small dots are, in this case, the data arrived at by scientific observation. However, the dots of reality are not numbered and more dots keep appearing as our knowledge expands. Moreover, it cannot be presumed that at any stage any system of linking will reveal the ultimate pattern. Yet if it is accepted that any system of linking is only provisional—and this is the attitude that Teilhard had towards his synthesis[24]—the system will not dominate man but can fulfill the function of integrating consciousness and experience by providing a relative pattern of intelligibility and so facilitate a greater contact with reality rather than insulate from it.

Three questions concerning metaphysics still need to be considered. The first is whether it is possible to have the kind of synthetic metaphysics suggested above and avoid its hardening into an absolutist world view. It has been suggested that such a system can mediate an encounter with reality and facilitate the process of assuming creative responsibility in history. If it is kept in this category, such a synthesis, like Marxism, can be valuable for emancipating the underdeveloped and exploited masses of the world by unifying, in this view, and mobilizing their energies in the cause of their own interests. However, history has shown how such a theory can soon harden into an incorrigible dogma. On the other hand the refusal to acknowledge the possibility of any significant synthesis resulting from the atomization of perception, sensibility, and society can be just as much an obstacle to an encounter with reality and the undertaking of creative responsibility for the world.

The second question is raised by Mircea Eliade.[25] He makes the claim, based on a phenomenological study of religion, that the propensity of man to resort to transhistorical structures, whether these are mythical or metaphysical, reveals the profoundly religious nature of man. This leads Eliade to assert that the contemporary situation of man who is urbanized, industrialized, and enveloped in technology, is isolated from the rhythms and the mystery of the cosmos, and consequently is incapable of developing the "religious" faculty or sensitivity which he claims is a necessary precondition for being a Christian. As a result of secularization, he claims, "the cosmos has become opaque, inert, mute: it transmits no message, it holds no solutions and offers no transcendental insights". Man is thus exposed to what Eliade calls "the terror of history". Pre-secular man escaped from the terror of history by abolishing time through various processes of participation in, identification with, or return to a transhistorical time. The various mythical and metaphysical manifestations of this process made it possible for "tens of millions of men . . . for century after century to endure great historical pressures without despairing, without committing suicide or falling into that spiritual aridity that always brings with it a relativistic or nihilistic view of history".[26] He reaches the conclusion that the horizon of archetypes and repetition cannot be transcended with impunity unless we accept a philosophy of freedom that does not exclude God.[27] The crucial question for modern man since Nietzsche has been whether the positive exclusion of God is a necessary condition for any philosophy of human freedom, and whether man can assume responsibility for history and still acknowledge even the possibility of God. However, the point at issue here is whether the propensity of man to resort to transhistorical structures is really an indication that man is profoundly religious by nature. To claim that it is an indication of the religious nature of man is too strong. The evidence produced by Eliade is explained by the less ambitious claim that man is by nature incurably rational, and in the face of the variety of history, has a recurring propensity to erect conceptual structures, to explain history and also to master it.

To a large extent the burden of Eliade's argument rests on the concept of the "terror of history", and for the religious tendency of man to reassert itself it would seem that many of the historical processes would have to be reversed. However, the kind of phenomenon which Eliade isolates could just as well be described as *the challenge* of history. Yet there is an ingredient in the phenomenon Eliade isolates which is very similar to if not identical with the problem that man has faced throughout history and continues to face: the problem of the edge of reality. What it is important to appreciate is that initially this is a rational, or more specifically, a human problem. It manifests itself in its most palpable and personal form in the fact of death, but manifests itself both more abstractly and comprehensively in the mystery of existence.

This point is worth emphasizing, for this "problem of the edge of reality" or "mystery of existence" seems to be the watershed of myth, magic, religion, and metaphysics. Each of these is in some way related to, or responds to, or arises from this human locus. The radical secularist response is that there is no problem. If it is acknowledged as a problem, myth, magic, metaphysics, and religion in various ways are responses to it.

The third question that poses itself is: what is the relation of metaphysics to religion? The answer will vary from religion to religion and within Christianity itself. If it is the case that religion is a response to this human problem, the function of metaphysics in relation to the problem is to analyse and state the problem in its most precise terms, indeed to examine whether or not the problem arises merely from our being "bewitched with language". A second function is the epistemological one which, by critical analysis of human knowledge, examines whether the problem and/or the specific religious solution are logically and ontologically possible. (The crisis theology of Karl Barth would repudiate this role of human knowledge in relation to revelation, but at the cost of the accusation that his theology is an intellectual exercise analogous to a system of geometry with no contact with the world of the real.) A third function, and this can be and has been fulfilled by myths, is to provide religion with a rational framework for the expression of its response.

The value of the phenomenon which we call the process of secularization has been to halt the proliferation of metaphysics and metaphysical entities, for in many ways metaphysics came to dominate life and thus inhibit the elements of spontaneity and creativity. Secularization eradicated the thickets of metaphysical jargon, to which ecclesiastics, especially, claimed privileged access, and from which it was possible to maintain a policy of mystification which proved an obstacle to the rationalization of vast areas of life. From the maintenance of the divine right of kings through to the strictures against birth control, metaphysics has often proved an obstacle to the process of rationalization. Secularization has also led to the abolition of the chronic dualism which has plagued Western thought.

However, secularization has come to be identified with a kind of uni-stratified monism. To the extent that it is defined as the abolition of metaphysics, it is incapable of accounting for the persistence of the threefold problem of the edge of reality, the reflective analysis of human cognition, and the human search for intelligibility (all of which can be described as metaphysical problems), unless it is made synonymous with secularism which repudiates these problems. As Robert Bellah points out:

In the world view that has emerged from the tremendous intellectual advances of the last two centuries there is simply no room for a hierarchic dualistic religious symbol system of the classical historic type. This is not to be interpreted as a return to primitive monism: it is not that a single world has replaced a double one but that an infinitely multiplex one has replaced the simple duplex structure. It is not that life has become again a "one possibility thing" but that it has become an infinite possibility thing. The analysis of modern man as secular, materialistic, dehumanized and in the deepest sense areligious seems to me fundamentally misguided, for such a judgement is based on standards that cannot adequately gauge the modern temper.[28]

THE NATURE OF RELIGION

In *Sex, Culture and Myth* Malinowski says: "Religion is a

difficult and refractory subject of study. It seems futile to question that which contains the answers to all problems. It is not easy to dissect with the cold knife of logic what can only be accepted with a complete surrender of heart."[29]

Any attempt to define "religion" is inevitably bedevilled by a wide variety of difficulties. The definition is likely to be different according to whether the person's perspective is from within religion or some particular form of religion, in which case the definition is likely to contain an evaluative component as to what religion ought to be, or from outside religion, in which case the definition is likely to contain an implicit judgment as to whether religion ought to exist at all.[30] From both of these perspectives the definition is likely to contain a distinction between what religion appears to be and what it *really* is. On the one hand the advocate of religion might want to emphasize the transcendent aspects of religion even though religion appears explicable in mundane terms. On the other hand the opponent of religion might want to reduce it to a phenomenon explicable in merely mundane terms.

In the first phase of the science of sociology of religion, there was a prevalent positivistic tendency to reduce religion to and define it in merely mundane terms. Comte, Tyler, Spencer and to some extent Frazer used a positivistic approach. As Parsons points out: "It is, however, a basic assumption of this pattern of thinking that the only critical standards to which religious ideas can be referred are those of empirical validity."[31] Parsons goes on to point out, however, that Pareto, Malinowski, and Weber, among others, moved away from this non-empirical reductionist assumption to a more objective attitude to religion, so that it was now possible to predict:

Any new philosophical synthesis will need positively to take account of these distinctions rather than to attempt to reinstate for the scientific level the older positivistic conception of the homogeneity of all human thought and its problems. If these distinctions are to be transcended it cannot be in the form of "reducing" religious ideas to those of science — in the sense of Western intellectual history — or vice versa.[32]

Indeed Max Weber thought it the best procedure not to attempt to define religion, or at least, not until the conclusion of a comprehensive study of religions in their specific social and cultural context.[33]

However, as secularization is often defined in terms of the

emancipation of man from religion, and as some theologians, following Bonhoeffer, speak of "religionless Christianity", it is necessary to attempt a working definition. Two questions immediately present themselves.

a) What should be the starting point of the definition? Can it be "religious experience"? The difficulty with this, first of all, is that any definition of religion based on it would violate the logical law of avoiding the use of the term defined in the definition. A second difficulty, as Joachim Wach points out, is that we do not have available criteria for distinguishing between what is religious and what is not.[34] Can it begin with the distinction between sacred and secular as Durkheim suggests?[35] Once again the difficulty is with criteria for distinguishing between these two categories, for amongst the peoples and the religions of the world, almost all objects have at different times and in different places been both sacred and secular. Can the community or the church which calls itself religious be the starting point? This has value for the science of sociology of religion but it is possible that the self-consciously organized community is merely an epiphenomenon of religion.

b) What should the procedure of the definition be? This question is important, for definitions of religion have often been based on or confused with accounts of the origin of religion, even when these attempts have not been overtly reductionist in intention. Hence it is possible to define religion in terms of its historical origins, as with Paul Radin, in terms of its socio-psychological origins, as with Georg Simmel, or in terms of its social origins as with Emile Durkheim.[36]

I want to suggest that the appropriate starting point of the definition of religion is the fundamentally human problem isolated in the last section. Religion is a species of response to this problem. Paul Tillich has said that religion is what concerns us ultimately. This description appears misguided precisely because religion is a *response,* one response among many, to what concerns us ultimately. In the last section, what concerns us ultimately was called the "problem of the edge of reality" or "the mystery of existence". It was pointed out that the most radical response to this problem is the philosophical response which claims that the problem is meaningless and that all responses to it are equally meaningless. Any fundamental vindication of religion would have to begin at this point.

Religion is a positive response to this problem. It can thus be defined: "Existential human behaviour directed towards or related to the non-mundane, as a response to the mystery of existence." The elements of this definition need to be amplified.

a) It is *existential* human behaviour, in the sense that it is a response of the person as a person, rather than a merely intellectual response as in the case of a philosophical or metaphysical explanation of the mystery of existence, and in this way religion is distinguished from metaphysics though it may also be closely related to it. In this way it is also distinguished from myth, for though myth engages the person more completely than does metaphysics, it does not signify the commitment of the person as does religion. However, as with metaphysics, myth may be intimately associated with religion as an epiphenomenal expression of it. In this way it is also distinguished from magic, for magic is the use of means, even though disproportionate, to achieve some specific end. If we use the traditional scholastic distinction it could be said that religion is an immanent activity, whereas magic is a transcendent activity. Yet here again, though religion and magic are distinguishable, this is not to say that they are not often or usually closely associated.

b) Rather more tentatively, the social component of religion would need to be included under the rubric of "existential". One reason for this is that man's total responses seem inevitably to be also social in some way or another. Another reason is that all religion seems to be community behaviour in some way or another as Durkheim pointed out,[37] though this does not entirely exclude the possibility and the problem of a merely private religion.[38]

c) *Non-mundane,* expressed negatively in this way, is capable of accommodating a wide range of religions from Buddhism, in which the religious behaviour is related to transcendent Nothingness, to forms of medieval Christianity, in which religious behaviour was directed towards a hierarchically structured and heavily populated celestial world. At the same time *non-mundane* is calculated to exclude the variety of so-called surrogate religions which positively exclude the possibility of anything but the mundane.

d) *Behaviour* remains as general as possible, to include ritual, theoretical expression and sociological expression. On the evidence presented by a comparative study of religion it seems difficult to say which of these three factors is the most basic. What can be said is that the religious response to the problem of existence has a ceremonial or ritualistic form, it gives rise to a theoretical conceptualization and/or justification and has sociological implications. The sociological implications are of two orders. The first order of implications is for the structure of the community which makes up this religion. The second order is for the society in which this religion exists. Each of these factors, ritual, theory, behaviour, individually or collectively, can give rise to religious experience, though it seems impossible to be able to analyse or describe this in terms distinct from what is explicable in merely mundane terms.

Cultural anthropology, comparative religion, and sociology of religion have shown that religions are profoundly conditioned by the culture in which they arise, first in considering the original problem as a problem (for modern Western culture tends to regard it as a pseudo-problem), secondly as to whether the response to the problem be religious or philosophical, thirdly as to the forms the ritual, the rationalization, and the sociological consequences take. Sociology of religion has also shown the effects that religion in all its manifestations can have on society.[39] Once a particular religion has been identified, the function of the sociologist is to examine the interaction of this social or "cultural system"[40] with the other social and cultural systems within the society as a whole, to estimate whether the action in each case is a reinforcing or a disintegrating one and to uncover latent or unsuspected interactions.[41]

In considering the effect of the process of secularization on religion it will prove more manageable to limit the discussion to Western Christianity. Three questions present themselves:

a) Is Christianity a religion? The question, as has been pointed out, was raised by Dietrich Bonhoeffer, but the pressure of a secular age evoked the expression of it. W. Richard Comstock summarizes what Bonhoeffer meant by "religion" and indicates, consequently, what "religionless Christianity" implies:

First, religion shares with metaphysics the orientation towards "other world". Secondly, it cultivates an inward or individualistic search for a salvation from this world and a retreat into an "other worldly" religious realm. Thirdly, religion posits a special sphere of holy ritual, private prayers, and monastic retirement within the world that is somehow considered to be more important than the mundane tasks of everyday life. Fourthly, religion uses the God of this other world as a "deus ex machina", as an illicit problem-solver.[42]

If this is a fair summary of Bonhoeffer's position, it must be presumed that talk about religionless Christianity is merely a rhetorical device to call Christians to assume their share of responsibility for the world, or that Bonhoeffer simply identified God with the world. If one wants to continue to speak about God, as Bonhoeffer did, one must put him in the category of the non-mundane, and unless Christianity is a matter of total indifference to any kind of relationship with God, and is regarded merely as a technique or programme for social and cultural change, it must be called a religion. The significance of the Bonhoefferian rhetoric and the consequence of the pressure of secularization on Christianity is that Christian theology has been forced to seek a new juxtaposition of the three terms "God", "man", and "world", in such a way that any relationship with God is established *through* the mundane.

b) The pressure of secularization was not, however, so easily avoided. The question still remained: why speak about God at all? The Christian theologians seemed to have surrendered the dualism that had appeared indispensable to the claims of Christianity only at the cost of the elimination of everything but the mundane. If "God" was to remain in the Christian lexicon, some provision had to be made for the realm of the transcendent. It is possible to distinguish two very different responses to this challenge. In an article entitled "Inspirational Religious Literature: From Latent to Manifest Functions of Religion", Louis Schneider and Sanford M. Dornbusch analyse a trend in popular religious literature over the last seventy-five years. Their claim is that the essence of this trend is the emergence of "spiritual technology" which has made certain "by products" of religious activity into "goals". At best it "instrumentalizes" God to make him the means to human mental health. At worst it advocates "faith", "belief", "prayer", and "ritual" without any objects, as useful for the achievement of wealth and emotional and physical health. In this literary genre: "The 'hero' appears more and more as the 'well-adjusted' man, who does not question existing social institutions and who, ideally successful both in a business or in professional sense, feels no emotional pain."[43] Independently of whether there is any object of faith or any God to whom prayer is addressed, these two "religious" activities are thought of as important as psychological and social integrators. At a higher level and in a more latent way, as Will Herberg and Robert Bellah point out, religion is allowed or made to function as an instrument of cultural and national integration and solidarity—for instance, Eisenhower's "Our government makes no sense unless it is founded in a deeply felt religious faith—and I don't care what it is."[44] The difficulty with this overall strategy, whether intended or not, is that it is bound, ultimately, to be self-defeating, for in the last analysis even the latent functions of faith and prayer depend on the belief that there is a God who is the object of faith and to whom prayer is addressed:

> The subjective benefits of prayer are so unmistakable that one who had lost all belief in any objective relation between the praying individual and a higher power, might very wisely continue to pray (if he could) purely for the sake of the reflex effects of prayer upon his own mind and character ... The question whether prayer is nothing more than a mind state having a certain subjective value ... or whether it is also an objective relation between the prayerful soul and some sort of "Higher Power" above ... —this is for metaphysics rather than for psychology. Psychology may and should point out, however, that the subjective effects of prayer are almost invariably due, directly or indirectly, to some real faith in the objective relation ... For since the subjective value of prayer is chiefly due to the belief that prayer has values which are *not* subjective, it will with most persons evaporate altogether once they learn that it is *all* subjective.[45]

A second and more sophisticated response to the challenge posed by the process of secularization to vindicate the realm of transcendence and hence allow for the possibility of God has been to make two further radical shifts in theological perspective. It was pointed out at the conclusion of (*a*) that under the influence of Bonhoeffer there had been a shift from ecclesiastical introversion to a tendency to seek God in and through the world. The two other shifts intimately related with this shift are the emphasis on seeking God not vertically but horizontally, not in the past but in the future. God is spoken of as "the absolute future".[46] He is the one who is to come. Is this a claim to knowledge about the future? J. B. Metz denies this:

> Christian eschatology is not an omniscient ideology about the future, but a "theologia negativa" of the future. This poverty of knowledge is rather the very wealth of Christianity. What distinguishes the Christian and the secular ideologies of the future from one another is not that Christians know more, but that they know less about the sought-after future of humanity and that they face up to this poverty of knowledge.[47]

The question that this evokes is: why speak about God at all? Why not just speak of the future? This could be simply a less vulnerable form of the type of mystification which the process of secularization seems suited to eradicate. This leads to the third of the three crucial questions which the process of secularization poses for Christianity.

c) Is Christianity an ideology? In an essay entitled "Christianity and Ideology", Karl Rahner describes an ideology as a total and closed system, an absolutizing of a partial aspect of reality; it can be a fully developed theory, an unreflective attitude of mind, or an arbitrary and voluntaristic mood. He goes on to distinguish three possible forms:

i) Ideology of immanence in which specific, limited areas of experience are absolutized and made the criteria or determinants of all areas of experience. Thus nationalism, racism, socialism, materialism, and empiricism would be examples of ideologies of immanence.

ii) Ideology of transmanence in which what is ultimate, infinite, and pervasive of all spheres of reality is absolutized in such a way that the penultimate and finite are minimized or ignored. Idealism, supernaturalism, personalism, fraternalism are examples. This kind of ideology is characteristic of metaphysics and many religions.

iii) Ideology of transcendence which seeks to discredit and dispel the claims of the other two forms of ideology and to absolutize its purely formal victory over their claims to validity. "Thus this ideology advocates a program of so-called boundless openness to everything in general with a scrupulous avoidance of a straightforward commitment to anything in particular." Examples of this would be many forms of "meta-evaluative" scientific perspectives when they become a life-style, a great deal of linguistic analysis, and some forms of existentialism.[48]

This definition and the subsequent distinctions will be of relevance when the inadequacies of science are examined later on. The question here is, does Christianity belong to any of these categories? In the not too recent past it could justifiably have been called an ideology of transmanence. However, "the penultimate and the finite" of the secular age have so completely dominated the scene that no longer can they not be simply ignored; they have appeared to have eliminated the "ultimate and the infinite". Some forms of neo-liberal Christianity have taken on a boundless openness to everything combined with the avoidance of a commitment to anything. But how can the commitment which is Christian faith be reconciled with the kind of openness which the avoidance of an ideology seems to demand?

The process of secularization has had two important effects on Christian theology:

a) It has convinced Christianity or the Christian church (in principle if not in fact) that it has no privileged access to a knowledge of the nature of things nor of the structure of reality.

b) It has led or is leading to a reformulation of faith in hypothetical terms rather than in dogmatic terms. In II Cor. 5:7 Paul says: "We live by faith (fistis), not by sight (eidos, gnosis)." Hebrews 11:1 says: "Now faith is the substance of things hoped for, the evidence of things not seen." "Substance" here means the grounds or the basis.[49] If Christianity is not an ideology, it is a hypothesis, not of the scientific kind to be verified rationally by experimental procedures nor of the logical kind to be verified by deductive procedures, but verified existentially, that is by the total commitment of the person.[50] It is still appropriate to press the question of the grounds for this commitment. The Christian would be constrained to reply that there was a twofold ground: the remote ground, viz. the problem of existence, and the proximate ground, viz. the phenomenon of Christ. The secularist would want to press the matter further to ask what the conditions are for the proper performance of this existential experiment and in what circumstances a resolution could be expected. The Christian would posit the rubric of altruistic love as the basic condition for the success of the experiment and claim that its final resolution would take place in the future.

One of the interesting features of this dynamic structuring of the Christian response to the challenge of secularism is that it has the shape which Lévi-Strauss claims to discover in myth. In the past, Christianity in its conceptual and sociological structure assumed a rigid pyramidal form. In this non-ideological hypothetical form it must be "read" and "lived" like an orchestral score in which there must be a simultaneous movement diachronically from past to future following the evolving melodic line and synchronically, that is, vertically, allowing the harmonic structure to be influenced by the horizontal development of the melodic line. For the Christian, as for all religions, there is a consciousness of this synchronical component of life. The fundamental issue between the secularist and the non-secularist, and this issue will emerge in the second section of the chapter, is whether the "score" of life is merely a unilineal one and thus must be read diachronically, or whether indeed the "score" is an orchestral score, and must therefore be read diachronically *and* synchronically.

It would seem that the process of secularization has thus forced Christianity to re-orient its perspective, to take on a much less dogmatic and more open-textured conceptual and behavioural pattern without necessarily forfeiting the factor of commitment. It has forced Christianity to forfeit the appearance of logical or ontological constraint which it assumed in the past. But when secularization comes to the point of challenging the very logical or ontological possibility of what faith is committed to verifying, then the epistemological and metaphysical assumptions of the process of secularization become the focus of attention.

THE ABOLITION OF ECCLESIASTICAL POWER

In the Western world the church has in recent centuries generally been regarded as the prime agent of sacralization and mystification. At the close of the Middle Ages the relationship of the Catholic church to the spheres of politics, economics, social mobility, and culture generally was a dominative, restrictive, and basically dysfunctional one. However, it would be possible to dispute and even refute this generalization in specific instances. The generalization would be less true as one progressed further back into history in the ages when, although the church, through the monasteries and ecclesiastical-civil administrators, dominated large areas of Europe after the disintegration of the Roman Empire, it nevertheless mediated the overall cultural development of the barbarian tribes up to the thirteenth century.

From the thirteenth century onwards, the Catholic church proved to be an obstacle to the development of the nation states, of economic rationalization, and of scientific progress. Max Weber and R. H. Tawney have shown the affinity between the rise of capitalism and the Protestant theology.[51] Yet the roots of capitalism and science must be traced further back into Christian history. As Alfred North Whitehead has pointed out:

The Middle Ages formed one long training of the intellect of Western Europe in the sense of order. There may have been some deficiency in respect to practice. But the idea never for a moment lost its grip. It was pre-eminently an epoch of orderly thought, rationalist through and through ... I do not think, however, that I have yet brought out the greatest contribution of medievalism to the formation of the scientific movement. I mean the inexpugnable belief that every detailed occurrence can be correlated with its antecedents in a perfectly definite manner, exemplifying general principles. Without this belief the incredible labours of scientists would be without hope.[52]

While this may be true, this kind of function of the church in relation to science tended to be a latent one. By the mid-nineteenth century the Catholic church appeared to be ideologically opposed to the clearly emerging secular, liberal, and scientific values and insights, and yearning for the cultural context in which it exercised greater power. But in spite of its often strident protests the world of politics, economics, and culture generally became emancipated not only from its dominion but also from its influence.

The actual situation, however, varies from nation to nation, and the relation of each church, denomination, or sect to the culture in which it exists varies enormously. Some of the churches which were agents of the emancipation of various social components and forces from the domination of the Catholic church soon established a dominative role of a different kind and in more limited spheres in their own right. It is possible to assert nevertheless that there has been a process of evolution which represents the decline of the power and influence, even in specifically religious concerns, of the formal ecclesiastical establishments. There are three important descriptions and evaluations of this decline:

a) Pitirim Sorokin sees the process in an unfavourable light for he regards it as having resulted in a "sensate" cultural orientation in which material values are regarded as the only real ones and the only significant aims: worldly success, power, and hedonistic gratification. He interprets the development of history from the high Middle Ages until the present as a process of decline towards complete irreligiousness mediated by the various forms of Protestantism. Nevertheless he repudiates an "ideational" cultural orientation in which unquestionable primacy is given to transcendental values and seeks an "idealistic" orientation in which a balance is maintained between the two sets of values.[53]

b) Robert Bellah on the other hand traces a process of religious evolution from the state of identification of religion with reality among the primitives, through the domination and legitimation of the existing social order in the Middle Ages to the modern situation in which he is almost "tempted to see in Thomas Paine's 'My mind is my church' or Thomas Jefferson's 'I am a sect myself' the typical expression of religious organization in the near future". His final evaluation is:

> This [freedom] has been characterized as a collapse of meaning and a failure of moral standards. No doubt the possibilities for pathological distortion in the modern situation are enormous. It remains to be seen whether the freedom modern society implies at the cultural and personality as well as the social level can be stably institutionalized in large-scale societies.[54]

c) Talcott Parsons sees the evolution of the relationship between the church and culture as involving two interrelated aspects —on the one hand a lessening of the tension between the church and the world precisely because many, even most, Christian values have become institutionalized in society itself; on the other hand "the principle of religious toleration, inherent in the system of denominational pluralism, implies a great further extension of the institutionalization of Christian values, both inside and outside the sphere of religious organization".[55]

While it is probably not true that the declining influence of the church represents a process of general cultural decline it is probably true that Bellah's and Parsons' assessment of the present cultural (in the comprehensive anthropological sense) situation is rather too euphoric. The important point however is not an assessment of the cultural standard but the relationship of the church to the culture. If it is the case that in the United States, as has been claimed,[56] there has emerged a political-social-economic leviathan, and if it is the case that Christianity is something more than a means for adjusting people emotionally and psychologically to a culture, the problem arises as to how the church maintains a *critical distance* from the culture. If each man is his own sect, or if denominational pluralism the ideal, it seems difficult to see how the church can avoid becoming completely assimilated into the prevailing cultural fabric. Even the critical distance provided by its futuristic perspective will not be sufficient to allow for any significant political and cultural leverage unless there is a minimum degree of ecclesiastical identity and coherence. The emerging situation of the last few years in America has revealed clearly the potential role of the church, not as a dominator of society but as a critic of or a stimulus to society. A complete atomization and destructuring of the church, so that the church no longer influences its members over against the culture of which they are part, results in its becoming merely a function of that culture.

The process of secularization has had a profound effect on magic, myth, metaphysics, and religion. It has highlighted many of the cultural dysfunctions of these phenomena. Yet in seeking to eliminate these, it tended also to eliminate or ignore some of the persisting problems to which these phenomena were responses.

B. The Positive Component of Secularization: The Rationalization of Culture

In this section the aim will be to examine the agents and the sources of secularization in its positive dimension. It is expected that a close scrutiny of the agents of secularization will reveal a peculiar ambiguity, namely that while acting as agents of the demystification of Western culture these agents revealed aspects which themselves called for secularization or demystification and thus led to fundamental doubts and misgivings about the process of secularization and rationalization of culture.

For the sake of tidiness the scope of this enquiry will be limited to the Western world since the thirteenth century, beginning thus with a "traditional" society dominated by a single religion.

Two orders of agents of rationalization can be distinguished. The first order of agents was of fundamental cultural movements without a high degree of reflective self-consciousness. These movements led to the break-up of the traditional society of Christendom with varying degrees of suddenness and violence and having a variety of time spans. Among these could be listed, extending to the middle of the twentieth century:

a) The geographical revolution, beginning with the Crusades, the great voyages of discovery, through to the conquest of space. The barely perceived consequence of this was a relativization of human religions, cultures, and values.

b) The economic revolution, which replaced distribution of goods according to traditional status by distribution based on the market mechanism and contract. This complex revolution, extending to the industrial revolution and the automation and cybernization of production, has in principle brought man to the stage where scarcity, economy, and the need to win his bread by the sweat of his brow are obsolete.

c) The political revolutions, which time and again overthrew the order of things blessed by tradition and religion. Until the nineteenth century these were often inspired by movements at least partly religious. Since then the more radical forms of political change have taken on an anti-religious complexion. As H. Richard Niebuhr has pointed out:

> It is a striking fact that the revolutionary tendencies of the poor in the nineteenth century were almost completely secular in character . . . In any other century of Christian history this failure to keep alive the promise of social amelioration through Christian ethics and by divine miracle might have had less far-reaching results.[57]

d) The social revolutions consequent on both the economic and political revolutions led to a radical acceleration of social mobility. Status depended less on birth than on worth.

e) The communications and educational revolutions made the information and the wisdom of the ages available to all and made more difficult the intellectual and spiritual domination of the many by the few. Education helped eliminate areas of privileged access to knowledge and thus helped eradicate the possibility of mystification.

The second and more proximate agents of rationalization were science and modern philosophy. This is not to claim that these were merely epiphenomenal to the cultural movements mentioned above. Often these movements arose from and depended on the discoveries of the scientists or the writings of the philosophers. Yet it was in and through science and philosophy that the attitudes and values implicit in or precipitated by these movements became more self-consciously delineated and articulated. In and through science and philosophy the process of rationalization was applied more systematically and came to scrutinize and criticize, and thus came into conflict with, the thought patterns of traditional society. Through science and modern philosophy, man developed that critical self-awareness and reflective consciousness of the biological, psychological, economic, and social laws which led him to the present century and to an awareness of his potential mastery over the direction all of these movements should take in the future.

THE EVOLUTION OF SCIENCE

By following briefly the course of the history of science it will be possible to see how it affected magic, myth, metaphysics, and religion as the prime agent of secularization, how it was instrumental in eroding them but how, in the last analysis, this process of elimination was not completely successful. An inductive historical approach is necessary to this topic because of the difficulty of defining science and of the still rather prevalent tendency to speak of it as "Science".

Herbert Butterfield has said of the scientific revolution that "it outshines anything since the rise of Christianity and reduces the Renaissance and the Reformation to the rank of mere episodes, mere internal displacements within the system of medieval Christendom".[58] This difference between our age and any other age is that the scientific way of looking at things is a dominant, all pervasive outlook. In previous ages, in traditional societies, a great deal of the knowledge necessary for survival and some control over the immediate physical environment was empirical knowledge, and distinguishable from magic, as Malinowski has pointed out. However, nearly always such scientific beginnings were drawn up into or made part of a world outlook which was mythical or metaphysical, an outlook which could not be modified by observation and hence which restricted the empirical and the technical to a limited area.

Some order in empirical knowledge appears in the records of ancient Egypt and Babylon — units and rules of measurement, simple arithmetic, a calendar of the year, the recognition of the periodicity of astronomic events, even of eclipses . . . But at an early stage, men almost universally took a wrong path. Led by the idea that like produces like, they tried by imitating nature in rites of sympathetic magic to bring rain or sunshine, or fertility to the teeming earth . . . The first to submit such knowledge to rational examination, to try to trace causal relations among its parts, in fact the first to create science, were the Greek nature philosophers of Ionia. The earliest and most successful of such attempts was the conversion of the empirical rules for land surveying, mostly derived from Egypt, into the deductive science of geometry . . . But with the rise of the Athenian school of Socrates and Plato, the Ionian nature-philosophy was superseded by metaphysics. The Greek mind became entranced with its own operations, and turned from the study of nature to look within.[59]

Before the scientific revolution, questions of fact were settled by the power of authority, whether the authority was that of the church, the Bible or the ancients, or by the power of the human mind to deduce the answers by a rational process which had little to do with the processes of observation. During the later Middle Ages the authority of Aristotle in every branch of learning was almost as powerful and all-pervasive as that of the church, and questions ranging from the structure and physiology of plants and animals to the behaviour of the planets were settled by reference to him. Indeed Alan Richardson has made out a very plausible case for the view that the opposition to science, "this entirely new venture of the human spirit", which developed at the time of Galileo Galilei arose specifically not from ecclesiastical sources but from the Aristotelian cosmologists.[60]

To understand, however, the significance of the revolution it is necessary to examine briefly some of the characteristics of the mediaeval mind. An examination of these characteristics will allow us to see remnants of the mediaeval way of looking at things not only where they could be expected to persist, namely among the churches, but also among the overtly secular institutions of contemporary culture. Johan Huizinga thus describes the mediaeval way of viewing the world:

The mental habits and forms characteristic of the high speculation of the Middle Ages nearly all reappear in the domain of ordinary life. Here, too, as we might expect, primitive idealism, which the schools called realism, is at the bottom of all mental activity. To take every idea by itself, to give it its formula, to treat it as an entity, next to combine the ideas, to classify them, to arrange them in hierarchic systems, always to build cathedrals with them, such, in practical life also, is the way in which the medieval mind proceeds.[61]

And again:

If the medieval mind wants to know the nature or the reason of a thing, it neither looks into it, to analyse its structure, nor behind it, to enquire into its origin, but looks up to heaven, where it shines as an idea ... Whatever the faculty of seeing specific traits may have been in the Middle Ages, it must be noted that men disregarded the individual qualities and fine distinctions of things, deliberately and of set purpose, in order always to bring them under some general principle. People feel an imperious need of always and especially seeing the general sense, the connection with the absolute, the moral ideality, the ultimate significance of a thing. What is important is the impersonal. The mind is not in search of individual realities, but of models, examples, norms. Every notion concerning the world or life had its fixed place in a vast hierarchic system of ideas, in which it linked with ideas of a higher and more general order, on which it depends like a vassal on his lord.[62]

In this way of viewing the world, it was very difficult for the data of experience to modify the conceptualized structure of the real. The data of experience were "allegorized". Any disparity between the formalized structure of ideas and the data of experience was bridged by the technique of allegory. Things did not represent themselves; events were not what they appeared to be. A lion, for example, held little interest as a lion, and because the reality was valuable only as an opportunity to provide an illustration of the order of things, it could serve equally well to represent Christ "the lion of Judah" or the devil "going about seeking whom he may devour". Fundamental to the scientific revolution, therefore, was the increasingly systematic process of looking at things in themselves and of examining them without reference to what someone else had said about them and without the literary or psychological transposition of these things to relate them to a theoretical order of ideas. It was inevitable, therefore, that as this systematic examination of things progressed, conflict would result with the prevailing theoretical order which had been built from materials deriving from biblical and Greek cosmology, Greek metaphysics and a wide variety of adapted mythological forms.

The scientific revolution can be said to have begun with the publication of Francis Bacon's *Novum Organum* in 1620 and Isaac Newton's *Principia Mathematica* in 1687. The leaders of the scientific revolution were Christians and in spite of the condemnation of Galileo by the Inquisition and the persecution of Johannes Kepler by the Protestant theology faculty at Tübingen, and in spite of the inevitable theoretical tensions which were developing, the early stage of the scientific revolution did not appear to be—to the scientists at least—fundamentally incompatible with the Christian faith.

The crisis of the scientific revolution, the first real confrontation, was precipitated, not by the scientists, but by the literary champions of science in the eighteenth century age of Enlightenment. The response of the churches to the challenge of the philosophers of the Enlightenment was basically negative and the science-religion conflict became increasingly polarized. However, to understand the nature of the conflict, how the conflict led to a profound modification of religious thought, and the possibility of the resolution of the conflict, it is necessary first of all to distinguish the three main stages in the development of science itself:

a) In the first stage, covering the period from 1620 until the mid-nineteenth century, scientific activity was concentrated on inanimate nature: chemistry, physics, and astronomy. Science seemed to offer, not just an area of human knowledge, but a paradigm for human knowledge in which exactitude, clarity, and certainty were possible, and thus offered an alternative to religious and philosophical forms of knowledge which led, especially during the wars of religion and the political revolutions, to violence and bloodshed. Science was confident that it could uncover the basic elements and laws of reality and that this knowledge could then be universally applied. In this phase scientism, rather than science itself, tended to be static, certain, and dogmatically materialistic and mechanistic.

b) In the second phase, the focus of scientific study shifted to include man with the development of a less polemical study of history, of the sciences of anthropology, economics, psychology, and sociology. There were, and still continue to be, attempts to reduce these sciences to elements which can be handled with the exactitude and precision of the physical sciences. The failure revealed the radical discontinuity between nature, whether inanimate or biological, and human activities. Even though the latter were approached with objectivity and with the methods appropriate to the physical sciences, clarity, unanimity, and certitude in the human sphere remained elusive. Though the "social" sciences have not achieved full recognition as sciences, and though, as sciences, they occupy an inferior position, nevertheless the failure of the social sciences to fulfill the ambition of clarity and certitude has blunted the eliminating cutting edge and the early brash dogmatism of scientism.

c) In the third phase even the physical sciences were stripped of many of their fundamental certitudes. The great theological synthesis of the Middle Ages had been built on the absolute foundation of revelation and authority. The great scientific synthesis of the nineteenth century had been built on the absolute foundation of the direct observation of the fundamental unit of matter, the atom. But a period of scientific revolution occurred at the beginning of the twentieth century.

In that enormous liberating revolution of the first twenty-five years of physics in this century, we came to realize that the very foundations of our subject were being removed from us. Physics had been built on the concept of mass and velocity, whose study is mechanics, and on the concept of ether and its electric forces, whose study is electro-dynamics; and on the concept of the continuity of measurement, so that it should be possible in principle to trace the gradual changes which come over any system or systems, and so illustrate the law of cause and effect. Stage by stage every one of these convictions has been stripped off us. Einstein's relativity showed us that there was no such thing as an absolute position, or an absolute velocity, and that the same body would not appear to have the same mass to two observers who were travelling at different speeds relative to it. The experiments of Michelson and Morley showed us that there was no substantial ether through which our solar system travelled, and that electric and magnetic forces depended on how the experimenter moved. Heisenberg's famous Uncertainty Principle underlined what every psychologist knew in his heart . . . that no one person could ever exactly repeat the same experiment, nor could two different people ever make exactly the same measurement . . . One reason why no measurement could be repeated, with exactly identical results, was that the act of measurement, whether in psychology or physics, altered the system measured. The observer was not, and could never hope to be, independent of the thing that he observed. To ask a question of nature was to affect her, to change her . . .[63]

Science, therefore, did not provide either a fixed immutable vantage point *from which* to criticize, nor an impeccable technique *with which* to criticize all cosmic and human phenomena. The increasing realization of the implications of Darwinian evolution, of the influence of the subconscious on all human activity revealed by Freud, and of the economic conditioning to which all human epiphenomena are liable described by Marx, have all had the cumulative effect of making men cautious about any claims to having an absolute criterion or an incorrigible critical device.[64]

This is not to claim, however, that science in all its forms has not had a profound clarifying and even scarifying effect on culture generally, and has not served to eliminate a great deal of the magical, mythical, metaphysical, and religious superstructure of human culture. It is not to claim that the very doubts to which science has in this century been subjected have arisen from metaphysical or religious sources primarily. They have arisen from the very development or evolution of science itself. In a way, science has been the agent of its own secularization and de-mystification. The development of science has led to a new understanding of what the process of "rationalization" entails. The question that needs to be examined is whether, in the last analysis, religion and science are proceeding on an either-or collision course, so that the latter inevitably, at least in principle or in the ideal human situation, demands the elimination of the former.

It should be illuminating, therefore, to examine more closely just what it is that any science does and how it goes about its task:

a) In the first place, the appropriate scientific stance or posture is one of detachment. The scientist must assume or create a distance from what he is studying. There immediately results a crucial difference between scientific activity and life, that is, specifically human life. This feature will be examined later on when the role of existentialism in relation to contemporary sensibility is examined. This perspective is necessary for scientific activity, but if it becomes a normative ideology for living or a life-style, the result can be analogous to the disparity between reality and results when a zoologist seeks to study the physiology of an organism by the exclusive use of dead specimens for his investigation.

b) What is the characteristic thrust and direction of science? Initially, as has been seen, science was the habit of looking at things as they were in themselves and a corrective of the mediaeval tendency to see things through an allegorizing prism. But science has since then resulted in an increasingly rapid ramification of specializations, an increased differentiation of consciousness and dissection of reality. Its basic objective is analysis and when a synthesis or "model" is constructed, its function is to facilitate further analysis, in pure science, or the achievement of a specific result in applied science or technology.

c) What does science get at, ultimately? Up until this century the physical sciences, at least, hoped to isolate and describe the behaviour of the basic units of reality. This hope has receded. As Werner Heisenberg has expressed it:

When we represent a group of connections by a closed and coherent set of concepts, axioms, definitions and laws which in turn is represented by a mathematical scheme, we have in fact isolated and idealized this group of connections with the purpose of clarification. But even if complete clarity had been achieved in this way, it is not known how accurately the set of concepts describes reality.[65]

This indicates the extent to which science has been subjected to a kind of secularizing process since the middle of last century. The difference between the symbol-creating activity of the scientist and that of the primitive is that the symbol system of the scientist produces better results and produces them more predictably.

d) It is of central importance to this chapter to understand the role played in science by symbol-creation. The mathematical symbol system has been, in many ways, the mythology of science. Initially it was thought that science would uncover the structure of reality and the ambition, in many ways fulfilled, grew of expressing this structure and the relationships within it with and in the clarity, accuracy, and precision of mathematical formulae. The tendency was to presume that the structure of the mathematical symbol system reflected the structure of the real. But then it was discovered at the beginning of this century that there can be different and conflicting mathematical systems, having fundamental axioms which contradict those of the other systems, being complete and coherent within themselves and capable of use as symbol systems in astrophysics and nuclear physics. Thus in astro-physics, "once criteria of congruence are agreed on, then the choice of a geometry becomes a completely empirical matter".[66] The principle of selection among mathematical systems becomes how best to manipulate reality, rather than reveal or represent it, to get the results desired or achieve prescribed goals.

Before the function of mathematics in science was realized, however, the tendency was to presume that what could not be reduced to a mathematical expression or its equivalent had no truth value. This was what could be called the reductionist phase in science. It is this aspect of the scientific revolution which leaves no room for myth, metaphysics, or religion, nor for poetry, drama, or literature. As we will see in the next section, it was this aspect of science which received its strongest expression in logical positivism. However, physical science now tends to see the reduction or transposition of the terms of a problem into mathematical symbols as a device to control, rather than an explanation of, reality.

e) It is also illuminating to recall from the history of science that scientific conclusions of importance have not been reached precisely by inductive and discursive processes. Many of the great scientific discoveries have involved "a leap of the mind", an intuitive element which appears out of character with the usual demand that an approach to the solution of a problem be scientific:

It is a popular delusion that the scientific enquirer is under an obligation not to go beyond generalization of observed facts . . . but anyone who is practically acquainted with scientific work is aware that those who refuse to go beyond the facts, rarely get so far.[67]

f) Closely related to (*d*) is the question of the relationship of the biological and social sciences to the physical sciences and especially to mathematical symbol systems. In many ways this problem is an expression of the problem of determinism versus freedom and nature versus history. The tendency of scientists with a deterministic outlook is to attempt to reduce the varieties of human behaviour to a higher and more complex instance of the forms of behaviour of the lower forms of biological or physical activity and to express it, if not in mathematical equations, at least in univocal terms. The reductionist tendency has declined primarily because reductionist attempts have failed on purely scientific grounds. There appear to be great discontinuities among the three levels of science. It seems that one's answer as to whether this situation will ever be different depends on whether one is inclined to a deterministic view of human behaviour or to the view that man has a radically unpredictable component called freedom. In the meantime:

Social science must have its own criteria of intelligibility, and these almost certainly will not be reducible to those of physics and chemistry. It makes its claim to being a science not because it can demonstrate its continuity with the physical sciences, nor even because it satisfies the oft quoted and very misleading definition "science is measurement", but because of the method it employs. *Science is fundamentally an attitude of mind, a way of approaching problems.*[68]

g) It would seem that science, and especially its application in technology, is related to an analysis or examination of what is given, of what already exists, or to the solution of problems about how goals are to be achieved. What is the function of science or technology in relation to the formulation of future goals or the direction that the human race, in conscious possession of the various forces revealed by science, should take? For Jacques Ellul in *The Technological Society,* technology has become the metaphysics of the twentieth century; it has eliminated ends in making mechanical techniques an all-pervasive end in themselves. "It is, in fact, the essence of technique to compel the qualitative to become quantitative, and in this way force every stage of human activity and man himself to submit to its mathematical calculations."[69] Ellul sees technology, the integrated and comprehensive complex of techniques ranging from politics to sport, as a monism eliminating the dimension of human freedom and responsibility. Man does not determine goals for society, the functioning of the mechanism is the only goal. "The complete separation of the goal from the mechanism, the limitation of the problem to the means, and the refusal to interfere in any way with efficiency; all this . . . lies at the basis of technical autonomy."[70]

This view tends to see the evolution of man as the change from domination by myths, then by metaphysics, then by mathematics, to the present domination by mechanical means or technology; it sees man's history not as progress, but as a journey into an increasingly arid waste land. Yet an alternative interpretation is possible, that the increasingly automatic means of production and control of the environment allows man the opportunity for genuine personal freedom and creativity. This more optimistic view, however, seems to exclude man from specifically social freedom and creativity by sharing in a determination of the general political, economic, and cultural goals of society.

The present cultural situation is therefore ambiguous. While it is possible to perceive a process of secularization of science at the more theoretical level, it is also possible, as Ellul suggests, that technology has become, in many countries of the Western world, the contemporary metaphysics.

Nevertheless it is possible to say that science has effected a prevailing attitude of mind and a way of approaching problems which is unique in history. In essence it is the *inductive* attitude of mind or approach to problems. It is an attitude which is appropriate to an evolutionary human situation. This inductive quality of human consciousness and sensibility has profoundly affected the Christian outlook and posture. Yet when the inductive approach is distinguished from the process of reduction used as an explanation rather than as an illustrative device, it need not necessarily be incompatible with Christianity. The difference would lie in the radically different kind of problem to which Christianity and science would respond by inductive procedures, and in the degree of personal involvement in the procedure. In science the person remains for the most part detached, only his analytical mind is engaged, whereas in religion the person is existentially engaged, that is, in every aspect and dimension of his being.

THE RISE AND DECLINE OF PHILOSOPHICAL POSITIVISM

British analytic philosophy of this century epitomizes, and states in the most formidable way, the challenge the secular age poses to religion of any kind. In logical atomism and logical positivism were distilled all the elements of the complex movements of the secular age calculated to erode the very foundations of metaphysics and religion. This philosophy in its most aggressive phase claimed that the problems to which religion purported to respond were ephemeral—illusions created by the ambiguities of language. It developed an epistemology which rendered all religions and/or metaphysical assertions either tautologous or meaningless. However, a process of secularization, analogous to that described in the recent history of science, a self-induced process, began to emerge to modify and dissipate the anti-religious and anti-metaphysical quality of this philosophical tradition. This philosophy had to come to terms with human complexity. " 'To be modern' in Europe and America is to give up simple explanations of man and the world, to embrace complexity once and for all, and to try, somehow, to manage it. Modern philosophy is a philosophy of complexity and of disillusionment."[71]

It is important to trace this process of disillusionment in the philosophy of positivism for two reasons. In the first place it has become the implicit, scarcely articulated ideology of many people in the Western world. In the second place, though the advocates of secularization such as Harvey Cox are careful to distinguish between secularization as a process and secularism as an ideology, there seem to be operating, though in a latent way, in the concept of secularization, important elements of the positivistic outlook and epistemology.[72]

It was the ambition of René Descartes in posing the critical problem of knowledge to develop a philosophy which would enjoy the clarity, the rigour, and the cogency of mathematics. Since the time of Descartes modern philosophy has fallen into two broad divisions: the idealistic, which in this century has been rather generally and unanimously repudiated as deductive metaphysics, and the empiricist or positivistic tradition. The mainstream of English philosophy is a continuation of the profound revolution initiated by John Locke and David Hume. It carries Hume's empiricism to its logical conclusions.

It is understandable that English philosophy, which has always shown a distinctly more empirical than metaphysical character, should at the beginning of this century have been rather deeply influenced by the progress of science. The first symptom of this influence was a strong anti-metaphysical tone. The second symptom was an enthusiasm for the belief that there are basic units of language and life, basic *atoms*. This resulted in the attempt to reduce language and life to these units. Dalton's atomic physics still prevailed. Rutherford's work had not yet shown, in the domain of physics, that this ambition was possibly futile. A similar ambition was to beguile English philosophy for most of the first half of the century.

In the first instance, the analytic movement in British philosophy was a reaction to the Neo-Hegelianism of F. H. Bradley, for Bradley was in a sense the last of the metaphysicians. At the same time, however, the growth in the number of scientists and the extent of science posed a challenge to philosophy to state clearly what it studied and the methods it used. As Gilbert Ryle pointed out:

This challenge was made all the more serious by the rapid advance of studies in the logic of mathematics, the logic of probable and statistical reasoning, the logic of induction and the methodology of the social sciences. The era which produced Boole, de Morgan, Mill, Jerons, Frege, Nann, Bradley, Pierce, Russell and Whitehead had been equipping itself with criteria of cogency which philosophical thinking would find it hard to satisfy. Sterile of demonstrable theorems, sterile of experimentally testable hypotheses, philosophy was to face the charge of being sterile.[73]

Faced with this challenge, British philosophers in this century have, with virtual unanimity, conceded that philosophy, qua philosophy, is factually uninformative, and concentrated their attention on meaning. Philosophers became progressively more aware of the difficulties in communication among people, even in the communication of factual information, which arise from language itself. Hence philosophy began to focus on language rather than on facts about the world, and more specifically on meaning. Philosophers sought the meaning, not of words or ideas, as Locke and Hume had done, but of propositions or statements. The method used to arrive at meaning was analysis. Hence the function of philosophy became the analysis of the meaning of language.

In 1914 Bertrand Russell published *Logic as the Essence of Philosophy* in which he claimed that if only we can succeed in understanding the way we talk and think about the ordinary world, we shall not be led to reject it for another world behind it. As we shall see, this opposition to the tendency to appeal to hidden realities, entities behind the scenes, a supra-sensible world to explain this one, is among the basic concerns of the British philosophy of this century.

Russell laid the foundation for an understanding of how we think and talk about this world in *Principia Mathematica,* written in association with A. M. Whitehead. In this book they demonstrated the incompleteness of the traditional Aristotelian logic and developed a new type of logic of which the Aristotelian logic was but a small section. This new logic was a logic of propositions or statements and not a logic of classes as the traditional one had been. It was based on and examined the connections between statements. The Aristotelian logic had examined the relationship between classes or categories. From this development emerged the claim that the inadequacy of Aristotelian logic had helped sustain the illusion of the validity of metaphysics.

Russell's work was revolutionary and exciting because it sought to show that mathematics is a part of logic and demonstrated that "natural" languages such as English have a basic structure similar to that of *Principia Mathematica*. However, he claimed, these "natural" languages are less precise and hence defective when it comes to philosophical analysis. This need for precise philosophical tools gave rise to the ambition of constructing a logically perfect language in which it would be possible to discourse with perfect clarity and understanding and which would not give rise to the confusions which some thought were the sources of the traditional problems of philosophy. Russell thus explains the advantages of a logically perfect language:

The purpose of discussion of an ideal logical language — which would be wholly useless for daily life — is twofold: first, to prevent inferences from the nature of language to the nature of the world, which are fallacious because they depend on logical defects of language; secondly, to suggest, by inquiring what logic requires of a language to avoid contradiction, what sort of a structure we may reasonably suppose the world to have.[74]

In the last part of the quotation, there is suggested the central element of Russell's philosophy, at this juncture, that his logically perfect language is a representation of the structure of the universe. This is made more explicit in his reduction of all sentences to atomic sentences. Russell claimed that though a logically perfect language could not be used, the molecular or complex statements of "natural languages" could be reduced to atomic propositions which in turn represent atomic facts.

Philosophical analysis in this scheme of things consisted in breaking down the molecular statements into their atomic components. However, some paradoxes were soon revealed. Sentences of the kind "The present King of France is wise" and "God exists" posed problems which Russell solved, or claimed to solve, in his theory of descriptions. Essential to this theory is the distinction between the grammatical form of a sentence and its logical form. Sometimes the grammatical form can confuse us about its proper logical form. Once we have settled on the appropriate logical form the process of analysis is less difficult. Thus in the case of "God exists", the proper logical form is that "God" is the predicate and "exists" is what Russell called a "logical quantifier" having the same function as an indefinite pronoun. Hence properly expressed in logical form "God exists" says: "something, and only one thing, is omnipotent, omniscient and benevolent". This process of analysis reveals the sentence "God exists" to be, logically speaking, a general sentence of an entirely different structure from that of an atomic sentence. As it cannot be analysed into an atomic sentence it tells us nothing about the world or about a real God.

This way of doing philosophy or this system of analysis is called logical atomism. It received its most complete and comprehensive statement in Ludwig Wittgenstein's *Tractatus Logico-Philosophicus* in which was developed the picture theory of meanings. For Wittgenstein, the ideal language mirrored the world just as a map mirrors the terrain—it mirrors the structure of reality. For every proper name in the language there is a corresponding entity, and for every predicate a corresponding property. The ideal language thus gives us the structure of facts since facts are composed of objects and their properties.

However, before long it became clear, and Russell was among the first to recognize it, that both Russell and Wittgenstein were no longer analysing language to find or clarify meaning. They were reducing language to categories and forms according to criteria they had selected as tests of meaningfulness. In selecting criteria, they were committing the same fault they set out to correct, namely, the making of metaphysical assumptions. The basic and most arrant piece of metaphysics was Russell's assumption that the structure of *Principia Mathematica* reflects the structure of reality.

For what Russell and Wittgenstein did in this period was to glimpse traces of a pattern in our experience, and then, taking their eyes off the facts, to develop this pattern far beyond what it warranted by the facts . . . The logical atomists, like other metaphysicians, were seeking clarity and order, and where they failed to discover clarity and order, they invented them.[75]

A new but somewhat complementary phase in British philosophy was the development of logical positivism. This began as a movement among a group of philosophers in Austria known as the Vienna Circle. It included Moritz Schlick, Friedrich Waismann, Rudolf Carnap, Otto Neurath, and Herbert Feigl. The movement was introduced to the English-speaking world in A. J. Ayer's *Language, Truth and Logic*. Logical positivism was militantly anti-metaphysical; it summarized, philosophically, the confidence and the dogmatism of science as an ideology, and gave a formula for the expression of this as an exclusive cast of mind. In one way or another and more or less explicitly, the philosophy of logical positivism has spread throughout the English-speaking world and continues to exert considerable influence.

Though it has been stated in a variety of ways, the basic tenet of logical positivism is that the meaning of a proposition consists in the method of its verification. If there is no method of verifying a proposition then it is meaningless. Logical positivists allowed only two kinds of cognitive or meaningful assertions:

a) Analytic propositions, definitions, or tautologies, that is, the propositions of logic or mathematics which contain in themselves their own meaning.

b) Synthetic propositions which can be verified empirically or reduced to observable phenomena.

There was no scope in this scheme of things for theological discourse, for the assertions of theology must be either tautologies or meaningless. In the last analysis, theological discussion can never even begin because the question "Does God exist?" cannot be asked. It is meaningless.[76]

Gradually, however, it became clear that logical positivism was the victim of its own harsh criteria of meaningfulness. Its fundamental weakness, in its strong and iconoclastic form, is the twofold weakness already observed in logical atomism. It is reductionist rather than analytic and its basic assumption is a piece of metaphysics. The verification principle, the basic criterion and eliminative device is itself neither a definition nor a synthetic proposition, hence must be meaningless. J. O. Urmson sums up the fundamental weakness of the logical positivist position:

> While abandoning the metaphysics of logical atomism, at least officially and in intention, the logical empiricists (positivists) retained substantially the same view of the scope and nature of analysis; but it was now conceived as revealing the logical structure of the language of science, of informative discourse, not of the facts with which science deals. Roughly the same propositions remained basic under both dispensations, whether they were said to picture facts or not, and roughly the same things remained as logical constructions.[77]

Some of the logical positivists, including A. J. Ayer, claimed that the verification principle was, indeed, merely a definition purporting to lay down the conditions which actually govern our acceptance and our understanding of common sense and scientific statements.

> This leaves it open to the metaphysician (and the theologian) to reply that there are other worlds besides the world of science and common sense . . . But then the onus is on him to show by what criterion his statements are to be tested: until he does this we do not know how to take them.[78]

Ludwig Wittgenstein, who is also regarded, in his early period, as a logical positivist, is more uncompromising in his attitude to the status of the verification principle:

> My propositions serve as elucidations in the following way: anyone who understands me eventually recognizes them as nonsensical, when he has used them — as steps — to climb up beyond them. (He must, so to speak, throw away the ladder after he has climbed up it.) He must transcend these propositions, and then he will see the world aright. What we cannot speak about we must consign to silence.[79]

A number of attempts were made to give an account of the language of theology and of religion in the context of an acceptance of the verification principle interpreted in its most rigorous sense.[80] These resulted in the reduction of religious discourse to rather extravagant and rhetorical ways of speaking about emotional states, moral intentions, or exhortations to follow a particular life-style. And yet there is a sense in which any religious discourse must conform to the requirement that the meaning of assertions should consist in the method of their verification. The meaning of all Christian theological assertions is contingent on the total commitment of the person and their verification eschatologically. The conflict arises first of all because Christians often think, or appear to think, that theological assertions are verified by reference to past events or by some kind of vertical and privileged access to another world of specifically religious experience. It arises secondly when positivists demand that these assertions be verified through a mode of personal disengagement and by the reduction of the terms of the assertion to mathematical or univocal symbols.

However, analytic philosophy moved beyond the phase of logical positivism, to the non-reductionist technique of the analysis of ordinary language developed by G. E. Moore. This technique approached the problems of the analysis of language aware of the pitfalls of reducing statements of one kind to statements of another kind or of condemning some classes of statements as meaningless, and cautions about applying implicit or explicit criteria based on metaphysical assumptions.

The basic insight and assumption of this group of philosophers is that "the fundamental task of language is human communication and not logical exactitude, that no logical analysis of language can ever approach the actual scope and flexibility of the language of everyday life. No abstract analysis can account for its changeability, its evolutions and its unpredictability."[81] The leaders of this school were John Austin, John D. Wisdom, Gilbert Ryle and the later Ludwig Wittgenstein.[82] There were no grand schemes, no attempts to arrive at a simple criterion of truth or meaning. Wittgenstein supplied the basic technique: "Don't ask for meaning, ask for use." In his *Philosophical Investigations* he introduced the idea of "language games". There are many kinds of language games played in everyday conversation. The task of the philosopher is to distinguish the various games, analyse their rules and classify their characteristics. His function is descriptive. He does not seek the essence of a language game or the essence of language or meaning. Confusion and pseudo-problems arise when games are confused or the rules of one game are introduced into another language game.

As a consequence of this new non-reductionist phase in British philosophy, theologians have the opportunity to speak without it being presumed that what they will say will inevitably be nonsense. John Macquarrie has observed: "This new approach to language at least gives religious language a reprieve."[83] The theologian has to make clear the rules of the theological language game and how this game is related to the other games which communicate in some way or another our experience.

The whole analytic tradition in philosophy has raised some crucial questions and issues for Christianity:

a) whether it is really possible to speak meaningfully about anything except what is intra-mundane

b) the danger of nonsense and mystification when there is any appeal to another world or to a specific experience as the foundation for the meaning of assertions called religious

c) the fact that in the past Christianity has permitted an extravagant baroque theological structure to develop by the logical and mystical interrelating of the various "mysteries" of the Christian religion without very much reference to experience or the careful use of words

d) whether it is possible to give assent or personal commitment to assertions made in another country, in another culture, in another age and under scarcely understood circumstances, and allow such assertions to exercise an important influence on personal decisions.

On the other hand, in this brief analysis of the recent history of positivistic philosophy, it is possible to detect a process of secularization, an erosion of the anti-religious and anti-metaphysical confidence which the empirical tradition displayed earlier this century. This process has revealed the ease with which metaphysical assumptions can underlie the most anti-metaphysical philosophy. It revealed the futility of reductive processes, for inevitably they rely on invalid criteria and eliminate dimensions of experience and the means of communicating them. Philosophy has thus been unable to reduce reality to a mathematically accountable simplicity. It has been forced to accept the complexity of reality, thought, and language while at the same time maintaining its right and its obligation to scrutinize and ruthlessly criticize each of these phenomena.

C. *Conclusion*

The process of secularization, therefore, is not essentially a negative, eliminating, and scarifying process. It can also be a humanizing and emancipating process. Interpreted in this way it can be seen as expanding the possibilities of being human by eradicating those factors which dominate and hence restrict the human potential. This does not necessarily mean the complete repudiation of rational or sub-rational systems in human life; it can mean that secularization leads to an appreciation of the proper role of rational systems, such as metaphysics, or myths in human life. Indeed, the uncovering of factors which dominate the human person is a process that is not likely to be finally accomplished at any given time. Just when man thinks he has been emancipated from the domination of myths and metaphysics, he often discovers that his autonomy is threatened by mathematics, cybernetics, technology or some other factor in life which almost surreptitiously takes on the character of an absolute. The history of recent human thought seems to teach that each technique in effecting some stage in the emancipation of man has appeared to be, in the first instance, an ultimate stage of human freedom, only to emerge a little later as itself also exercising an imperialistic dominion over the human person and creating its own myths.

At the close of the Middle Ages, the rationalization of human relationships through the exchange and distribution of goods in the open market effected the abolition of the myth of a person's value being determined by birth. In our century the open market itself has become a political and cultural myth, as has been demonstrated by John Kenneth Galbraith in *The New Industrial State,* and by the Catholic "new left" in *Slant Manifesto*.[84] The advocates of the process of secularization invariably describe the developed nations of the Western world as having achieved a democratic control over their internal and external environment in this century. Michael Harrington in *The Accidental Century*[85] in effect describes this conviction as a myth encouraged in the interests of the few. For the Slant group, the emancipation of the mass of people in the Western world from the crude exploitation of the early phase of the industrial revolution has given way to a more insidious form of *cultural* exploitation. More insidious, because whereas bad working conditions, poverty and hunger were likely to provoke rebellion, cultural exploitation—exercised through the mass media—is calculated to increase consumption and passivity:

The mass media, therefore, underpin capitalism: they confirm the worker in his passivity and alienation, and act as a safety-valve for his disruptive desires and emotions. They also feed him the kinds of social values and responses which result in acceptance of the capitalist status quo.[86]

For Galbraith, it has been in the interests of the new technostructure to maintain two important myths, that of the entrepreneur, "individualistic, restless, with vision, guile and courage . . . the economists' only hero", [87] and that of the source, in man's needs and desires, of economic motivation:

> This source of economic motivation is still celebrated in the formal liturgy of the system. But the system, if it accommodates to man's wants, also and increasingly accommodates men to its needs. And it must. This latter accommodation is no trivial exercise in salesmanship. It is deeply organic. High technology and heavy capital use cannot be subordinate to the ebb and flow of market demand. They require planning; it is the essence of planning that public behaviour be made predictable — that it be subject to control.[88]

And yet even this apparently closed monolithic system can lead, in a way analogous to that described in the development of science and positivistic philosophy, to a process of demystification and demythologization. As Galbraith goes on to point out:

> . . . while the commitment of the culture, under the tutelage of the industrial system, to a single-minded preoccupation with the production of goods is strong, it is not complete. Rising income also nurtures a further artistic and intellectual community outside of the industrial system.[89]

It is possible that the Hippie movement and the widespread student unrest throughout the world are symptoms of the refusal to accept the production-of-goods-consumption-of-goods culture which itself made this refusal economically possible and will prove to be the agent of its own demystification.

A similar process of analysis could be followed in relation to prevailing political myths and policies of political mystification. In Russia there is the enormous disparity between the political reality on the one hand and the authentic Marxist political and economic theory invoked to bolster and reinforce the reality on the other hand. In America there is the enormous disparity between "the American Dream" and the facts of American poverty, racial discrimination, crime, and war which never really count against the dream.

The point is that the process of secularization is an ever human task. When it is realized as such it can be appreciated as being, not an automatic and inevitable progression, but a conscious human duty through which man saves himself from the tutelage of the products of his own cleverness or from the consequences of his foolishness.

The levelling of man's world and the horizontalizing of his perspective does not necessarily lead to the exclusion of a "depth" or complexity of experience nor to the exclusion of the possibility of unique experiences which could be called "religious". What it does lead to is the elimination of factors totally transcending experience which are invoked to dominate or direct it. We can begin to see, therefore, that a positive and dogmatic atheism which is claimed to be an inevitable consequence of the process of secularization is not a quality of secularization as such but an ideological interpretation of the process of secularization. It is the claim that the full, free, and totally personal human experience *cannot* lead to or result in a relationship with or an awareness of a God. This is the kind of metaphysical domination from which the process of secularization is supposed to deliver us.

The final question is whether "secularization" is now an adequate term to describe some important and what could prove to be central cultural processes. In the first place, as Ronald Gregor-Smith has pointed out, the word has almost incurably anti-religious and anti-Christian overtones and associations.[90] Harvey Cox, Arend van Leeuwen, and Friedrich Gogarten claim that secularization has its sources in, and is a continuation of, the Judaeo-Christian tradition.[91] For Cox, the Genesis account of creation emphasizes man's dominion over creation, his responsibility for it and his task of continuing this work. Man is made in the image and likeness of God the creator. Cox calls the creation story "the disenchantment of nature", a cultural phenomenon unique to the Hebrews in a world where all men were in thrall to the powers of nature. He sees the Exodus story as the "desecularization of politics", the separation of the realm of the sacred from the realm of political activity.

Political change depends upon a previous desacralization of politics. The process is closely related to the disenchantment of nature. Since nature always repeats itself, while history never does, the emergence of history rather than nature as the locus of God's action opens a whole new world of possibilities for political and social change.[92]

Finally, in the covenant of Sinai, there is effected "the deconsecration of values". The function of Israel was to acknowledge the one true God and reject all idols. The effect of this covenant, according to Gabriel Vahamian, was to ensure

> a depletion of man's natural inclination to deify himself, or his society, or the state, or his culture . . . a relentless exposing of the manifold, constant proclivity to elevate the finite to the level of the infinite, to give the transitory the status of the permanent, and to attribute to man qualities that will deceive him into denying his finitude.[93]

But in spite of the claim that secularization has biblical sources, its development, at least since the Enlightenment, has proceeded in the context of Christian opposition. Nevertheless, as Shiner says of Gogarten:

> Although it is hard to accept as historically accurate Gogarten's contention that Christian faith stands in a causal relationship to secularization, his theological argument that faith is not only compatible with secularization but demands its continuance, remains intact.[94]

The real difficulty with the concept of secularization is not whether it is derived from or compatible with the Judaeo-Christian tradition, but whether it is an adequate conceptual tool for the dual task of creative criticism of the Judaeo-Christian tradition on the one hand, and the cultural context of this tradition on the other.

The claim I want to make is that it is an inadequate conceptual tool for the following reasons:

a) It implies a unilineal, diachronical perspective and tends to depend on an historical typology which functions as a set of metaphysical assumptions, as was pointed out earlier.[95]

b) It implies a reductionist propensity, for definitions of secularization do not usually acknowledge the important self-induced modifications which have eventuated in science and positivistic philosophy in recent years. The process of secularization is invariably defined on the one hand in terms of the elimination or reduction of human phenomena which are not described in univocal language, and on the other in terms of rationalization, as involving a strict logico-mathematical-univocal language.

c) It seems to rely on a concept of time to the exclusion of space. This exclusive time focus could be shown to be intimately associated with the unilineal perspective and the reductionist propensity of secularization. Indeed, the advocates of secularization draw attention to the historical fact that metaphysics was dominant in an age when the conceptual focus was on space, and time was represented in spatial terms, i.e. cyclically. The advocates of secularization, however, seem to think of time in the almost exclusively geometric pattern of a straight line. Now, in the first place, it is probable that the Greeks and some primitive tribes thought of time as a sequence of oscillations between opposite poles as Edmund R. Leach has pointed out.[96] Their world view was not primarily spatial, nor their representation of time cyclic. Greek and Roman festivals varied between formality and masquerade, sometimes taken together, forming a pair of contrasted opposites. Greek and Roman thought varied between the formality of metaphysics and the formlessness of becoming. In the second place, as J. J. C. Smart points out, "It is a consequence of Einstein's special theory of relativity that the notions of space and time must be fused together into the notion of space-time."[97] It is significant that Teilhard de Chardin nearly always spoke of space-time and advocated a metaphysics which was arrived at inductively and held provisionally. The point is, that if time is ignored, metaphysics tends to dominate; if space is ignored, as seems to be the case with the advocates of secularization, metaphysics is eliminated, while if use is made of space-time as a conceptual perspective, metaphysics in at least one of the senses described above is possible as a conceptual integrator, as a mediator of contact with reality and as a device for the projection of desirable human goals and the mobilizing of creative activity to achieve them.

d) Secularization, as the rationalization of thought, human relations and activity, involves "the withholding of emotional participation in thinking about the world".[98] It demands a degree of non-involvement in and disengagement from the world, but as this increases, it can also entail both a de-humanization of the world and a fragmentation of human sensibility.

None of these four defects is decisive, and the concept or definition of secularization can be interpreted to cope with and thus nullify the force of those four objections. Yet they do raise questions about the usefulness of the term in the present cultural context. One of the features of recent human cultural history is the phenomenon of existentialism, and it is necessary to examine this briefly to appreciate the human significance of a secular life style which is founded on "the withholding of emotional participation" and before suggesting an alternative to secularization as a conceptual tool.

Paul Tillich, in *The Courage to Be,* distinguishes between the existentialist *outlook* and the *philosophy* of existentialism.[99] The existentialist outlook or attitude is one of involvement in life and existence, not in a detached or theoretical way, but with the whole of one's being. It could be described as the readiness to think, not just with the brain, but with the heart, guts, and every fibre of one's being. As Tillich says: "A self which has become a matter of calculation and management has ceased to be a self. It has become a thing." The existentialist philosophy, on the other hand, is the rational and discursive framework in which this outlook and attitude seeks form.

Existentialism arose as a protest against the de-humanizing and de-personalizing forces of the twentieth century. These, the existentialists claimed, were of two main kinds:

a) Metaphysical systems, abstract systems of essences which render life sterile and static and which dominate life to the detriment of the intuitive, the creative, and the spontaneous.

b) Positivism in all its forms which theoretically or practically result in the reduction of all the dimensions of human life to the empirically observable, the technologically manageable, the statistically computable, the sociologically significant, the politically manipulable or the economically profitable, in such a way that the human person is regarded and treated as a thing or an object.

It represents the demand for freedom from political, social, economic and ideological restrictions to lead an authentically human and personal existence. It is the demand that *bios*—"life", prevail over *logos*—"reason", where *bios* represents human life in all its dimensions, complexity, and richness and where *logos* implies a systematic, abstract, and detached process, theoretical or practical, imposed on life to restrict it.[100]

Existentialists have a definite preference for the new, original, a-typical and emotionally charged complexity of situations in which the true existential condition of the free person is manifested at its best . . . Their emotional dispositions — concern, anxiety, dread and loneliness — condition them to be prepared to expect and to experience the irrational, dangerous and disrupting dimensions of existence. All these attitudes are negatively reinforced by a profound dislike of and contempt for the well organized, safe, secure, systematic, conservative, traditional and philistine way of life led by the majority.[101]

The expression of existentialism has taken a wide variety of forms. Its appropriate medium of expression is non-philosophical. Thus the existentialist outlook has been most cogently and forcefully represented in theatre, cinema, and novels. Jean Paul Sartre's first play, *Les Mouches,* is almost an existentialist thesis in dramatic form. But existentialism has its philosophical expression in forms as diverse and disparate as the history of philosophy itself. In practice, therefore, existentialism can result, and has resulted, in an explicit and highly elaborate metaphysical system, such as that of Martin Heidegger on the one hand, or a cynical despair about being able to say anything of significance which takes on the status of an implicit though negative ideology, on the other hand. It can range from the deep individualistic pessimism of Sartre, demanding that man, stripped of all his illusions, face the nausea and utter futility of existence, to the relative optimism of Gabriel Marcel who sees in "person-engagement-community" a basis for human hope and meaning.

Existentialism as an outlook and attitude has features which are disconcerting: it tends to be concerned with the experience of the present rather than with the creation of the future, it tends to be individualistic, concerned with private issues and somewhat morbidly pessimistic. However it is possible to distill the following characteristics of this philosophical and literary phenomenon which indicate that it has acted as a reaction to and an antidote for the reductionist tendencies manifest in science and philosophical positivism and rather latent in the process of secularization:

a) It highlights the futility of explaining man in the terms of and according to the methods of the physical sciences. Existentialism "saves us from the extravagance of trying to construct a philosophy without first scrutinizing in all its accessible dimensions the *locus* in which all philosophizing takes place—our own human existence".[102]

b) Existentialists insist on the primacy of life over systems of thought which tend to dominate it. Such systems are necessary, but as aids to the living of life and the full participation in it and not as frames to dominate and constrict it.

c) The whole of the existentialist movement testifies to the primacy of *the human person* and his right to freedom and proclaims the challenge to individual persons to live lives that are authentic.

d) Truth in the existentialist view is not primarily a question of the objective verification of propositions or assertions, but something apprehended on the ground of total existence. It is opposed to the dissection of the human composite and the separation of man from the totality of objects which make up the arena of his experience. As Karl Heim says: "A proposition is existential when I cannot apprehend or assent to it from the standpoint of a mere spectator but only on the ground of my total existence."[103] This principle of totality is an important breakthrough in contemporary sensibility.

e) Finally, in the quest for meaning, existentialism emphasizes the role of the individual in creating his own goals, values, and lifestyle. Man is not an object; his role is not merely passive. Even in the pessimistic view of Sartre, man has to be creatively involved if he is to find meaning in or impose it upon his existence.

In the light of existentialism as an important and pervasive influence in contemporary sensibility, it is possible to suggest an alternative to "secularization" as a conceptual tool of cultural analysis and criticism. This can be done by suggesting an alternative historical typology to that advocated by those who use "secularization". Cornelius van Peursen has suggested that there have been three periods in the history of man: the mythical, the ontological, and the functional.[104] In the first period living powers and forces "behind the scenes" influenced and even dominated man's life. Magic, he claims, was used at this stage to control his environment. In the ontological stage, man's understanding of the world was more rational, but essentially philosophical. No longer did living powers loom behind the scenes, but they were replaced by entities, values, substances, and natures which both explained and determined man's behaviour. Immersed in or dominated by this network of ontologically or theologically motivated substances, man could not be ultimately responsible for his destiny. In the third stage, the functional period, man lives and acts according to the data revealed to him by observation and according to the creative possibilities opened up by the data. In this situation, van Peursen claims, man lives pragmatically.

In *Christianity and World History,* Arend van Leeuwen suggests a twofold division of world history into the ontocratic period and the technocratic period. In the former, the apprehension of life is part of a cosmic totality whether this is mythological or ontological. In the latter, life is conceived as an open-textured process of discovery and use.

In *The Secular City* the periods of human history, divided by van Peursen and van Leeuwen into philosophical categories, are divided by Harvey Cox into sociological categories. Corresponding to the mythical period he posits the period of the tribe, corresponding to the ontological period he posits the period of the town, and corresponding to the functional period he posits that of the city. Thus for Cox, while secularization describes the content of man's coming of age, the process of urbanization describes the context of man's coming of age.

The alternative historical typology suggested below must not be considered as an evolutionary-eliminative one, but an evolutionary-inclusive one, so that the dominant features of each period are not repudiated and replaced but are subsumed in various ways and in varying degrees into the most recent category. Thus this typology would have three main periods:

a) The *Mythological* period, corresponding to the tribal stage, in which man conceptualized his awareness of reality in terms which were comprehensive, vivid, concrete, and in general characteristic of the literary mode of an oral tradition or literature. The characteristic thought patterns of this period were *pre-personal*.

b) The *Rationalistic* period, corresponding in a general way to the period of the town in which man conceptualized his awareness of reality in more abstract, objective, and univocal terms. While these conceptualizations were an advance on the pre- or sub-rational expressions of the mythological period, they were, nevertheless, *sub-personal* and tended to dominate and hence restrict the achievement of the full range and scope of the potentialities of the human person. There are two distinct periods within this rationalistic period:

i) The *deductive stage,* corresponding more specifically to the period of the town, in which metaphysical and religious systems predominated. These systems attempted to account for reality and the richness and variety of human experience, in terms which were logically coherent but usually empirically inadequate.

ii) The *reductive stage,* corresponding to the period of the city, which ensured the ascendancy of the empirical method, but established criteria which tended to make empirical methods and technical devices so universal as to eliminate areas of human experience. This could also be called the secularist phase.

c) The *Personalist* period, into which we could now be entering. The term "personalist" here should not be confused with "individualistic". Jacques Maritain distinguishes both the meaning and the sources of the distinction between the idea of "person" and the idea of "individual".[105] "By the very fact that each of us is a person and expresses himself to himself, each of us requires communication with the other and with others in the order of knowledge and love. Personality, its essence, asks for a dialogue in which souls really communicate."[106] Hence understood in this way the term personalist entails also the notion of social. This personalist period into which there are indications we are entering would correspond to the emergence, not of the urban or national community, but of the international or world community. It involves an inductive approach to life in which the person is not dominated by, but uses empirical procedures, technical devices, mythical and rationalistic frameworks as instruments to achieve an extension of creative experience and as various means of expressing it.

Hence the conceptual tool suggested for cultural analysis and criticism instead of "secularization" is the dual concept of "personalization-socialization". The term "socialization" calls for explanation. It is used in Vatican II to indicate the contemporary phenomenon of the multiplication and complexification of social relationships in human society:

Thus a man's ties with his fellows are constantly being multiplied. At the same time "socialization" brings further ties, without, however, always promoting appropriate personal development and truly personal relationships ("personalization").[107]

The explication of socialization from personalization provides a corrective to the existentialist tendency to personal individualism and privatization. At the same time the idea of personalization establishes the human person as of prime importance over against the various mythical and rationalistic systems which have tended to dominate him in the past and the impersonal technical systems which tend to submerge him in the present.

No proof can be given of this typology, but some indications of its validity can be given and some reasons for espousing it as a goal can be thereby suggested. For Cox, secularization describes the content of man's coming of age and urbanization describes the context. One of the problems of today is that of urban decay. One of the obstacles to peace is, as Arnold Toynbee has pointed out, the still all too prevalent religion of nationalism. This same factor of nationalism can prove to be an immediate obstacle to "man's coming of age". Hence it could be that the real *context* of man's coming of age is not the secular city which seems afflicted with chronic decay but the world community which transcends less universal considerations.

The League of Nations and the United Nations are probably no more than rather abortive attempts to mediate international disputes, rather than indications of genuine trans-national emotions, attitudes, or perspectives. The same cannot be said of student unrest throughout the world. It is the result of the fusion of a complex of issues and sentiments, but one of the strongest of the issues and one of the most persistent of the sentiments is a disenchantment with and a refusal to accept values and attitudes circumscribed by national or nationalistic political and economic considerations.

It would be possible to exaggerate the significance of this supra-nationalist perspective if it were not paralleled by the phenomenon of modern communications. If Marshall McLuhan's work is interpreted as an insight into contemporary sensibility and not as epistemology, it can be taken as an indication of the technological underpinning of the emerging cultural context. If moreover, his central insights are valid and his "probes" accurate, it becomes increasingly clear how inadequate the unilineal device of secularization is for cultural analysis. Some brief extracts from his work can serve to illustrate this point:

The family circle has widened. The whirlpool of information fathered by electric media — movies, Telstar, flight — far surpasses any possible influence mum and dad can now bring to bear. Character is no longer shaped by only two earnest, fumbling experts. Now all the world's a sage.

Electric circuitry has overthrown the regime of "time" and "space" and pours upon us instantly and continuously the concerns of all other men. It has reconstituted dialogue on a global scale. Its message is Total Change, ending psychic, social, economic, and political parochialism. The old civic, state, and national groupings have become unworkable. Nothing can be further from the spirit of the new technology than "a place for everything and everything in its place". You can't *go* home again.

> The new electronic interdependence recreates the world in the image of a global village.

> The shock of recognition! In an electric information environment, minority groups can no longer be contained — ignored ... Our new environment compels commitment and participation. We have become irrevocably involved with, and responsible for, each other.

> When faced with a totally new situation, we tend always to attach ourselves to the objects, to the flavour of the most recent past. We look at the present through a rear-view mirror. We march backwards into the future. Suburbia lives imaginatively in Bonanza-land.[108]

If this last observation is true it could be extended to say that secularists live intellectually in the Gutenberg age, dominated by the alphabet and the line: "Until writing was invented, man lived in acoustic space: boundless, directionless, horizonless, in the dark of the mind, in the world of emotion, by primordial intuition, by terror. Speech is a social chart of this bog."[109]

In conclusion it is important to stress the essential ambiguity of the present cultural situation. It is possible to emphasize the values of a proliferating technology, cybernation and bureaucracy in allowing man greater control of his environment and the rationalization which provides him with the affluence, the leisure and the freedom to create an eminently personal existence. On the other hand critics such as Marcuse claim that this very environment has already destroyed the possibility of man's freely creating his own personal existence because he has already been determined by the cultural context. The personalization-socialization tool does not allow us to solve the problem, but it is a conceptual tool that is less dependent on the immediate cultural situation it can be used to criticize.[110]

Contemporary Conceptions of Church

> The Catholic Church is the only thing which saves a man from the degrading servitude of being a child of his own time.
>
> *G. K. Chesterton*

> Man can never jump out of time, but has only to choose whether his present is determined by the past or the future.
>
> *R. Bultmann*

Introduction

In an article entitled "Catholic Ecclesiology in Our Time", the late Gustave Weigel pointed out:

Ecclesiology as a formal theological discipline was born in the sixteenth century as a direct result of the Protestant Reformation. But the tractates on the Church all suffer from one common defect. Catholics and Protestants were engaged in bitter polemics. It was the time of controversial theology, in many ways fruitful but essentially quarrelsome.[1]

A relatively non-polemical ecclesiology began with Johann Adam Möhler in the late eighteenth and early nineteenth centuries. He dealt with the church, not in relation or opposition to the churches of the Reformation but "from the inside out, so that it represented an efflorescence of the presence and activity of the Holy Spirit".[2] This constructive and positive ecclesiology grew in strength. Clement Schroeder and Jean-Baptiste Franzelin prepared the "Primum Schema de Ecclesia" of Vatican I in which the church is described as the Mystical Body of Christ. Leo XIII in the encyclicals *Satis Cognitum* and *Divinum Illud* concentrated on the influence of the Holy Spirit in the church. The classical works on the positive theology of the church in this phase, *The Whole Christ* and *The Mystical Body of Christ,* were written by Emile Mersch, and this trend culminated in the formal statement of the doctrine by Pius XII in the encyclical *Mystici Corporis Christi* of 1943. In 1951 Charles Journet published the first volume of *L'Eglise du Verbe Incarné*, a monumental work attempting to analyse the church according to its four causes, material, formal, efficient, and final. By the time of Vatican Council II, therefore, Catholic ecclesiology had progressed through three stages:

i) that of a theologically unreflective life of the church in which concepts and definitions of the church were contained implicitly in the theological considerations or the canonical structure

ii) that in which the church was defined apologetically, juridically, and hierarchically over against the churches of the Reformation

iii) that in which the church was *defined,* by reflective analysis in terms of its own formal constitution.[3]

The one important defect in Catholic ecclesiology at this stage of its development was that it had not made explicit the relationship of the church to the world. The "world" or the "modern world" had no intrinsic role to play in this phase of the church's consciousness of itself. Initially the second Vatican Council did not intend to alter radically the conception of the church in relation to the world. The problem was thought of in terms of a "communication gap" between the church and the world, of bridging this gap by adjustments in the language of the liturgy and of theology, by some changes in structure, and by the church's addressing itself more directly to some of the pressing problems of the modern world. The documents *Lumen Gentium* and especially *Gaudium et Spes* did more, however, than solve the problem of the communication gap between the church and the world. They laid the foundation or at least provided the occasion in the post-Vatican II period for a new phase in the theology of the church.

The process of "Aggiornamento", however, had a number of unforeseen consequences. As Anna Morawska has pointed out: "The idea that the church is not only reformable after all, but actually needs reform badly, and that at least some typically 'secular' thinking has been proven right . . . produced a sort of chain reaction in the Catholic world at large."[4]

Vatican II either generated or revealed a state of "anomie" in the Catholic church. Yet, with the benefit of hindsight, it is possible to appreciate that this was inevitable because of the apparently innocuous characteristics of the Council: the change in the language of the church and the "pastoral" ambition of the Council. As Leslie Dewart has pointed out in *The Future of Belief*[5], once the church gave up the Latin language "it could not retain its long-traditional cultural form and would therefore ultimately undergo more than an 'accidental' change". The same kind of consequence can follow from the use of the word "pastoral". As Edward Schillebeeckx points out in *Vatican II: The Real Achievement,* for some, "pastoral" means "a practical, apostolically affected attitude which is less concerned with dogmatic or moral truth than with a soothing and encouraging approach to man" which leaves the substance of the truth unchanged. For others, however, "pastoral" means a concern for and a dynamic interaction with the world which can have a substantial modifying effect on theological truth and on the church.[6] As a consequence of these diverse conceptions of "pastoral", "the gap between the genuine and, in part at least, truly creative Catholic thinking and official church theory and practice, which seemed to be bridged at the beginning of the Council, was thus created again and is still growing".[7]

It seems therefore that there is an increasing "anomie" in the Catholic church, and the Christian church by and large, in the sense that there are symptoms of social disintegration and the breakdown of old cultural forms with a subsequent loss of solidarity and value-consensus. The antidote to this malaise is a conscious search for a new sense of community created by new goals and values.

The Problem of Definition

The peculiarly contemporary form of the problem of a definition of the church was articulated first and most pungently by Dietrich Bonhoeffer. In his *Ethics* he asked the question: "What is the significance of a Church (church, parish, preaching, Christian life) in a religionless world?"[8] In his *Letters and Papers from Prison* he replies: "The Church is the Church only when it exists for others ... The Church must share in the secular problems of ordinary human life, not dominating, but helping and serving."[9]

In a sense the Christian church could claim that it has always existed for humanity. But the crucial question now is, *how* it exists for humanity. The context in which the question is asked has changed radically and this changes the nature of the question. The cultural context of the church in the past was either polytheistic or theistic. Consequently the church defined itself primarily in relation to God or in relation to Christ as sent by God. The apologetic task was always that of arguing that this group, that is, this church, was really the representative of God, or validly communicated the *grace* of God or the *word* of God. The contemporary cultural context is atheistic. The church no longer has, as its primary task, that of demonstrating that it is vindicated or mandated by God. Its primary task has become that of vindicating the very existence of God. Consequently, it cannot be defined primarily in relation to God but must be defined in relation to the world.

This then will be the *specific aim* of this chapter, to analyse contemporary conceptions of the church according to the way they relate the church to the world. In other words, in our cultural context, the church must be defined in terms of the world and not in terms of God and/or the Holy Spirit. There are a number of reasons for this approach to the problem:

a) The theological reason. As J. B. Metz points out in an article entitled "Unbelief as a Theological Problem",[10] unbelief or atheism is not simply a problem of the cultural context of the church, but is central and essential to the very consciousness of the church itself. If it is true that unbelief is as fundamental a problem within the church, then this would appear to disqualify the church from defining itself over against an entity which is essential to its own problematic. Put in another way: the theology of the Christian church today is essentially an *apologetic theology*. In the past, apologetics was the technique of defending a body of beliefs, from a position of theological certitude, with more or less philosophical and anthropological weapons, against the attacks of those outside the church. Today, theology has taken on the character of a ruthlessly honest reappraisal (and with the hope of reassurance) within the church. This arises partly from a positivistic tenor of contemporary culture which has influenced the church, but it leads ultimately, in reductionist terms, to two tangible entities in the sociological sense: the church and the world.

b) The logical reason. In the past the church has tended to define itself in terms of God, and the world in terms of the church. In the Aristotelian process of definition, this procedure is logically odd. God is not in any category, so definition in terms of him must prove to be ultimately futile. Moreover, the definition of the world in terms of the church, of the clergy in terms of the hierarchy, and of the laity in terms of the clergy, reverses the order of defining things in terms of generic and specific difference and leaves the laity and the world with very negative and attenuated functions. The appropriate logical procedure is to begin with genus world and define the church in terms of some specific difference which distinguishes it from all the other material or sociological entities which make up the world.

c) The procedural reason. In seeking the specific difference between the church and the world, it is important to develop not an entitative conception, but a functional one. Do not ask what the church is; do not ask what the essence of the church is; ask what it is meant to do. William Horosz has pointed out in an essay entitled "Religion and Culture in Modern Perspective":

> The fact is that the modern mind is readily more concerned with the processes, activities, and functions of experience than it is with entities which reflect static forms and fixed structures. The happenings in experience are more amenable to reflective scrutiny because they radiate their energy, potency or dynamism in the context of human experience more than entities of a more substantial nature. Having to grasp the topics of religion and culture functionally, by relating them to the individual, to the group, and to the social techniques and circumstances that give rise to these functionings, the modern man can more properly evaluate the social and cultural roots of religion as well as the spiritual and intentional aspects of the cultural order. In brief, the truth seems more accessible from the functional standpoint than from a more substantial point of view.[11]

The Vatican Council pointed out that the desire of Christians should be to "serve men of the modern world even more generously and effectively". Many Christian writers have stressed the role of the church in relation to the world as that of *diakonia*. But what specifically is this service and how does it differ from the variety of services that the world itself offers?

The Meaning of "Church" and "World"

One of the dangers in a theology of the church is to set about looking for the "essence" of the church or an essential definition of the church. As Hans Küng points out in *The Church*,[12] the essence and the actual historical or sociological form of the church can never be separated. Hence rather than talk about "an ideal church situated in the abstract celestial spheres of theological theory" it is better to "consider the real church as it exists in our world and in human history".[13] For Küng, the question is not, what is the church? The real question is, does the church have a future or *ought* the church to have a future?[14]

It is easy to identify the church today as a sociological entity. It is not as easy to identify the boundaries of the church. The mediaeval city was walled and presented a clear-cut distinction between itself and *rus*. The city of today gradually fades into suburbia and then into the countryside. So it is with the church. The large churches and denominations are clearly the church taken in the comprehensive sense, but gradually, both in individual terms and collective terms, what can be included under the term "Christian church" is less easy to determine at the edges. Among the churches there are discontinuities and failures in communication. It is difficult to say at any particular time where the "creative centre" is. It is precisely, however, a clearer understanding of the role of the church in relation to the world which could mediate the post-ecumenical age. Such an understanding could then lead to a removal of the discontinuities (though not necessarily the "cultural" diversities) and the development of effective channels of communication.

In one sense the meaning of "world" is quite straightforward and univocal: it is all that is. Yet the word has been used in a wide variety of ways in scripture,[15] in theology,[16] and in sociology.[17] Troeltsch and Bellah, in the process of developing typologies of church and religious evolution, tend to take "world" in a somewhat univocal sense. Bellah's intention is to elaborate a theory of religious evolution in terms of world rejection or world acceptance, but though he carefully defines his use of the terms "religion" and "evolution", he seems to accept "world" as a constant even while acknowledging that the world is an evolving one.[18] This leads him to a rather simplistic linear conception of religious evolution in which Catholicism is characterized as world rejecting and Protestantism as the initial phase of world acceptance by religion. The difficulty is that the "socialization" process of the world of today which began with the rise of the towns, the growth of trade, and the emergence of nation states during the late Middle Ages is fundamentally different from the disintegration of the Roman world in the context of which Augustine's *The City of God* was composed, and from the world of early feudal barbarism over against which the monasteries represented the "world" of knowledge, education, science, progressive agriculture, technology, and even sophisticated forms of government. To *leave* the world, in that context, meant to abandon the sphere of the feudal joust and the warrior culture to adopt what was then the civilized world of the church. With the progressive emancipation of the sphere of the secular, this situation certainly changed and the monasteries and the church generally took on the character that Bellah ascribes to them. A second difficulty is that today Christian theology (both Catholic and Protestant) is entering a new phase of *world rejection*. But this term is really inadequate to account for the range of attitudes that it has been used to include.

It seems necessary to distinguish between world *re*nunciation and world *de*nunciation. World renunciation is capable of including the precept that Christians be in this world but not of it, that they maintain a concern for and an involvement in the world of politics, economics, social movements, and cultural processes while at the same time maintaining a "creative distance". It will emerge in the following typology that this "creative distance" takes different forms in different historical contexts.[19] World denunciation, on the other hand, is the kind of description appropriate to sects which repudiate any involvement in mundane affairs. World denunciation has generally been regarded by the church as heretical, because it regards the world as incorrigibly evil.

A General Historical Typology of Church

To deal with the specifically contemporary conceptions of

church it is necessary, first of all, to survey briefly the main conceptions of the church which have prevailed in the past. Before dealing with these conceptions a few clarifications are called for:

a) The term "church" will be used in the sense in which Troeltsch uses it and will refer to the main body of Christians throughout the last two thousand years.

b) This survey deals only with the church in the West and does not take the Eastern church into consideration.

c) The typology will be based on the way in which the church thought of its relationship to the world, while allowing for the varieties of the understanding of "world".

d) This typology is devised to clarify issues and facilitate discussion about contemporary conceptions of church, hence it neglects certain aspects not adequately accommodated by the church-world basis of the typology.

Using this church-world relationship as a basis, it is possible to distinguish three main phases: the pre-Constantinian phase, the autocratic phase and the modern phase.

PHASE ONE: PRE-CONSTANTINIAN

In this phase it is possible to distinguish two stages. Immediately after the ascension of Christ the early Christian community waited for the imminent second coming of Christ. Its outlook was essentially eschatological in the sense that it was a community expecting *the end*.

> The eschatological view of the world taken by the young church, which was strongly influenced by the spirituality of later Judaism, was very largely negative because it looked forward to the consummation of the reign of God in the immediate future. "This world", "this age" in Pauline and Johannine terminology and in most of the terminology of the New Testament, is a disastrous phenomenon, ruled by the powers of sin and death ... stands in opposition to God and is thus heading for its end.[20]

However, this community did not withdraw from the world as did the community of Qûmran. Rather it saw itself as sent into the world to preach the good news of salvation; it had the task of testifying to the love of God through its love for man.

The second stage of phase one differs mainly in emphasis or degree. When the second coming of Christ did not occur, when the eschaton was not immediately realized, it exercised a less dominant influence than in the first phase, and the problems of appropriate responses to the mundane institutions in and through which they lived began to emerge. From this point until the Edict of Milan the eschaton recedes and the idea of the Kingdom of God, present on earth, at no stage absent in some form in the early church, begins to gain strength. As Ernst Benz points out, the orientation and expectation of the coming of Christ in the early church did not suddenly collapse so that it had to be replaced by a new one. The change came slowly, probably without being noticed by most people.

From the beginning, the Christian expectation of the end of time had two foci like an eclipse. One focus was the joyous conviction that the Kingdom had arrived . . . The other focus was the belief that the time of complete fulfilment was imminent. In the early Church, a development occurred by which, imperceptibly, the point of gravity shifted from an expectation of imminent fulfilment to a consciousness of present salvation.[21]

The component of inclusive loving community and the missionary pressure to preach the good news involved the early church in the world. Two factors kept it at a "creative distance" from the world: the anticipated eschaton and persecution by the world which the church could not embrace entirely while an alien god (the Roman imperium) ruled that world. When the Christian God ruled that world this distance would be diminished.

PHASE TWO: THE CHRISTIAN AUTOCRACY

The acceptance of Christianity under Constantine and its virtual establishment as the religion of the Roman Empire by Theodosius makes it possible to focus on the beginning of a new relationship between the church and the world. Without entering into the intricacies of the origin and the precise nature of this relationship it is possible to say that it is the relationship of virtual identity described by the term "Christendom", presided over at its zenith by Innocent III and defended by Boniface VIII's *Unam Sanctum*.

The relationship and its special quality had three fundamental sources:

a) Political. Initially in the use, by the Emperors, of Christianity as a principle of unity for a disintegrating empire; later in the use of the ecclesiastical organization in the West by Constantinople to compensate for deficiencies in the civil administration; later still in the special theocratic character of Celtic monasticism as it spread through northern Europe; and again in the "myth", created in the ninth century by Charlemagne, of the Holy Roman Empire.[22]

b) Cultural or philosophical. Even in the New Testament

writings there is evidence of the shift from the Hebrew conception of time, in which the eschatological expectation gained most significance, to a Greek conception of space in which the Christian message and mission was expressed in thought patterns which were fundamentally philosophical. The culmination of this process came with the ecumenical councils of the fourth to the seventh centuries.[23]

c) Theological. Augustine's *City of God* crystallized a trend in the conception of the church since the non-appearance of the parousia and expressed the fundamental conception which would influence Christianity for a thousand years, not just in forming the idea of the Roman Catholic Church, but also by influencing its would-be reformers Luther and Calvin.[24] "Augustine replaced the early expectation of the end of time by an ecclesiastical positivism which equates the visible Catholic church with the kingdom of God. The visible Catholic church, built upon an episcopal constitution, is the true mediator of redemption."[25]

The church was thought of as the Kingdom of God, visible on earth and mystically continuous with the Kingdom of God in heaven. The world came to be thought of as a church world, though with a kind of ambivalence. The church maintained its "creative distance" from the world mainly through monasticism, though sometimes every aspect of life, even warfare (as in the case of the military orders) seemed to become monasticized. Yet up to a critical point this was a creative process even in mundane terms.

The characteristics of this relationship between the church and the world, briefly stated, were:

a) it existed in a theistic cultural context

b) the Christian message was objectified in philosophical categories

c) the grace and the means of grace were ontologized—came to be thought of in rather static substantive terms

d) the church was institutionalized and became the purveyor of sacred entities

e) as a consequence the element of progress and acceleration in time towards the eschaton was greatly diminished, though it emerged at various times among "enthusiastic" and "apocalyptic" sects and preachers.

It is important to realize that in terms of this typology, the churches of the Reformation remain quite clearly in phase two because the Anglican, Lutheran, and Calvinistic concepts of the relationship between the church and the world remained, fundamentally, those of virtual identity. The world in each case was more limited geographically and richer in autonomous secular activities. But each of these churches retained the characteristic of claiming to be the authentic purveyor or retailer of a supernatural entity, Grace, the Word, or Salvation.

The Reformation was a symptom of, and at the same time mediated, the emancipation of the sphere of the secular from ecclesiastical control into the autonomy of the dynamics of politics, economics, social change, and cultural freedom. In its religious aspect, the Reformation destroyed the monopoly of Catholic hierarchical control, substituted the Bible for the scholastic synthesis, and freed the world and many Christians in both life-style and liturgical practice from the monastic hegemony. But the Reformation churches remained basically pre-secular and ontocratic in their conception of themselves and their function.[26]

The complex process, which began at the height of the Middle Ages, which was the economic revolution, the rise of the nation states, the Renaissance, the geographical expansion, in other words, the emergence of the modern world, initially did not change *basically* the relationship of the Reformation churches to the world. It was a different kind of world. But unlike the Catholic church they could continue to maintain a species of "sacral" relationship with this new world, for they had helped to emancipate it, if not create it.

PHASE THREE: THE MODERN WORLD

There are three main stages in this phase of the history of the church: the pre-secular, the secular, and the post-secular stages. In general the characteristics of this phase of history are the increasing emancipation of the world of politics, economics, social change, science, and the arts, first from ecclesiastical control and then from ecclesiastical influence, and the accelerating complexification of these spheres. Many post-Reformation Christian churches and sects approved of and contributed to this process and were instrumental in creating that characteristically modern phenomenon, the pluralist society. However, in the interests of simplicity, in dealing with the pre-secular stage, only the Catholic church will be considered.

1. The Pre-secular Stage

The immediate consequence of the Reformation was a struggle

among the churches to establish which one was mandated by God as the authentic mediator of supernatural entities. The precise nature of the entities purveyed by the church was, of course, central to the dispute and the dispute had political as well as theological manifestations and consequences. The religious wars of the seventeenth century were in large part responsible for the complex cultural phenomenon called the Enlightenment. It could be described as the conscious movement of "the world" to emancipate itself from ecclesiastical and religious domination. In its philosophical dimension it represented an attack on the concept of the supernatural; in its political dimension it represented, especially in France and Italy, the elimination of Catholic clerical influence in the secular sphere. The cultural context was initially anti-clerical, but gradually became increasingly agnostic. This stage of the modern period I would want to call the pre-secular stage, extending from the eighteenth to the twentieth century.

From the point of view of the Catholic church, this stage had two distinguishable periods. The first can be called that of *dialectical dualism,* the second, that of *interrelated dualism.* In the first period, the conflict between the Catholic church and the world was critical. The church saw itself attacked, not just by the churches of the Reformation, but by nearly everything that the modern world stood for, and this attitude received its classical expression in the *Syllabus of Errors* of Pius IX. And yet in this period there was not, in practice, though there was a great deal of it in theological rhetoric, a denunciation of and withdrawal from the world. The eighteenth and nineteenth centuries saw the proliferation of religious orders dedicated to education, medical care, and welfare work, representing a creative thrust into the neglected areas of human concern. The evolution of religious life from the monasteries of the early Middle Ages through the mendicant orders of the twelfth and thirteenth centuries, through the Jesuits of the seventeenth, the charitable, educational and missionary orders of the eighteenth and nineteenth centuries, to the secular institutes of the twentieth century, represents, at the same time, the maintenance of a distance from the world (which has also proved *creative* and which should be called "renunciation" rather than "denunciation") and the search for increased mobility and flexibility to keep a creative contact in and with the world.

However, the prevailing tone of the relationship between the

Contemporary Conceptions of Church

church and the world in this period was one of conflict. Religion became a sphere of specifically private concern and the church felt itself threatened by and alienated from the important political, economic, social, and cultural developments of the age.

In the second period (of the pre-secular stage of the modern phase of the church-world relationship) the church achieved a species of compromise or working relationship with the modern world. In this period the relationship could be described as one of *co-existing dualism*. The church continued to regard itself as primarily the purveyor of supernatural entities or commodities; religion remained essentially a private component in the increasing "socialization" of modern life, but in the twentieth century, since the time of Pius X and especially under Pius XII (in spite of *Humani Generis*) a more positive acceptance and appreciation of the world developed in the Catholic church.

The relationship could even be described as schizophrenic or Machiavellian in the sense that most of the members of the church lived, in effect, in two worlds: the world of their everyday life, which had, for the most part, only negative relevance or implications for their supernatural lives (i.e. provided they did not violate the ten commandments), and the sacred world of the church in which they received Grace, or the Word, or Salvation.

However, a number of important qualifications need to be entered here. With regard to the Catholic church, the social encyclicals and statements of the Popes from Leo XIII to Pius XII, though relatively marginal in the consciousness and life of the church, did both manifest and stimulate a Christian interest in and influence on the social question. In the second place, the growth of Catholic Action represented a positive movement to influence the world in a Christian way which was different from the dominative influence of the sacral age. However, the movement often became an instrument by which the institutional self-interest of the church was served rather than a creative Christian influence in the world. In the third place, the rapprochement between the Catholic church and the secular Western world has shown symptoms of deriving from their mutual fear of and antipathy to communism. This raises the issue, to which it will be necessary to return later, of the ways in which the secular world has used and continues to use the church for its own ends,[27] even in a cultural context which is fundamentally secularist and radically atheistic.

2. The Secular and Post-secular Stages

Here we have the cultural factors coalescing to pose a critical challenge to all that the church, in any of its forms, appears to stand for. Each of these factors has a long history of development and it is difficult to give a precise date or even to name the century when the challenge became critical. Yet it is the present consciousness of the characteristics of this challenge and of its importunity which have given rise to what can be called the specifically contemporary conceptions of church among theologians.

The essential feature of secular and post-secular conceptions of church which distinguishes them from all the pre-secular phases and stages is that the church is no longer thought of and defined primarily by its relationship to God, but by its relationship to the world; it is no longer thought of as the retailer of supernatural commodities, but as having a function which can be described—though not completely—in mundane terms.

It is important first of all to try to enumerate, briefly, the characteristics of the modern world, of the contemporary cultural context, so that it is possible to speak more coherently of a definition of the function of the church in relation to this world. Most of these characteristics were listed in the opening section of the Vatican II document *Gaudium et Spes*.[28]

a) It is self-consciously evolutionary. Everything is expected to change. "The decisive turning point for an understanding of man and history came when the idea of evolution, as developed by natural science, penetrated into nineteenth century anthropology."[29]

b) It is, as a consequence, relativistic, in the sense that there is a fundamental distrust of absolutes of any kind, and all institutions and theories tend to be treated as provisional.

c) Its approach to problems is *inductive,* so that there is a deep antipathy to appeals to authority, privileged insight or deductive (metaphysical) procedures. A corollary of this feature, as has been pointed out above, is a preference for functional conceptions rather than structural conceptions, and a deep anti-metaphysical bias.

d) Its orientation and fundamental concern is with the future. As J. B. Metz points out: "The men of this era are attracted and fascinated *only* by the future, that is, by that which has never been . . . The golden age lies not behind us, but before us: it is not re-created in the memories of our dreams, but created in the desires of our imagination and heart."³⁰

e) Its methods are increasingly technological. This technological character of the contemporary situation provides "the element of progress and the element of acceleration" which, Benz points out,³¹ the imminent expectation of Christ exercised on the early church.

f) Its ambition is creative. This ambition arises from man's consciousness of his technological prowess, but it is seen or has been seen as threatened by both Christianity and its God. The ideal of absolute human autonomy has formed itself in contrast with what appeared to be the demands of the Christian God for human docility, passivity, and conformity. Thus: "Nietzsche's perception of the urge in human nature to create something beyond itself, to find self-realization in a higher form, is of truly prophetic character." Nietzsche's idea of the goal of man's creating something beyond himself was the superman. Yet "the image of the superman, as described by Nietzsche, shows only a definite, strictly limited selection of perfectly normal human qualities. The principle of their selection itself is entirely negative. It is nothing but the elimination of all those qualities which are, in some way, connected with Christian ethics."³²

g) Its prevailing mood is atheistic. Atheism today "has not only ceased to be the esoteric privilege of the sophisticated . . . it has become the spiritual attitude of many people . . . It is no longer a world view or a philosophy of life *in opposition to God* but rather the presentation of a positive possibility of existence *without God*."³³

Many of these features need refinement and clarification. Some of them do not seem to apply to many people's attitudes or institutions even today. Yet such disparate sources as the Vatican Council and the theologians of the death of God regard them as characteristic of our age, hence these features must inevitably dictate the terms of the problem of talking about the church today and elaborating a functional definition of it, even though they might not impose the *limits* of the scope and function of the church. It is hoped that both the refinements and clarifications of these features, on the one hand, and the ways in which the scope and function of the church can possibly transcend their limitations, will emerge in the subsequent typology.

In general, the secular stage in the history of man represents a horizontalizing of man's perspective and a radical shift in focus from God to man. The word "secular" itself indicates a shift in the focus of man's concern from a Greek spatial conception of the world (indicated by the Latin *mundus*) to a more time-conscious conception of the world (indicated by the Latin *saeculum*).[34] However, within this modern tendency it is possible to distinguish two conflicting trends. The first, which can be called secularist, is a trend to *reduce* the apparent complexity of man's experience to simpler terms, usually to the terms of what can be expressed in univocal and/or mathematical forms. Such attempts at reduction often derive from an implicit secularist ideology.[35] The second, which can be called the post-secularist or non-reductionist trend, allows for the complexity of reality and of human experience and seeks both to investigate and expand it.[36]

This framework allows us therefore to discuss the various contemporary conceptions of church: the two main categories are pre-secular conceptions and secular conceptions; within the class of secular conceptions of church it is possible to distinguish secularist conceptions and post-secularist or non-reductionist conceptions. However, a number of difficulties present themselves when it comes to putting the various current conceptions of church into appropriate categories:

a) Many contemporary theologians, especially Protestant theologians, have not made explicit, in their theology, the function of the church. The same applies to philosophers or sociologists whose basic term of reference is "religion".

b) The categories do not necessarily occur in chronological order.

c) Sometimes, it seems, theologians can and should be included under two categories either because the categories themselves are not totally or adequately distinct or because the theologians give their conception of church different emphases in different situations.

At this stage of the development of a renewed ecclesiology, however, the suggested typology is in some ways more important than accuracy in categorizing theologians, for it seems that one of the basic needs in contemporary ecclesiology is precisely the development of a frame of reference or a typology against which, or in terms of which, the fundamental issues can be raised and clarified.

Contemporary Conceptions of Church

PRE-SECULAR CONCEPTIONS

In most ways the conception of the church taught by the Vatican Council is a pre-secular conception because in most of the documents it tends to speak of the church as a retailer of sacred entities or commodities. Yet the document on the church itself is ambivalent and in future will probably be looked on as ringing down the curtain on the ecclesiology which came to its climax in *Mystici Corporis Christi* and opening the way to an ecclesiology which is authentically secular. The general ambition of the Council to make contact with and become more vitally involved in the world (history) and the description of the church as a pilgrim people eschatologically oriented[37] indicates a new threshold of the church's conception of itself which can be described as secular. However, the church continued to define itself in relation to the world, rather than in terms of it.

The view of the church which Charles Davis tilted against in his *A Case of Conscience* is not the church which the Vatican Council describes, though there are many still far from dormant vestiges in both the documents and the reality.[38]

In Protestant theology, conceptions of the church based on, or deriving from, what has been called "crisis theology" or "the theology of the Word" are pre-secular. The modern exponents of this theology are Karl Barth, Emil Brunner, and Oscar Cullmann. The church in this view is the minister of the Word of God, of the revelation of God, which allows no vital contact or interaction with or influence by anything but the undiluted and gratuitously given revelation itself. This revelation, the Word, is independent of and impervious to the exigencies of human history except in a very attenuated and negative sense. In this conception of revelation, of Christianity and the church, there is posited a fundamental incompatibility between the church, when fulfilling its true function, and the world.[39]

SECULAR CONCEPTIONS

Secularist Conceptions

The characteristics of these conceptions are:

a) The acceptance of a reductionist epistemology which

claims, in effect, that only what is empirically verifiable, in a rather mathematically limited sense, is real.

b) The world, as experienced in the *"now*-sense", defines the limits of the humanly possible.

In the early phase of the secularist challenge, Liberal Protestantism and Catholic Modernism were seen not just as attempts to come to terms with the challenge but as a craven capitulation to it. It is beyond the scope of this chapter to verify or refute this still popularly held claim.

A more obvious instance of this category is the attempt to explain religion, Christianity and the church as epiphenomena or manifestations of merely mundane and empirically observable and explicable phenomena. Thus for Emile Durkheim, ceremonial and ritualistic institutions, such as the church, function as the disciplinary, integrating, vitalizing, and euphoric forces of any given society;[40] for Karl Marx religion is part of the ideological superstructure precipitated by the basic economic and class structure;[41] for Sigmund Freud the church is the institution for nurturing the transcendent illusions which many need to compensate for psychological immaturity and which protect them from the harsh and, for the immature, destructive realities of an incurably contingent existence.[42]

The most recent forms of the secularist conception have been expressed by R. B. Braithwaite and Paul van Buren. For Braithwaite, talk about God has no cognitive significance, but merely ethical significance. For him, "the primary use of religious assertions is to announce allegiance to a set of moral principles". The function of the church is to promote and foster "the intention to follow an agapeistic way of life", as a human—in terms of genesis and consequences—ideal.[43] Van Buren attempts to give an account of Christianity and the Christian church within the terms of the philosophy of logical positivism, which demand ultimately that Christ be regarded as the human paradigm and that the function of the church be that of recommending Christ to the world as a human paradigm. The church is "the company of those sharing (a common) perspective" and its mission is to "claim the world for Christ".[44]

In general, dissatisfaction with secularist conceptions stems from two opposite sources. Almost invariably, reductionist enterprises are based on implicit assumptions which themselves fail to satisfy the reductionist criteria. In the second place, the reductionist claim to uncover what religion or Christianity or the church *really* is in psychological, sociological, or economic terms has proved both inadequate and ultimately unconvincing.

Post-secularist Conceptions

The characteristics of this category of conceptions of church are:

a) An attempt to relate Christianity and Christian living in some intrinsic way to the mundane, to the dynamics of existence, and to the flow of history.

b) A concern to "horizontalize" the Christian perspective and eliminate the chronic dualism of Christianity.

c) At the same time, a refusal to accept the secularist premise that the complexity of reality and the human experience of reality can be reduced to terms explicable within the limits of the empirically observable.

It is possible to distinguish three main classes within this category: the existentialist, the incarnational, and the eschatological conceptions of church.

The Existentialist Conception of Church

The existentialist movement, in its negative aspect, represented a strong reaction to the dominance of *logos* over *bios,* to the restrictions on human freedom and the fullness and spontaneity of human life imposed by both metaphysical systems and a positivist or technological outlook on life.[45] As Paul Tillich pointed out: "A self which has become a matter of calculation and management has ceased to be a self. It has become a thing."[46] Though it is difficult to generalize, this outlook championed a more spontaneous response to life, the pre-eminence of personal values and the need for a sense of community.

The existentialist conception of the church has two main sources which can be given different emphasis. The first source is in the philosophy of personal being, especially that of Martin Buber, which insisted that what is important is "not the quantitative maximum of life, not its flourishing condition in the world, nor its power, but the quality of it, its intensity, its moving and pathetic character".[47] Yet for Buber, this quality of life cannot emerge in isolation or escape from life, but must take place in and through everyday life, especially, even essentially, through personal relationships with other persons. The person and the quality of the life of the person have to be developed in and through the development and multiplication of *I-Thou* relationships so that "the various 'Thous' with which we come into relation may be thought of as constituting a perspective, the extended lines of which meet in the eternal 'Thou' or God".[48] The second source of this conception of the church is in the more synthetic and systematic of existentialist philosophers and theologians such as Martin Heidegger, Rudolf Bultmann, and Paul Tillich. In some ways Bultmann, whose philosophical background is that of Heidegger, could be called a reductionist theologian; for the criteria he brings to bear in the process of "demythologizing" the Bible appear often to exclude the possibility of anything not explicable in terms of the merely mundane. Both Tillich and Bultmann, however, see the world of today as posing the peculiarly contemporary problems of personal existence to which revelation or the Word must be made relevant. Tillich "tries to correlate the questions implied in the situation with the answers implied in the message".[49] Tillich presumes that the answers are contained virtually—in the existential rather than the logical sense—in the Word. But immersion in the world as it is raises the questions which determine both the relevance and the style of the answers.

From the coalescing of these two influences there emerges a conception of church as a community dedicated to the evoking of the authentic self in the context of and over against contemporary situations and the development of true personal relationships through which a relationship with God is established. In this conception of the church (which is more a prevalent attitude than a specifically enunciated conceptual form) there is a strong anti-organizational anti-institutional bias as well as a deep antipathy to conceptual clarity.

It is this conception of church which has replaced the pre-Vatican II conception among many Catholics. This conception is more implicit than explicit. It is an attempt to make Christianity more relevant to life and put it in more vital contact with history, but as J. B. Metz has pointed out, it continues in the direction of the "privatization" of the church,[50] for the emphasis is on the authenticity of the person and the effective warmth of the community. It tends to be uncreative in the affairs of the secular world because its anti-metaphysical bent inclines it to accept the givenness of the world and even the problems of the world as the occasion for the relevance of the Word and the emergence of the self in the web of relations of the community. In the existential conception of the church a "distance" is maintained from the world, but this is because the Western world does not provide the sense of community which this kind of church hopes to provide. But this distance has not proved to be a "creative distance". It is possible, then, to summarize the defects of this conception of the church even though it could prove difficult to attribute it to anyone in particular:

a) It "writes off history in favour of a dialectics of the moment . . . theologians, concerned with the problem of existential decision in the present, had forgotten to inquire into the meaning of the future".[51]

b) Related to this defect is that of the *purpose* of the community. If in this community God is revealed or experienced, this conception of church suffers from the problem of pre-secular conceptions of church. On the other hand, if it does not want to espouse this facet of the pre-secular church then it has the task of clarifying the *purpose* of the community.[52]

c) Because the community seems to have no purpose beyond itself and its own religious experience it must inevitably be conditioned and shaped by historical circumstances rather than contribute towards determining the direction of history.

d) While it recalls the importance of personal relationships and the value of community versus institution in Christianity, it neglects that element in biblical tradition which stresses man's relationship to the cosmos and his responsibility for it. Hence, it sees the problems of technology only in the negative sense of providing a threat to personal and community values.

Probably the prime example of this conception of church is the "underground church". Yet it is necessary to distinguish among: (a) elements which are forced underground through circumstances of local ecclesiastical prohibition of the effective implementation of the liturgical provisions of Vatican II and/or ecclesiastical proscription of valid and necessary social and political action of Christian groups; (b) elements which in spite of the liturgical and structural reforms of Vatican II are seeking a "more authentic ecclesial community" in the context of which they seek "more intense and valid religious experiences"; (c) non-geographical parishes which may not have an existentialist conception of the church at all.

It is the second group which illustrates the defects of this kind of idea of church. Father Caporale, the Italian sociologist, pointed out two characteristics of this group:

a) It tends to be composed of people of very similar social and educational backgrounds;

b) It shows little indication of issuing into significant social action or creative movement of any kind.[53]

It is important to note that the existentialist contributions have acted as an antidote to the over-institutionalized ideas of the church of the past. The conceptions of the church which follow do not necessarily exclude these positive insights, though in going beyond them they might also neglect them.

The Incarnational Conception of Church

In general, this conception of the church and of the role of the Christian in the world is much more extroverted than is the existentialist conception. The role of the church is to be, or to mobilize its members to be, involved in specific secular issues. The theological emphasis is less on God and the religious experience of him, than on Christ as the man involved in secular issues. It is identified for the most part with the theologies of secularization, which claim that the biblical tradition is the source of secularization in the Western world. Love cannot be reduced to I-Thou relationships but extends to and must include functional relationships.[54] God manifests himself in history, at the creative centre of political, social, economic, and cultural change, and it is here he must be contacted.

At the same time, this conception of the church and of the function of the church is not, at least overtly, secularist or reductionist. While being anti-mythical and anti-metaphysical, it is in general ambivalent and even positively ambiguous about the possibility of the transcendent and therefore about the existence of God. The function of the church usually is thought of as reducing all else to the status of relative, provisional, and transitory, by contrast with the absoluteness of God; as reminding man of his responsibility for the world and of his obligation of creative action in history.

It is possible to distinguish three main classes in this incarnational conception of the church: the annihilatory conception, the kenotic conception, and the political conception.

The Annihilatory Conception of the Church. This view is held by the death-of-God theologians, especially by Thomas J. J. Altizer.[55] The death of God is more than just a cultural fact. For Altizer it is an ontological fact which took place on Calvary in Christ. He sees the present cultural fact of the death of God as an historical actualization in the consciousness of all men of an event which happened on Calvary when Christ cried "My God, my God, why hast thou forsaken me?" The movement of the cosmos is from the divine, the reality of God, into the secular. Spirit is immersed in and sacrificed to flesh so that "rather than promising the disclosure of the sacred in the negation of the profane, it dramatizes the movement of the sacred into the profane".[56]

For Altizer the function of the church is to announce the death of God and his immanence in the secular. Moreover, in an article entitled "Catholic Philosophy and the Death of God" he claims that the outlook of the Catholic church makes it the best suited for this function:

To be Catholic is to recognize the presence of the Church wherever there is revelation and salvation . . . The Catholic Christian must inevitably assume that God's movements are reflected in human consciousness and experience, if only because of his belief in the analogical or positive relationship between God and the world. Thus, if human consciousness, including most certainly the explicitly Christian consciousness, has progressively been moving in the direction of abandoning a former ground in the life-giving power of the name and the image of God, the Catholic Christian can only conclude that God Himself is in some sense moving through a process of self-negation or self-emptying of His former epiphany or self-manifestation.[57]

This view has affinities with the secularist view. However, it differs from it in acknowledging the existence of God at some previous age; there *was* a God. His incarnation in, and immolation for, the world has made the secular sacred and absolute.

The Kenotic Conception of the Church. The whole tendency towards an incarnational conception of church has been profoundly influenced by, if not entirely derived from, Dietrich Bonhoeffer's *Letters and Papers from Prison*. Bonhoeffer, even in his earlier works, was deeply concerned that the church—for him the Lutheran church— had become the retailer of "cheap grace". The church had failed to advocate grace won by following in Christ's footsteps in the world. Yet the church could effectively imitate Christ only when it *emptied* itself of all the trappings, ideological, theological, social, political, and cultural which kept it apart from and frustrated its being of service to the world. The germinal passage of the incarnational and kenotic conception of the church runs as follows:

> The Church is the Church only when it exists for others. To make a start, it should give away all its property to those in need. The clergy must live solely on the free-will offerings of their congregations, or possibly engage in some secular calling. The Church must share in the secular problems of ordinary human life, not dominating, but helping and serving. It must tell men of every calling what it means to live in Christ, to exist for others.[58]

The church has failed and continues to fail to communicate with and serve the world because its primary aim has been self-preservation. It can fulfill its functions only when it forgets itself and empties itself. "The church must reassess the context and the compass of redemption and come to a more realistic appraisal of . . . (the fact) that God's primary concern is with *this world*. It must be willing to risk its own existence for the sake of the world."[59]

This theme of Bonhoeffer's was taken up and developed by Bishop John Robinson in *Honest to God* and, with regard to the church, in *The New Reformation*.[60] Robinson is concerned in the latter book with a starting point for theology. In the chapter entitled "Towards a Genuinely Lay Theology" he seeks a starting point for talk about the church and about theology generally which begins with secular or worldly issues. Fundamentally, Robinson is concerned with two issues that are not quite integrated in his writings: the problem of God and the problem of how the self-perpetuating and fundamentally introverted structures of the church, whether these be theological or administrative, can be dissolved or at least mobilized in the interests of the world.

The same kind of concern appears in the writings of two Catholic theologians, Robert Adolfs and Ivan Illich.[61] Adolfs' intention is limited. He demands the emptying of all the traditional claims of the hierarchy of the Catholic church as a condition of its entering into any kind of significant communication with or influence on the modern world. Illich, referring to the position of the Catholic church in South America, and speaking as a sociologist, sees the self-immolation of the church as an indispensable condition for the necessary social, political, and economic changes that must come there. In the interests of social justice, and in imitation of Christ, which it claims to represent, the church must dissolve itself or be destroyed in its present form, for otherwise it will continue to reinforce the obstacles to the correction of the rampant poverty, injustice, and social inequality in South America. He *believes* that, theologically speaking, from this act of immolation a new form of the church will arise. Illich does not even concede the church a role in effecting this necessary social change, though this is not so much a question of whether the church in South America *should* be an agent of social change as of whether in its present form and with its historical background and traditional associations with aristocratic power elites it *could* ever be an agent of social change and reform.

The function and even the definition of the *church* in terms of *social* and *cultural change* represents an important new phase in the conception of the church. In Robinson the emphasis is on the church as "the Accepting Community".[62] The first phase in the process of achieving an extroverted perspective in the church was to accept the world as God's world, to be of service to this world. But when the question of the specific service which the church was to offer to the world arose, being satisfied with mere acceptance was not enough and the role of the church as a witness to and agent of the absoluteness of God and the transience of all created things became more clear.

Harvey Cox's *Secular City* represents this turning point. On the one hand he argues for the Christian's and the church's acceptance of the fact, the values, and the cultural implications of the secular city. He bases his case for this on the coincidence of some of the central features of the secular city with some important—and somewhat forgotten—characteristics of the biblical message, namely the "disenchantment of nature", the "desacralization of politics", and the "deconsecration of values". On the other hand, he outlines a theology of social change, and in this process of social change sees the role of the church as that of "God's Avant-garde". And yet in Cox's conception of the church, the determinant is basically "world acceptance": "A church whose life is defined and shaped by what God is *now* doing in the world cannot be imprisoned in such antiquated specifications. It must allow itself to be broken and reshaped continuously by God's continuous action . . ."[63] The disadvantage of this conception is that it seems to under-emphasize the role of *creative* responsibility for the world and demand that the church be the interpreter of God's action in history rather than the creative agent of it.

In an article in *The Secular City Debate*,[64] Bernard Murchland suggests that Cox tends to identify the secular city with the City of God and succumbs to the pitfall of investing the relative cultural standards of an age with ultimate sanctity. He invokes Reinhold Niebuhr's indictment of liberal Christianity: "A religion which capitulates to the prejudices of a contemporary age is not very superior to a religion which remains enslaved to the partial and relative insights of an age already dead."[65] However, though Cox does seem to make the secular city a kind of cultural terminus and therefore to make the vanguard role of the church that of championing its values, he must be seen primarily as attempting to do three important things:

a) exorcize the church of a neurotic preoccupation with itself and an attachment to outmoded structures, conceptual forms, and values

b) relate the church to the world and get it to accept the positive values of the contemporary world

c) define the role of the church as the agent of secularization, which need not necessarily end with the secular city but which is conceived essentially as an on-going process.

The role of the church as the agent of social change and specifically as the agent of secularization emerges much more clearly in the work of Arend van Leeuwen. In the final chapter of *Christianity in World History* he points out that it

is in the West that a civilization liberates itself—and with itself other civilizations—from provincialism and self-perpetuation and comes to grips with the future of mankind ... At last, in the rise of modern technology, the way is opened for a new pattern to break through with irresistible power, thrusting the temple once and for all from its place at the centre.[66]

He claims that Christianity was the cultural matrix of the technological age and that it must avoid the temptation to develop a religious hegemony against all that technology stands for. Its function rather is to pave the way for the technological age, the age of "the fourth man", the "post-Neolithic man", even though this means the abolition of religion and Christianity itself.

Technology is an integral, even the essential, component in

the process of secularization and hence of social and cultural change. Ernst Benz says that the Christian church needs to ask, in seeking its contemporary function:

Does technology form part of the history of salvation and, if so, in what sense? Is it, as Augustine taught, an expedient, a crutch, given man to make his life easier despite original sin, or is it itself, as Hugo of St. Victor claimed, a remedy against original sin? Is it, as Teilhard de Chardin explained, the springboard of man's evolution into the superhuman?[67]

The Political Conception of the Church. One of the defects of the conceptions of the church which define its relation to the world in terms of the agent of social change is that they are vague about the criteria for social change and the direction it should take. The most specifically described role of the church amongst the incarnational conceptions is that which aligns the church with (and hence defines it in terms of) definite political issues or even with definitive political theories or forms.

In an article entitled "Putting the Liturgy in Its Place", Daniel Callahan claimed that the persisting tendency within the Catholic church to give a kind of magical primacy to the liturgy is "the most important of the church's failures to carry out its Christian work and witness in the world". He claimed that the church is trying to say two things simultaneously: that we find Christ in the liturgy and that we find him in the world. Yet, at least psychologically, the emphasis on the first effectively nullifies the second. If the liturgy were made a function of involvement in a real secular need, a rite celebrated by workers in a poverty programme, or a peace movement or a race relations project, then it would be desacralized and yet be more relevant.[68] The difficulty with this view is that if there are a number of viable Christian options or alternatives in any of these specific issues, the danger is that the church will become identified with one among several equally good possibilities and thus a divisive force rather than a reconciling agent. Its "catholicity" could be impaired.

An interesting form of a contemporary political conception of the church is proposed by Alex R. Vidler in *Soundings*.[69] He argues for a continuation of the "establishment" of the Anglican church in England. This nexus between the church and the state "helps keep the church aware of its obligation to serve the whole people in all areas of their need . . . it is a safeguard against ecclesiastical inbreeding . . . since it brings an independent influence to bear upon the church, one that is directed to the interests of the nation and the laity". The link between church and state he sees as providing a twofold service to the world:

a) It serves to stand "witness to the fact that man, every man, is a twofold creature with a twofold allegiance, whether he realizes it or not".

b) It serves as "a sign that the authority of the state is neither final nor absolute".[70]

The disestablishment of the church would reduce it and all of Christianity to the role of a denomination, a merely optional category in the varied life of secular man. These two functions could be said of the phenomenon of "civil religion" in America.[71] Though there is no established church, this comprehensive, though nebulous, religion acknowledged by the political and social structures of society serves to validate the various specific choices amongst churches, which in a more indirect way than in England would automatically prove a corrective against investing the merely mundane or the state with absolute value.

It is with the *Slant* group in England that we find a relatively fully elaborated political conception of the church. Politics is defined as "the grammar of human relationship",[72] but not in the personal sense. The Slant conception of church is based on a cultural criticism of the Western world as having been subject to a process of perceptual, linguistic, and cultural fragmentation.[73] Their claim is that "we are served by the degree to which we create community in the world", where community is "a number of men who bring each other into selfhood through shared and equal relationships".[74] This community is seen as the whole complex of social, economic, political, and cultural relationships among men. The basic question that the Christian church has to ask today is: which socio-economic order is more suitable for nurturing this ambition of community, the capitalist order which posits as basic the rule of *competition* among men, or the Marxist order which bases the socio-economic community on *co-operation* among men? Or in another way: does the church of the Last Supper have more in common with the individualistic capitalist ethos or with the communal Marxist ethos? The Slant group claims that the second of the alternatives is true, though it is careful to indicate that Communist states as we know them are quite untrue to the Marxist ethos.

The Slant group claims that the church has been concerned

with the working classes only in its own interests. An analysis of recent centuries reveals "the slow jive Capitalism and Christianity have danced through history", culminating in John XXIII's *Mater et Magistra*.[75] The church has helped capitalism by itself being "a major ideological instrument in the whole process of mystification, persuading men to interiorize capitalist morality, either by direct teaching, or by transposing specific attitudes into grandly cosmic formulae".[76]

The manifesto is: *"Slant* stands for a positive engagement by Catholics in the affairs of the contemporary world." But this engagement is a specific one expressed in the socio-politico-economic form of Marxian socialism. The church is thus described as "the Sacrament of a socialist society", that is, it is both the symbol and the agent of the Marxist vision of the community of men. In the last chapter of this book, Lawrence Bright points to the eschatological character of the church but in the context of asserting that the Bible does not distinguish two worlds.

Thus the Slant group sees the function of the church as working for an earthly community through social change. Its programme is at once radical and specific.

A brief review of the features and defects of the incarnational views of the church is called for:

a) Many of them simply take the existence of God and/or the authority of the Bible for granted.

b) In the kenotic view of the church there is an implicit belief that though the church empties itself, it will rise phoenix-like in some new and more vital form.

c) There is a process of evolution in the idea of *service* to the world from "world acceptance" to that of agent of social change.

d) The forms of social change range from the rather vague advocacy of the process of secularization to the adoption of the specific theory of Marxism.

e) In general, there is an indifference if not antipathy to institutional forms of the church.[77]

f) Though reductionist or secularist ambitions are by no means overt, they sometimes remain implicit, as for example, Cox's elimination of any function for metaphysics and in the general skepticism about the possibility of the realm of the transcendent.

g) Perhaps the greatest defect of the incarnational conceptions of the church is the failure to maintain or describe some form of "creative distance" from the world. We saw that the existentialist conception of the church maintained a distance that was uncreative. The incarnational conceptions, especially those advocating that the church be an agent of social change, involve the church creatively in the world, but do not make clear how it can avoid becoming ultimately immersed in and identified with it. Some would reply that allegiance to the absolute God or reliance on the Word provides this distance. But this takes us back to a pre-secular conception or outlook, for God and the Word are central to the contemporary problematic of the church, and cannot be simply assumed.

The Eschatological Conception of Church

In the not so distant past the church maintained a "creative distance" from the world by defining its role as the dispenser of otherworldly goods, or by monastic or quasi-monastic institutions and ecclesiastical styles, or by seeing in a past and more Christian age the ideals for mankind for which it yearned. In the eschatological conception of the church, the creative distance is not spatial but temporal. The church refuses to accept entirely or become completely immersed in this age, in its institutions and values, because it stands for and is a symbol of the *future*. The future has come to exercise a revolutionary influence in theology and consequently in contemporary conceptions of the church. It is in terms of the eschaton that the function of the church must be defined, yet not in the way it was defined in the early church, as a future event coming from above the world, "Christ in the clouds", but as a future "event" coming *through* the world. The contemporary Christian does not occupy himself in the world announcing this coming "event" while *waiting* for it to happen. Involvement in the world means both announcing the "event" and working towards it.

These two interrelated ideas, involvement in the world with a view to the future, appeared in the Vatican Council as a germinal, though not a dominant theme, and much more strongly in the World Council of Churches Conference on Church and Society in Geneva, 1966.[78]

This trend has gathered momentum as a result of the confluence of five powerful factors in contemporary Western consciousness: the influence of Bonhoeffer already discussed; the impact on the church, after almost a hundred years of the Darwinian revolution, of the realization of the radical evolutionary character of everything that is human and created; the tremendous forces for social change since World War II in the third world, and among these forces the influence of Marxism as a theory driving towards a *future* resolution of social and economic inequalities; the influence of the insight of Nietzsche "of the urge in human nature to create something beyond itself, to find self-realization in a higher form"[79] and the present technological capacity to achieve this; the increasingly felt and expressed need for what could be called a "post-secular form of transcendence". The influence of Marxism, especially, has been quite significant in this decade and it has come from two sources: the ecumenical dialogue between Christians and Marxists in Europe, which has resulted in an increase in the evolutionary-future oriented component in current European theology,[80] and the Christian missionary experience of the Marxist revolutionary dynamic in the developing world.

Some elaboration of the need for a "post-secular form of transcendence" is called for. The thrust of Western thought since the Enlightenment has been towards the elimination of the transcendent, conceived in vertical terms. The culmination of this process was the secularist or reductionist phase in science, philosophy, and theology. The implications of this phase and its consequences for a post-secularist perspective are analysed by Thomas F. O'Dea in an article entitled "The Crisis of Contemporary Religious Consciousness":

Ivan Karamazov commented that without God, everything is possible. Modern man has experienced in his sorrow what this can mean. But it is also true that without God nothing is possible; man can now also experience what this can mean. In the development of technology a great bureaucratic structure has been elaborated. All men, except the "culturally deprived", fit into this structure; they have become parts of a great social machine. The social relationships and institutions formed to enable men to control the world of nature have become a second nature controlling them. Modern man finds himself consuming in order to work, reversing the ancient causal formula; in a hundred ways he adapts himself to the social leviathan he has brought into being. Mastery over nature has become objectified into a social structure that controls all men . . . Having lost transcendence, he finds himself without practical leverage in effectively changing his world. Without God or his memory in Enlightenment philosophy, he no longer knows what it means to be man, and hence, cannot utilize his enormous capacities to humanize the conditions of his life.[81]

This passage need not be taken as a repudiation or even an

expression of regret at the complexification of modern social and economic life nor at the proliferation of man's technological competence. But it does indicate the loss of a dimension and more importantly the elimination of a fulcrum for leverage in effecting social change and progress. The post-secularist phase puts the transcendent element in the future. This development has a number of advantages:

a) God is thought of more as a hypothesis to be verified eschatologically, rather than as an entity whose reality is vindicated horizontally by revelation or by logical processes. Recent biblical scholarship has shown this postponement to the future of any positive manifestation of God. The fulfillment in Christ, the apotheosis of the risen Christ, have yet to achieve their full perfection. Christ has yet to come.

b) The shift of perspective to the future allows greater scope for what Bishop Robinson calls "inductive faith". He describes doctrine as "the definition of experience".[82] The Jewish people and especially the Christian people have had experiences, especially of the Christ-phenomenon, which have been objectified in doctrinal forms and patterns. In the ontological age these experiences were expressed statically. In an evolutionary age the dimension of the biblical promise of the future, of the exodus impulse, has come to the fore again.

c) The eschatological perspective allows the church to maintain a new form or style of "creative distance" from the world while being fully involved in it. It is maintained through the goal of the future by means of a sceptical, provisional, relativistic attitude to contemporary cultural forms. Yet a dynamic balance is required to avoid Manicheeism, a balance between an acceptance and celebration of the present that is good and a drive towards what is better, entailing a questioning attitude and creative work.

In general, therefore, the eschatological conception of the church defines the church as the symbol and the agent of the *future*. Its function is to work, horizontally, through the world to achieve, and not merely to wait for the future.

Immediately, however, four important questions arise:

1. Is not this shift of focus to the future by theologians a rearguard action against the whole secular enterprise to dispose of God and any specific function for the church? It is beyond the scope of

this chapter to examine this question, but the basis for hope in the future is not merely a symptom of naïve wish-fulfillment, nor the objectification of the mere logical possibility of there being an Absolute of some kind. It is based on the historical fact of Christ and of the early Christians' experience of and response to what Christians call the resurrection of Christ.

2. Can there be anything more than the mundane, even considered in terms of what is yet to come? Fundamentally this is the epistemological question which has not been explicitly raised and faced even in post-secularist theology. While the positivists and the secularists have been repulsed, no cogent synthetic alternative has been constructed to vindicate the possibility of the Christian knowledge of something more.

3. What is the nature of the eschaton? Karl Rahner has defined Christianity as "the religion of the absolute future".[83] But how does this differ from what will be in 1984 or 2084 and so on? As Daniel Callahan asks: "How then, does a man know *now* that his authentic goal is the absolute future, not merely a projection? He cannot envisage an absolute future; all he can envisage is the projected future."[84] The theological problem of the nature or significance of the eschaton is beyond the scope of this chapter. Karl Rahner deals with it in depth in two essays entitled "The Hermeneutics of Eschatological Assertions" and "Christianity and the 'New Man' ".[85]

4. Closely associated with the last question is that of the continuity of this world with the absolute future. Will the eschaton be a continuation of human history as we know it, will it cross a threshold into a new age, or will there be a radical disjunction between the two?

This question leads to a division of eschatological theories which provides a framework for distinguishing among various eschatological conceptions of the church. The church in this form of contemporary theology is an eschatological symbol. But what the symbol stands for needs to be clarified.

One of the consequences of the debate which followed the publication of *The Secular City* was the shift by Harvey Cox from a basically incarnational conception of Christianity to an eschatological conception: "Though my critics have not given me much help in solving this problem, they have dislodged me from the ground on which I once stood, and for that I am grateful. They have pushed me along the most promising path I could find. They have turned my face towards the future, where if man meets God again, that encounter must take place."[86] In an article entitled "Evolutionary Progress and Christian Promise",[87] Cox distinguishes three different ways, inherited from Christianity, of perceiving the future:

a) The *apocalyptic,* deriving from ancient Near Eastern dualism, foresees imminent catastrophe, produces a negative evaluation of this world, and often believes in the elite which will be snatched from the inferno when everything else dissolves.

b) The *teleological,* derived mainly from the Greeks but adopted by Christianity, sees the future as the unwinding of a purpose inherent in the universe itself or in its primal stuff, the development of the world towards a fixed end. It provides the basis for philosophies of social evolution.

c) The *prophetic* is the characteristically Hebrew notion of the future as the open field of human hope and responsibility. The Israelite prophets did not, as many popular misconceptions would have it, "foretell the future". They recalled Yahweh's promise as a way of calling the Israelites into moral action in the present.

To these three categories can be added another, the pneumatic, to include those eschatological conceptions which are less related to social change than the ones mentioned above.

The Apocalyptic Conception of the Church. In the article referred to above, Cox distinguishes two kinds of contemporary apocalypticism: the one places emphasis on the elitist age that will be ushered in, the other on the catastrophe which will mediate it. Popular Christian preaching of the evangelical kind has used the threat of nuclear holocaust as the contemporary catastrophic apocalypse. There is an apocalyptic element in Bolshevist Marxism. Yet Christians generally have recently ignored the apocalyptic imagery of the Bible. However, some Christian theologians deeply involved in social problems in under-developed countries have thought of the church as an agent of revolutionary social change and its task as that of precipitating dramatic and therefore "apocalyptic" social and economic crises. Thus Richard Shaull regards Christianity and the church as continuing the biblical tradition of being at home in the midst of revolution:

The gospel introduced . . . a revolutionary God, whose righteousness, according to the Psalms and the prophets, means that he lifts up those who are bowed down and humiliates the oppressors . . . In Isaiah especially, central attention is given to his role as a political revolutionary, an emphasis that breaks forth in the New Testament in the *Magnificat*. In the life, death and resurrection of Jesus, the messianic theme of destruction and restoration finds new meaning and focus . . . As God's action in the world aims at its transformation, the coming of Christ and the work of the Holy Spirit release new and disturbing forces in history that affect the process itself . . . those who participate in God's work cannot seek refuge in old ways nor draw back from the front lines because the situation is becoming increasingly dangerous. For it is in this struggle that the battle for the future of man is being waged; it is in the midst of apocalyptic events that we perceive signs of imminent victory.[88]

The Teleological Conception of the Church. In this conception there is a basic continuity between the past, the present, and the future. The eschaton will result from the unfolding of the immanent evolutionary process of the world. The most notable exponent of this view is Teilhard de Chardin. He sees the process of evolution as one of the increasing complexification of matter and with this increasing complexification an increasing spiritualization and personalization. Yet at different stages of this process, new levels are reached and new thresholds are crossed. The first great threshold was the appearance of life; the second was that of "hominization" when the evolutionary process became conscious of itself, and man became its spearhead. With the development of reason the "biosphere" becomes enveloped in the "noosphere" or mental envelope which includes not only men, but all their works. Teilhard extrapolates this process, already observed, into the future when it will converge on the "omega-point", a suprapersonal unity of all things in God who is tangential to this point and this process.

The phenomenon of Christ is the beginning of a new threshold, that of "amorization". Christ is the reflection into the heart of the evolutionary process of the omega-point which stands at the end. The reality of the omega-point is assured by Christ by actualizing it in our midst. The church or the Christian society is the symbol and the agent of "amorization", of self-transcending love, of the end already at work in the midst of the noosphere.

Teilhard's conception of a process moving towards the omega-point may appear deterministic at first and result in an uncreative passivity on the part of the Christian, allowing events to take their course. However, he does stress[89] that one of the features of this phase of the development of the noosphere is the "cosmic vertigo" man feels as he realizes that the development of the world of the future, including man himself, is entirely in his own hands. Up until now the process of evolution has been an unconscious one; man has not been fully aware of the social, cultural, and psychological laws which have led him to his present state. But now he must act in a fully responsible, conscious, and creative way to determine the future. Hence this makes Christ as the symbol and first phase of amorization of central importance for the future of man.[90]

The Prophetic Conception of the Church. This describes the most recent development among eschatological conceptions of the church. In general it is called the theology of hope and is represented by Jürgen Moltmann, Wolfhart Pannenberg, and Johannes B. Metz. They differ from Teilhard in eschewing the teleological elements in the historical process and see the function of Christianity as calling man to creative activity to develop the future. Metz in a recent lecture at Harvard wanted to distinguish his theology from the theology of hope but did not make the distinction clear. He calls his theology "a political theology". In all probability the difference arises from the different ecclesial backgrounds. In Moltmann and Pannenberg the emphasis is on the theology of the Word and there are elements of crisis theology. In Metz, the emphasis is on the sociological fact of the church, and its capacity to influence the direction of social change.

For Jürgen Moltmann

"Revelation" . . . has not the character of *logos*-determined illumination of the existing reality of man and the world, but has constitutively and basically the character of promise and is therefore of an eschatological kind. "Promise" is a fundamentally different thing from a "word-event" which brings truth and harmony between man and the reality that concerns him. "Promise" is in the first instance also a different thing from an eschatologically oriented view of reality as universal history. Promise announces the coming of a not yet existing reality from the future of the truth . . . On the other hand, it does not merely anticipate and clarify the realm of coming history and the realistic possibilities it contains. Rather, the "possible", and therewith "the future", arises entirely from God's word of promise and therefore goes beyond what is possible and impossible in the realistic sense. It does not illuminate a future which is somehow already inherent in reality. Rather "future" is that reality which fulfils and satisfies the promise because it completely corresponds to it and accords with it.[91]

In Moltmann's view there seems to be a radical disparity between reality, that is, the mundane, and the promise. The task of the Christian is that of a restlessness in the mundane context, a hope of finding a correspondence with the promise which would constitute the future in the present. The "promise"

> contradicts existing reality and discloses its own process concerning the future of Christ for man and the world. Revelation, recognized as promise and embraced in hope, thus sets an open stage for history and fills it with missionary enterprise and the responsible exercise of hope, accepting the suffering that is involved in the contradiction of reality, and setting out towards the promised future.[92]

The basis of the hope and the promise is in history, but at the same time defies history. This tension, even a contradiction, gives rise to the Christian missionary dynamic:

> In expounding the promises in the Christ event in terms of latency and tendency, we discovered a historic process of mediation between subject and object, which allows us neither to assign the future of Christ to a place within some system of world history and of the history of salvation, and thereby make this event relative to something that is foreign to it, acquired from other experiences and imposed upon it from without, nor yet to reflect the future of Christ into the existentialistic futurity of man. The history of the future of Christ and the historic character of the witnesses and missionaries condition each other and stand in a correlation of *promissio* and *missio*.[93]

The parousia of Christ "as a result of its eschatological promise, causes the present that can be experienced at any given moment to become historic by breaking away from the past and breaking out towards the things that are to come". The way in which the future operates on the present without becoming the present and without its being a mere interpolation of the present is examined by Wolfhart Pannenberg in an article entitled "Appearance as the Arrival of the Future".[94] As far as the Christian is concerned, "obedience to God . . . became turning to the future of the Reign of God. But wherever that occurs, there God already reigns unconditionally in the present, and such presence of the Reign of God does not conflict with its futurity but is derived from it and is itself only the anticipatory glimmer of its coming."[95]

Moltmann speaks of the church as "the exodus church", as "the pilgrim people of God", and he asks what these concepts of hope, and of promise, and of the future "mean for the social shape of Christianity in 'modern society' and for the task it has there to fulfill in the field of social ethics?"[96] Modern society seems to offer little or no scope for peculiarly Christian obedience or activity. But the question also arises whether "Christians can become an accommodating group, or whether their existence within the horizon of eschatological hope makes them resist accommodation and their presence has something peculiar to say to the world."[97] In the last part of the book Moltmann through a process of cultural analysis reveals that though modern society acquired its nature and power through emancipation from religion, nevertheless it is maintaining itself, and the present, against the openness of the future by exploiting religion in three ways. He describes modern society "as the cult of the absolute" and in this context religion has become:

a) the cult of the new subjectivity
b) the cult of co-humanity, and
c) the cult of the institution.

The social significance of the church is that of "an institutionalized (subjective) non-committal outlook. This, too, is a religious movement within the limits of a social standstill. It is Christianity as prescribed by the social milieu."[98] Moltmann claims that only when Christians become critically aware of this prevailing symbiosis can the church begin to challenge "the things that are socially axiomatic" in the interests of what the world is meant to be.

Only when they appear in society as a group which is not wholly adaptable and in the case of which the modern integration of everything with everything else fails to succeed, do they enter into a conflict-laden, but fruitful partnership with this society . . . Hope [embodied and nurtured in the church] alone keeps life — including public, social life — flowing free.[99]

The Christian church has not to serve mankind in order that this world may remain what it is, or may be preserved in the state in which it is, but in order that it may transform itself and become what it is promised to be.[100]

The coming lordship of the risen Christ cannot be merely hoped for and awaited . . . Hence mission means not merely propagation of faith and hope, but also historic transformation of life.[101]

Both Moltmann and Pannenberg see the resurrection of Christ as the anchor of hope in history. "The end of history is present prophetically in Jesus of Nazareth. In his resurrection the final end of universal history has been anticipated."[102]

However, some misgivings arise about this outlook:

a) It is not clear that it is not nonsense to talk about the future in the terms used by these theologians. "All words, images, models, concepts, paradigms, predictions, projections, and prophecies with which people deal with the future, if they wish to be understood, come from the past."[103]

b) The God Moltmann speaks of is the God of Abraham, Isaac, and Jacob, but we do not know *yet* what he is like. The knowledge of God is an inductive thing, but he does not make it clear why we should speak or want to speak of God at all. Yet God is not ultimately the basis of hope; the source of hope is the risen Christ who spoke about God.[104]

c) Moltmann refuses to compromise the "openness" of the future in any way. As Martin E. Marty asks:

> How can we make so much of the "If Christ has not been raised, then your faith is in vain" motif from I Cor. 15 and say so little about conventional Christian hoping in the light of another theme from the same chapter: "If for this life only we have hoped in Christ, we are of all men most to be pitied." He tends to bracket questions about afterlife hopes because they seem to contradict his view of completely open futures in the face of the God of hope.[105]

d) Moltmann, while providing a theological stimulus to and an ecclesiological context for action in the world in terms of social and cultural change, does not provide any clear goals, ultimate or penultimate, which can give direction to this action. He is content to say: "In despair, men anticipate a destructive end of history. In presumptuousness, men anticipate a perfected end of history. But effective hope is courage for history *before* its end and a courage to endure in the midst of ambiguities."[106]

It is probably to provide a more tangible base for social action and a specific focus or objective for social change that Johannes B. Metz calls his theology a "political theology" and sees the church as a palpable agent for social and political change. For Moltmann, "The future is open. It can bring everything or nothing, heaven or hell."[107] There is more than a tinge of gloom in this. In Rahner and Metz, there is a slightly greater emphasis on optimism. Rahner sees the church, as does the Vatican Council, as "the sacrament of the salvation of the world".[108] However, Rahner does not give sufficient emphasis to the futuristic quality of salvation to make the church a credible agent of social change.

Metz seems to subscribe to the substance of Moltmann's theological outlook but is concerned to give it more concrete embodiment in a programme for the church and in terms of penultimate goals. Concerning the goals for Christian activity, he recalls that Aquinas insisted that man has only one ultimate end, the future promised by God:

In relation to mankind's future one distinction disappears, which theology uses, and all too readily uses: the distinction between the natural and the supernatural . . . The two dimensions converge in relation to the future. The hope which relates Christians to the future cannot ignore the world and its future.[109]

Nor can the church merely express a pious hope about the future. It must critically and actively concern itself "with the great political, social and technical utopias, with the promises of universal peace, universal justice and the universal liberation of man for which our society longs".[110] It must deal, with specifically human tools of analysis, with the concrete goals each culture, or theory, or civilization offers. It has no privileged access to the future, hence does not offer an "ideology of the future", but more "a hope against all hope".

One of the features of Metz's theology is its reaction to the "privatization" of Christianity, against the "transformation of salvation into a private matter through transcendental, personalistic, or existential factors". The salvation which is the object of Christian hope "is related not simply or primarily to the salvation of the individual . . . but to the salvation of the covenant, of the people, of the many."[111]

When Metz calls his theology a "political theology" and when he speaks of one of the functions of the church as being a "political function", he acknowledges that this is unfortunate and somewhat misleading terminology. He does not want the church to be an established church nor to be allied with a particular political party, theory, or programme. He uses the term to indicate that the church must be vitally concerned about and involved in real, mundane issues. But its political theory will be negative in the sense that it must keep a critical and creative distance in the interests of the future.

Hence it is possible to summarize the features of Metz's conception of the church:

a) "The church is not the goal of her own movement; this goal is the Kingdom of God."

b) "The Church . . . lives always from the proclamation of her own provisional character and her progressive historical surrender to the coming Kingdom of God towards which she moves like a pilgrim."

c) "The hope to which the Church bears witness is not a hope which bears upon the Church herself, but upon the Kingdom of God as the future of the world."

d) "Thus the relationship of the Church to the world is not chiefly one of place but of time. The Church is not simply the not-world, she is that world of men who draw their stimulus and inspiration from the future promised by God and who call into question the world which is emerging from the present and human possibilities. She offers to the self-confident world with its hopes and dreams a liberation and a positive critique."

e) "How does the Church realize this mission for the future of the world?" Not by mere contemplation! Not by mere passive waiting, but by action "that must be essentially creative and militant and must be realized in a creative-militant eschatology". The goal for which Christians strive is not ready-made ahead of us, already there, but must be created by human initiative.[112]

In one way this ecclesiology is very positive in that it horizontalizes the perspective of the church, it defines it in terms of social and political change and leaves the nature of the Kingdom and of the existence and nature of God to be discovered inductively in the future. It distinguishes carefully between the political function the contemporary church should have and its political role in the sacral age. It leads Christianity out of the sphere of the individual and the private into that of the social and the public. However, inevitably, it leaves the goals undefined and is rather sanguine about the possibility of mobilizing any of the churches under the banner of this programme because they have been, in the past, forces of reaction and conservatism. This problem can be considered in the concluding section.

The Pneumatic Conception of the Church. One of the basic characteristics of the prophetic eschatological conception of the church is that it comes as close as possible to satisfying the secularist demands without actually capitulating to the inherent reductionist metaphysics of those demands. The prophetic conception of the church, especially in Metz's theology, centres on four relatively palpable entities: Christ as a historical person, the church as a sociological fact, the world of which the church is part, and the future. While eliminating the almost chronic dualism of traditional religion, it has maintained, against secularism, the complexity of reality and our experience of it. Its tone in using the traditional language of Christianity, God, the Holy Spirit, the Word, is tentative and provisional. Its procedure is radically inductive and it expects the traditional Christian lexicon to take on significance and value in relation to creative involvement in the world in terms of the future of which the function of the church is defined.

The post-secularist pneumatic conception of the church is not as accommodating. While maintaining a typically contemporary evolutionary perspective, it recalls two features of the teachings of Joachim of Fiore (1132-1202), and of the other eschatological sects since the beginning of Christianity: his anti-institutional fervour and his concept of the Holy Ghost as a creative power initiating a new phase of the history of salvation. For Joachim of Fiore, the Trinity manifests itself progressively in three successive periods of the history of salvation. Each period is dominated by or manifests a person: the first period of salvation is that of the Father; the second period, the age of Christ, is that of the Son; and the third and eschatological period is that of the Holy Ghost.[113]

In an essay entitled "Post-Christian Aspects of Radical Theology"[114] Maynard Kaufman claims that the Christian God died, that is, became no longer tenable, mainly because this God was spoken of as revealed in Christ. It was no longer possible to speak of God because it was no longer possible to speak of Christ. He suggests that "the failure of Christology implicitly preceded the so-called death of God, but that it became explicit only afterwards, and that the contemporary theological situation should therefore be positively affirmed as post-Christian. It is possible to be a post-Christian theist rather than a Christian atheist."[115]

Kaufman sees the return to theism through the process philosophy of John Cobb and Alfred M. Whitehead, for this kind of philosophy "enables a reappropriation of divine immanence in nature".[116] This philosophy allows a religion of creativity to reflect the Christological religion of redemption and allows man greater freedom to contribute to the process of the revelation of the Holy Spirit. The Holy Spirit is not an abstract or disembodied Spirit; it is "the spirit of life and vitality, and it is manifest as freedom and creativity". Only "a theology of the Third Person of the Trinity can provide the basis for a more constructive radical theology".[117]

This leads to a radical or discontinuous transition from the age of Christ to the age of the Holy Spirit which would, presumably, be manifested among those whose creativity is greatest. Kaufman does not apply this theology in terms of an explicit ecclesiology.

Indeed, throughout history, the "enthusiasts" who have invoked the Holy Spirit have dispensed with the church as of any but merely worldly significance. His post-Christian theism, however, does make it possible to identify and characterize a trend.

Rosemary Ruether's *The Church Against Itself*,[118] though differing in important ways from Kaufman's position, is nevertheless cast in a similar mould. Her perspective is eschatological; her antipathy is institutional religion and she defines the church in terms of the relationship between people and the Holy Spirit. The aim of the book is either covertly or overtly to seek the essence of the church, and this entails describing what the church *is not* in terms of the church as we know it. "The fault of the church is not necessarily signalled by gross immorality . . . [it] resides in a misappropriation of its relationship to God and man".[119] As a consequence "the church becomes its own chief theological problem".[120]

The chief theological problem or the chief paradox, for Ruether, is that "the very instrument for the proclamation of man's freedom from the law of death [is] itself most deeply entrenched in the law of death".[121] Without considering the accuracy of this superlative comparison with other institutions under the law of death, the question arises, how could it be otherwise than that a human institution is under the law of death? The difficulty is that Ruether wants the church to be seen as its "broken, finite, relative self",[122] but when these characteristics take the very typically human form of a tendency to absolutize itself, Ruether takes the church too seriously. Surely the very propensity of the church to absolutize or deify itself is a symptom of its broken, finite, relative self.

What then is the church? Ruether gives two definitions of the church, one of the *true church,* the other of the function of the institutional church:

The church, in its true nature, is not detached from history but vitally relevant to history and progress, and stands at the very heart of the creative ferment of history. It is wherever history is experienced as "kairos", as the decisive moment of conversion and as the breakthrough of new powers and possibilities.[123]

Each generation begets the next. Without the historical institution—the tradition—the material means by which faith is ever born anew would disappear. In this sense the Catholic tradition is quite right when it makes the structure—the outer means—indispensable to the inner grace. What it fails to see, however, is that this inner grace is not born through cause-and-effect relation with the outer means. They provide only the occasion and the possibility, while the inner continuity with the pneumatic reality of the Church is recreated again and again by each generation's direct encounter with the Spirit.[124]

Ruether is intent on affirming the creative efficacy of the Kingdom about to break into human history, but she fails successfully to resolve the problem of the church; indeed, for her, the church's dilemma is hopeless.[125] But the central difficulty with this conception of the church is that, though it is radically eschatological, it is fundamentally pre-secular. The theological underpinning is that of crisis theology which sees a radical discontinuity between history and salvation. There is a primitive dualism inherent in the inner-outer dichotomy of the church. The Holy Spirit and the serving Word are treated as given, and as absolutes when, as has been pointed out, the very existence of God is central to the problematic of the church today. Moreover, Ruether does not explain, given the influence of the Holy Spirit and the acknowledgment by the church of its own relative and provisional character, why the Holy Spirit could not possibly use this historically conditioned institution as a *cause* of inner grace.

Ruether seems to speak from a vantage point that allows for an outside, and hence privileged, perspective on the relation of the absolute Holy Spirit to the institutional structure which "expels the Spirit because it claims an absolute possession of it",[126] on the one hand, and to the creative few who experience *kairos* on the other. In a way there is nothing new, for the church has always distinguished in theory between the sheep and the goats in its midst. What is odd, if not altogether new, is the unwillingness to accept this ménage of sheep and goats as the church. This unwillingness stems, in turn, from a radical distaste for political action within the church to make it what it is meant to be or symbolize. Yet this unwillingness reveals an ambivalence in the attitude of many Christians similar to that indicated by Irving Howe in his criticism of the cultural style of the American "new left".

The "new leftist" . . . asserts his rebellion against the deceit and the hollowness of American society . . . But in the course of his rebellion he tends to reject not merely the middle-class ethos but a good many other things he too hastily associates with it. He tends to think of style as the very substance of his revolt, and while he may, on one side of himself, engage in valuable activities . . . he nevertheless tacitly accepts the "givenness" of American society, has little hope or expectation of changing it, and thereby, in effect, settles for a mode of personal differentiation . . . [Indeed he] is frequently trapped in a symbiotic relationship with the very middle class he rejects, dependent upon it for his self definition.[127]

It may not be accurate to apply this to Rosemary Ruether but it can be transposed to describe a Christian style which defines itself by appeal to the pneumatic through a repudiation of the institutional church. The consequence is that the exponents of this style provide themselves with a substitute for hard-headed political action within the church to make it an effective agent of social change in the world. The anti-institutional style tends to become a guarantee of *really* belonging to the essential or pneumatic church.

In an article entitled "Pie-in-the-Sky Theology?" Daniel Callahan describes the basic moves in the search for *the* reality of the church and the "complex legitimations of this reality":

These moves are three:
1) Deny that the apparent reality is the genuine reality
2) Point out the personal and intellectual deficiencies of those who notice only the apparent reality
3) Assert that the genuine reality can only be espied by the eye of faith.[128]

He goes on to claim that Rosemary Ruether carries this process to new heights. She repudiates almost all that the Christian and especially the Catholic church stands for, but

All the confidence she takes from us concerning the church, she saves up and heaps on the person of the Holy Spirit . . . [But] how she got hold of such certainties about the workings of the Spirit is not explained. Nor are we illuminated about why the very concept of "Spirit" should not be subject to the same kind of critical dissection she accords almost everything else Christian.[129]

Though the pneumatic conception of the church claims to be "an existentially descriptive ecclesiology which grasps the church's eschatological essence, not apart from, but in and through the profound and tragic dichotomies of its historical existence",[130] nevertheless it must introduce and appeal to an extra-mundane, ephemeral and in the last analysis, gnostic factor to make a grasp of the church's essence possible. In the first place this conception is pre-secular. In the second place it would have a debilitating effect on the possibility of the church's having any creative eschatological influence on the world for two reasons:

a) A great deal of energy would be dissipated on distinguishing between the historically conditioned institution and the pneumatic essence of the church.

b) The only *palpable* focus of concerted and creative action on the world, the institutional church, instead of being a symbol of eschatological hope, would itself be a classical instance, in Ruether's view, of the hopelessness of the human condition. It is also difficult to see how such an institution could possibly be "the material means by which faith is ever born anew".

The peculiar thing is that just at the time when the churches are showing signs of a profound reassessment of their values, goals and allegiances, the church should be described as that institution "most deeply entrenched in the law of death". What must be noted, however, is the effect that radical pneumatic influences have had on the church throughout history in stimulating it to a process of renewal.

Conclusion

Two central and interrelated problems emerge from a consideration of the contemporary conceptions of the church. The thrust in theology and ecclesiology has been towards dealing with tangible mundane terms and entities, such as Christ, church, world, and future, without accepting the reductionist exclusion of the possibility of personal and divine transcendents. Theologians seem content to allow talk about the traditional Christian categories to emerge from an inductive awareness developed in the context of Christian social action in the world. The two immediate ecclesiological problems, therefore, are:

a) What specifically is the *function* of the church in and towards the world in which it finds itself?

b) In the light of this function, how can the *structures* of the church be adapted to achieve the optimum capacity to fulfill this function?

These two problems and the context in which they arise have important ecumenical implications. An awareness of the evolutionary character of human and, therefore, of ecclesiastical existence, an appreciation of the consequent relative and culturally conditioned character of doctrinal formulations and ecclesial structures and especially a sensitivity to "the pressure of the future", all result in the de-ontologizing of Christian conceptions and can lead to the dissolution of barriers among the various churches.

If the church today is to be defined in terms of its action for political and cultural change in the world under the influence of "the absolute future", two problems concerning the structure of the church arise:

a) It is important to distinguish among (a) the organization which any sociological entity must have, to be a sociological entity at all; (b) the current sclerosis which probably affects many of the structures of the church, either the people who occupy the posts or the elements in and disposition of the posts themselves; (c) the institutions, such as schools, hospitals, real estate, etc., which are peripheral to the structure of the church, which bind it to specific cultural, social, and economic forms and which can function to ally the church too closely with the world.

b) It is important, secondly, to distinguish between the processes of *multiplication* and *complexification* of structures in any organism or organization. Robert Bellah gives the following definition of evolution:

Evolution at any system level I define as a process of increasing differentiation and complexity of organization which endows the organism, social system or whatever the unit in question may be, with greater capacity to adapt to its environment so that it is in some sense more autonomous relative to its environment than were its less complex ancestors.[131]

The structural problem for the church is whether it should break with the past and form a more simple adaptive non-structure, as the existentialist and pneumatic conceptions of the church seem to demand, or work towards greater complexification while avoiding multiplication of structures.

In all probability the church must do two things to ensure its future effectiveness. It must sever its umbilical relationships with non-ecclesial structures and then consciously set about the process of complexification. At the moment the danger is one of multiplication, both within the churches and among the churches. The Vatican Council and the World Council of Churches were both attempting to achieve similar goals in their conventions. But the duality is reminiscent of the development of two sets of cerebral cortices in the dinosaur. The cerebral lobes multiplied instead of complexified and the dinosaur was doomed to extinction. It no longer had the mobility and flexibility for adapting to a changing environment.[132] On the other hand the iconoclastic ambition of some Christians to eliminate all institutional churches would leave Christians without a formal and empirical term of reference, apart from Christ, for their theological lexicon, and deprive them of any substantial fulcrum in the interests of the future.

Part of the reason for the antipathy to the institutional church, especially in the Catholic church, is the aversion for the bureaucratic forms the institutions have assumed. However, as Harvey Cox points out:

> Bureaucracy is headed for extinction, not only in the church but in society. Warren Bennis, of the Sloan School of Management at M.I.T., says that bureaucracy, with its well-defined hierarchy of authority, its insistence on impersonality in work relations, and its emphasis on technical competence alone, is on the way out . . . It will not do for a period of accelerated scientific and social innovation. It is too rigid to cope effectively with the growing role of information feedback and ceaseless organizational self-analysis. Bennis foresees in industry the emergence of what he calls the "organic-adaptive structure" to replace bureaucracy. It will be based on different views of power, of man and of the meaning of organization itself. It will maximize the inclusion of persons in decision-making processes which affect their lives . . . If the society itself needs a new style of social organization, perhaps the church can serve the world by experimenting in its own life with unprecedented new forms of corporate existence.[133]

The Vatican Council, in enunciating the principle of collegiality, explicitly of the bishops, but by implication, collegiality of the priests and the laity in the church, also enunciated the principle on which inclusive, non-bureaucratic, decision-making, "organic-adaptive" structures could be organized. This principle is already being implemented in the Senate of bishops, bishops' national conferences, priests' senates, and parish councils. What has yet failed to materialize is a structure which will be inclusive of all the churches.

However, the structures will arise only as a result of an agreement among the churches of the basic ecclesiological perspective and goals. The World Council of Churches' 1966 conference on Church and Society clearly indicated its consciousness of its role in social change, especially in the final press statement entitled "An Impatient World's Challenge to the Church".[134]

There are important post-secular elements in the ecclesiological goals stated by Vatican II. Among many pre-secular conceptions and statements it describes the church:

a) As "at once a sign and a safeguard of the transcendence of the human person"[135] *b*) **As the sacrament of the unity, the reconciliation and the salvation of all men.**[136]

Most important is the eschatological perspective of the church:

> The present historical situation is leading humanity into a new stage. As the salt of the earth and the light of the world the Church is summoned with special urgency to save and renew every creature. In this way all things can be restored in Christ, and in Him mankind can compose one family and one people.[137]

The ambition of the reconciliation and unity of all men is the penultimate goal of the church. The church remains, however, unclear about how this goal is related to the ultimate goal:

> We do not know the time for the consummation of the earth and of humanity. Nor do we know how all things will be transformed. As deformed by sin, the shape of this world will pass away. But we are taught that God is preparing a new earth where justice will abide and whose blessedness will answer and surpass all the longings for peace which spring up in the human heart . . . Therefore, while we are warned that it profits a man nothing if he gain the whole world and lose himself, the expectation of a new earth must not weaken but rather stimulate our concern for cultivating this one. For here grows the body of a new human family, a body which even now is able to give some kind of foreshadowing of the new age.[138]

Part Two

THEOLOGICAL PROBES

The Too Subtle God

God's my god . . . But I find him rather too subtle . . . I don't know where he is nor what he wants.
Robert Bolt
A Man for All Seasons

"But perhaps we should love what we cannot understand."
"No, Father, I've a very different idea of love. And until my dying day I shall refuse to love a scheme of things in which children are put to torture."
Albert Camus
The Plague

Atheism seems to be the inevitable consequence of the process of secularization. If man is to be effectively emancipated from ecclesiastical domination and from the control of mythical and metaphysical systems, it would seem that he must also be rid of any acknowledgment of or dependence on God. The Vatican Council described atheism as "among the most serious problems of this age", yet it was sympathetic in its approach to and treatment of the causes of atheism. It claimed that "atheism results not merely from a violent protest against the evil in this world, or from the absolute character with which certain human values are unduly invested, and which thereby accords them the stature of God". The Council even attributed some of the responsibility for atheism in the world today to Christians themselves.

> Yet believers themselves frequently bear some responsibility for this situation. For taken as a whole, atheism is not a spontaneous development but stems from a variety of causes, including a critical reaction against religious beliefs, and in some places against the Christian religion in particular. Hence believers can have more than a little to do with the birth of atheism. To the extent that they neglect their own training in the faith, or teach erroneous doctrine, or are deficient in their religious, moral or social life, they must be said to conceal rather than reveal the authentic face of God and religion.[1]

Sometimes atheism is merely the result of men becoming so involved in the trivia of life that they never ask themselves any ultimate questions. Sometimes "men form for themselves such a fallacious idea of God that when they repudiate this figment they are by no means rejecting the God of the gospel". More often, today, the reductionist tendency manifests itself when it is claimed "that everything can be explained by this kind of scientific reasoning alone".

However, the Council recognized the basic grounds for the systematic atheism of today. It is a necessary condition of man's freedom "to be an end unto himself, the sole artisan and creator of his own history . . . This form argues that by its nature religion thwarts such liberation by arousing man's hope for a deceptive future life, thereby diverting him from the constructing of the earthly city."

The task for the Christian, therefore, is to take seriously the insights, the values, and the achievements of the modern world, examine the case against God and decide to what extent it is still possible to acknowledge, believe in, and talk about God. Perhaps it is the case that some kind of intellectual and spiritual justification taking the form of atheism is required for the establishment of an authentic and vital relationship with God. It could be that contemporary experience will reveal to us that the kind of creative autonomy advocated in the secular age is the condition of developing an awareness of God.

Werner Pelz has pointed out that "when we use the word 'God' we are talking about something which no longer connects with anything in most people's life, except with whatever happens to be left over when all the vital connections have been made".[2] The claim I will want to make is that when we use the word "God" we are talking about someone we relate to, and even become aware of, only when all the vital connections in life have been made. We can even begin to suspect that the very conflict between the theists and the atheists is a phase of the conflict between advocates of ecclesiastical power and their opponents. It is possible that ecclesiastics have propagated an image of God which poses a challenge to the creative autonomy of man when it is their duty to acknowledge the total, free, and creative activity of man as the proudest boast of God and the condition of man's relationship with him. We are reminded of the epigram of Voltaire: "If God has made us in his image, we have certainly returned the compliment." Churches which aimed at dominating the world instead of serving it, presented to the world an alien God which sought to command man by his transcendence, power, and majesty. It is their duty to present to the world an immanent God who inspires the world with his love, and challenges man in Christ to live life to the full.

The need for a radical purification of the image of God is not new to biblical faith nor to Christianity. The question is, will the kind of purification which is demanded in a secular age make it possible ever to talk about God again? William Hamilton has said: "God is dead. We are not talking about the absence of the experience of God, but about the experience of the absence of God." This experience of the absence of God is testified to in the literature and art forms of our age. The films of Ingmar Bergman trace the gradual disappearance of the experience of God, from the Middle Ages to our day, until in "The Silence" the absence of God is a palpable and threatening thing.

Some Christians have accepted the complete absence of God, the impossibility of talking about him, and the futility of referring to him as among the basic data of contemporary Christian experience. They take as the starting point of a theology for our age the famous passage from Dietrich Bonhoeffer's *Letters and Papers from Prison*:

So our coming of age leads us to a true recognition of our situation before God. God would have us know that we must live as men who manage our lives without him. The God who is with us is the God who forsakes us . . . The God who lets us live in the world without the working hypothesis of God is the God before whom we stand continually. Before God and with God we live without God. God lets himself be pushed out of the world on to the cross. He is weak and powerless in the world, and that is precisely the way, the only way, in which he is with us and helps us.[3]

And yet, for this passage to make sense, it cannot be taken literally, for the passage wants to speak about God. Hence, it is not good enough just to agree not to talk about God if one is to cope in any way adequately with atheism today.

For practical purposes we can speak of contemporary atheism as implying a threefold incapacity for or disavowal of God: a logical disavowal, a cultural disavowal, and, in the case of Christian atheism, a theological disavowal of God. In some ways these three aspects or phases are interconnected and overlap. However, collectively they pose the question whether belief in God has been finally disposed of, or whether, in some ways at least, contemporary experience has merely repudiated a figment promoted by the self-proclaimed champions of God.

The traditional division between natural and revealed theology prevailed in a context of the ascendancy of the timeless ontocratic world view. It is less easy to use this division when our appreciation of reality is radically evolutionary and when the prevailing consciousness is not metaphysical but historical. Revelation is described in the *Catholic Encyclopedia* as "the communication of some truth by God to a rational creature through means which are beyond the ordinary course of nature". The difficulty lies in deciding, using natural criteria, what the limitations of nature are. As Anthony Flew observes in *God and Philosophy*;

The crunch comes over the problem of identification. The great temptation is to assume that we have some natural (as opposed to revealed) means of telling that something, notwithstanding that it did actually happen, nevertheless could not have happened naturally (in that sense). We have not. Our only way of determining the capacities and the incapacities of nature is to study what does in fact occur. Suppose, for instance, that all previous observation and experiment had suggested that some performance was beyond human power; and suppose that we find, to our amazement, that after all some people can do it. Still this by itself is a reason, not for postulating a series of infusions of supernatural grace, but for shaking up the psychological assumptions which these discoveries have discredited.[4]

This dichotomy between natural and supernatural, between nature and revelation, has its source in the attempt to transpose the New

Testament contrast between flesh and spirit into the terms of Stoic and Neo-Platonic philosophy. The transposition results in a difference of levels of being, whereas the New Testament contrast is concerned with different modes of being at the same historical level.[5]

The Logical Disavowal of God

The process of the contemporary disavowal of God began with the publication in 1779 of David Hume's *Dialogues Concerning Natural Religion*,[6] in which he attempted to dispose of the argument for the existence of God from the design of or order in the universe. Hume pointed out that any universe is bound to have the appearance of being designed. The theist would be bound to describe the sort of universe that could possibly exist without this appearance. Secondly, the analogy between the universe and the human artifact is inadequate in the argument, because we know exactly what the artifact is designed *for,* whereas, in the case of the universe, we cannot tell, if it *is* designed, what it is designed *for,* and yet it is essential to know this, to know that it is in fact designed. This objection becomes rather more acute in an age which is more consciously evolutionary. In an age in which the general assumption was that reality was a complex of relatively static interrelated entities, it was more feasible to entertain the idea of an ordered universe. Now there is a sense in which the theological argument can be stated so that its focus is less the relationship between things and more the interdependence of their existence. This is the general thrust of the "ways" of Aquinas and to these I will return later. In his *Critique of Pure Reason*,[7] Emmanuel Kant criticized the Cartesian form of the ontological argument. This argument, originally stated by Anselm, had been criticized previously by theists including Aquinas. However, the Kantian critique introduced a factor which appeared to strike at the very heart of the more discursive proofs for God's existence elaborated by Aquinas. Kant rejected the basic assumption that existence is a predicate, which something can either have or lack. For Kant, the idea of existence does not add anything to a particular thing or kind of thing. When we assert that something exists, Kant claimed, we are merely applying the concept of the thing to things as they are. Hume in *A Treatise of Human*

Nature[8] was to apply this in a way embarrassing to the theistic proofs by claiming that the existence of something implies nothing about the existence of anything else.

This point has been driven home by Bertrand Russell in his analysis of the word "exists". According to his theory of descriptions, although "exists" is grammatically a predicate, logically it performs a different function, which can be illustrated by transposing "Cows exist" into its logically correct form: "There are x's such that 'x is a cow' is true." Russell's claim can be and has been questioned but we can allow the matter to rest here for the moment.

In both Anglo-Saxon and Continental philosophy, the various attempts to establish a natural and reasoned basis for talk about God, either in the direct experience of God, or by some form of proof, were subjected to an increased volume and intensity of criticism. That the criticism was not initially decisive was due to a number of factors. First of all, there was very little effective communication between the theists and the philosophers. Secondly, the theists claimed different epistemological stances from those of the critics so that divergences of opinion about the validity of grounds for asserting the existence of God had to be pursued, almost endlessly, into the intricacies of a variety of theories of knowledge. Thirdly, though the philosophical challenge to theism became increasingly serious, the cultural climate was such as to protect the theistic viewpoint, for a time, from the full thrust of the challenge. Fourthly, theists, in one way or another, found devices for withdrawing assertions about, or proofs for, the existence of God from the arena in which the ordinary logical criteria prevailed. A recent example of this is the claim of Professor John Macquarrie that the question of God is not a logical question. "We must remember that our question is the *religious question* of God, and that it has an *existential* structure." That is to say, "it is not a theoretical or speculative question, raised by the intellect alone, but a practical question posed by the whole being of man who has to exist in the world and decide about his existence."[9] Partly because of the dynamics of its own development and partly as an attempt to eliminate metaphysics, a great deal of Anglo-Saxon philosophy became concerned with the problem of meaning. This development in the twentieth century intensified the challenge to the champions of theistic assertions, for it appeared to outflank the difficulty of diverse epistemologies and also to pursue the theists onto whatever ground they were willing to defend themselves on. They were asked for the meaning of the terms they were using.

In the first instance, however, they were not asked. They were told that all talk about God was nonsense. In the heyday of logical positivism, the claim was not that the proofs for the existence of God were invalid. It was not that the various answers to the question "Does God exist?" were misleading. It was the much stronger claim that the question could not even be asked, because the question itself was meaningless. Thus A. J. Ayer says:

> And our view that the utterances about the nature of God are nonsensical, so far from being identical with, or even lending support to, either of these familiar contentions, is actually incompatible with them. For if the assertion that there is a God is nonsensical, then the atheist's assertion that there is no God is equally nonsensical, since it is only a significant proposition that can be significantly contradicted. As for the agnostic, although he refrains from saying either that there is or that there is not a God, he does not deny that whether a transcendent God exists is a genuine question. He does not deny that the two sentences "There is a transcendent God" and "There is no transcendent God" express propositions one of which is actually true and the other false. All that he says is that we have no means of telling which of them is true, and therefore ought not to commit ourselves to either. But we have seen that the sentences in question do not express propositions at all. And this means that agnosticism is ruled out.[10]

The technique by which the logical positivists determined which assertions or questions had meaning was the application of the verification principle. In its strong form it demanded as the condition of a meaningful statement that it be, in principle, empirically verifiable. Thus the nadir of atheism was achieved. One could not even broach the topic of the possibility of the existence of God without running the risk of eccentricity, and this climate prevailed in Anglo-Saxon philosophy until it was realized that the verification principle itself was an arrant piece of nonsense. It did not satisfy its own criterion of meaning. However, there were a number of "theistic" attempts to explain the use of "God-talk" within the limits of the criteria of the logical positivists. The most notable of these was R. B. Braithwaite's *An Empiricist's View of the Nature of Religious Belief*.[11] In this he attempted a non-cognitive account of theological language and reduced talk about God to language which is ethically but not factually significant. Thus he claimed that "the primary use of religious assertions is to announce allegiance to a set of moral principles" and the Christian's assertion that "God is love" is an expression of the "intention to follow an agapeistic way of life".

A more recent and more spectacular attempt to reconcile the traditional language of Christianity with the criteria of logical positivism is that of Paul van Buren's *The Secular Meaning of the Gospel*.[12] However, both of these books are forced into the situation of saying what Christians *really* mean when they use certain words and make theological assertions. They *reduce* uncomfortable assertions to a more convenient class, thus eliminating the disquieting elements in them. A second disadvantage with this kind of enterprise is that it is now recognized that they capitulated rather too easily to the demands of logical positivism, just at a time when some of the important features of logical positivism were being discredited.

An important step in the logical disavowal of God came with the statement of Anthony Flew's now famous "Gardener parable". Flew used this parable to refine the technique of attempting to come to grips with the meaning of assertions about God, but instead of demanding that they be empirically verifiable as a condition of their being meaningful, he asked the theists to state the situation which would have to prevail before they would consider a theological assertion false. In this way Flew aimed to put the onus of establishing the meaning of these assertions onto the theists. The principle he invokes amounts to this: if a person wants to assert that God exists, he should be able to say what would count against the assertion. Now if nothing is acknowledged as being able to count against an assertion such as "God exists" or "God is good", then the assertion must be factually meaningless.

Flew is disturbed by the traditional ability of theologians to continue to distinguish and qualify what was in the first instance a bold assertion, until it suffers "the death by a thousand qualifications". However, it seems that the theologians are never prepared to admit that the original bold assertion has been logically interred. Flew's parable was meant to precipitate a showdown and effect once and for all the logical disavowal of God.

The parable,[13] which is an adapted and tightened version of John Wisdom's parable related in his haunting and revelatory article "Gods", runs as follows:

Once upon a time two explorers came upon a clearing in the jungle. In the clearing were growing many flowers and many weeds. One explorer says, "Some gardener must tend this plot". The other disagrees, "There is no gardener". So they pitch their tents and set a watch. No gardener is ever seen. "But perhaps he is an invisible gardener". So they set up a barbed-wire fence. They electrify it. They patrol with bloodhounds . . . But no shrieks ever suggest that some intruder has received a shock. No movements of the wire ever betray an invisible climber. The bloodhounds never give cry. Yet still the believer is not convinced. "But there is a gardener, invisible, intangible, insensible to electric shocks, a gardener who has no scent and makes no sound, a gardener who comes secretly to look after the garden which he loves". At last the sceptic despairs, "But what remains of your original assertion? Just how does what you call an invisible, intangible, eternally elusive gardener differ from an imaginary gardener or even from no gardener at all?"

The believer in the parable illustrates for Flew "the peculiar danger, the endemic evil, of theological utterance", for so often "a fine brash hypothesis may thus be killed by inches, the death by a thousand qualifications". This leads Flew to argue that

anything which would count against the assertion, or which would induce the speaker to withdraw it and to admit that it had been mistaken, must be part of (or the whole of) the meaning of the negation of that assertion. And to know the meaning of the negation of an assertion is, as near as makes no matter, to know the meaning of that assertion. And if there is nothing a putative assertion denies, then there is nothing that it asserts either.

Consequently Flew puts the question to anyone asserting the existence or the goodness of God: "What would have to occur or to have occurred to constitute for you a disproof of the love of, or of the existence of God?"

In *A Man for All Seasons* Wolsey chides Thomas More with the remark: "You're a constant regret to me, Thomas. If only you could just see facts flat on, without the moral squint." This parable of Flew's is demanding that the theist see facts "flat on" without a theological squint. The difficulty is that the "facts" cannot be stated as clearly as Flew's parable would have. In the symposium which the parable introduced, R. M. Hare conceded that "on the ground marked out by Flew, he seems to me completely victorious". However, this could be a rather too easy surrender.

John Hick takes up Flew's challenge by questioning whether the notion of verification is a purely logical one or whether it is both logical and psychological.[14] "Verification is thus primarily the name for an event which takes place in human consciousness. It refers to an experience, the experience of ascertaining that a given proposition or set of propositions is true."[15] The question then arises as to how public the process of verification must be. When one person alone has concluded that an assertion is true, can the assertion be said to have been verified? The question then is, how can the verifying experience be communicated?

Part at least of the process of communicating the experience is the communication of the conditions in which the experience can be verified, for as Hick observes,[16] "verification is often construed as the verification of a prediction", and indeed, "when we are interested in the verifiability of propositions as the criteria of their having factual meaning, the notion of prediction becomes central". The conclusion of this line of reasoning is that just as the "logic of 'molecule' determines what you must do to verify statements about molecules" so "the logic of 'God' determines what you must do to verify statements about 'God'."[17]

Now if it is the case that the logic of "God" entails a statement of the conditions for the verification of statements about God, then an accurate account of these conditions is essential both to the ultimate verification and to the meaning of the statements. If part of the logic of "God" has been an insistence on or an attitude to the world which is static, radically antipathetical, conservative, and uncreative, when in fact these are not the appropriate conditions, then it is understandable that a widespread refutation of this logic will prevail, and atheism will be the result.

A second misgiving that Hick has about Flew's demand is that he presumes that verification and falsification must be related symmetrically. It is possible to imagine, for example, a proposition which could at some future time be verified, but which could never be falsified. Thus if a person claims that after death he will have conscious experiences, we can see that while this proposition can be verified by the actual persistence of consciousness after death, it cannot be falsified if there is no consciousness after death.

This now allows us to see how Flew's parable distorts the difference between the theist and the atheist. In the parable, the difference between the two is of the kind, why this and not that. Flew's theist wants to posit the invisible gardener as that which makes the difference between jungle and clearing. But the traditional Christian notion of God is that of Creator, he who makes the difference not between this and this, but between this and nothing. For this reason Aquinas maintained that there was no incompatibility between the notion of creation and the eternity of the created universe.[18] Hence to the non-believer's question, "Just what would have to happen not merely (morally and wrongly) to tempt but also (logically and rightly) to entitle us to say 'God does not love us' or even 'God does not exist'?" Flew's believer should have answered: "The annihilation of all goodness and all existing things." It is precisely because things *exist* and there *is* goodness that the believer wants to say that "God exists" and "God is good". It is not precisely because they are of this kind or quality rather than that kind or quality. Hence, while the technique for verifying the assertion "God exists" would have to be indicated as part of the foundation for the meaning of the assertion, in this view, the assertion could never really be falsified.

A second and relatively minor defect in Flew's statement of the case is the role of the explorers. In the parable they are observers arguing about a problematical state of affairs of which they are not part. This illustrates one of the deficiencies of the merely logical approach to the question of God and allows us to share some sympathy with John Macquarrie's description of this question as "existential" rather than "logical". In fact the explorers are part of the problem. The explorers are part of the situation which has to be accounted for and explained. They are, moreover, not merely part of the garden or the jungle. Whether the world is described as garden or jungle, the men who ask the questions are themselves gardeners and this further complicates the issue, for as Brian Wicker points out in *Culture and Theology*:[19]

. . . the sharp distinction drawn by former thinkers between subjective consciousness and the external world is simply a rationalization . . . That we are already inserted into the world, before even our most primitive concepts of subject and object arise, is the basic condition on which all knowledge and understanding of the world itself rests.

However, these observations are meant to show that Flew's parable does not decisively dispose of the traditional Christian notion of God. They do not establish that there is a creator in the way that Flew wanted it established. What they do establish, however, is an area of reference as a foundation for the use of the term "God". This area of reference is what is called, misleadingly, "Existence". There is not the space here to delve into the intricacies of the logical problem as to whether existence is a predicate. It is true as Hume says, "The idea of existence, then, is the very same with the idea of what we conceive to be existent. To reflect on anything simply, and to reflect on it as existent, are nothing different from each other."[20] Nevertheless, the assertion of existence is the assertion of something more than a logical licence to include a subject in a certain class of things, as Bertrand Russell claims. "Peter exists" is at once descriptively empty but ontologically complete, for it does not assert "This is Peter and not Paul", nor does it assert "This is Peter and not a corpse". If one wanted to say the latter, one would say "Peter is alive". What it says is "This is Peter and not nothing". This point was made by G. E. Moore in his paper "Is Existence a Predicate?"[21]

> I cannot help thinking that in the case of anything, to point at which and say "This is a tame tiger" is significant, it is also significant to point at it and say "This exists", in some sense or another. My reason for thinking this is that it seems to me that you can clearly say with truth of any such object "This might not have existed", "It is logically possible that this should not have existed".

Bertrand Russell's transposition of "Cows exist" into "There are x's such that 'x is a cow' is true" does not dispose of the ontological significance of "exists". His attempt to reduce "exists" to the category of logical quantifier is a symptom of the eliminating tendency of logical atomism and logical positivism. As H. S. Leonard has pointed out: "The extent to which modern logic has left tacit its commitments relative to singular existence, is indicated by the fact that it does not offer a generally available symbolism for affirmations of singular existence."[22]

The difficulty is that "exists" is at once absolutely necessary and also beyond categories and description. "Existence is presupposed to any predication of attributes; it is the 'toujours-déjà-là' of all knowledge . . . It is given with and present in and coaffirmed with all attributes. It is so much everywhere that we do not notice. It is so familiar that we take it for granted."[23] Existence cannot be defined, we can only assert it in a factual statement. As soon as we begin to speak *about* it, to call it "it", or "existence", or a "predicate", the emphasis shifts from the *existence* of the thing to the thing itself or its attributes, and this "quality" of the thing evades us. The reason for this, as Etienne Gilson points out, is that the intellect "dislikes the undefinable, and because pure existence is undefinable, philosophy does all it can to avoid it".[24] G. A. Paul analyses this "hidden quality" of things. It is not something behind the scenes or under the surface.

> We are bewitched by an inadequate concept of what it is for something "to be hidden". What we are looking for is indeed "hidden"; but not by being behind something else, or difficult to dig out, or difficult to discriminate sharply from something else, or transparent. What is hidden in that way is of no interest to us. We have overlooked a no less common way in which a thing, or movement, may be concealed from us. The decisive movement in the conjuring trick has been made and it was the one we thought quite innocent.[25]

The cryptic remark of Wittgenstein's, "Not *how* the world is, is the mystical, but *that* it is," could be recruited to illustrate this point. "How the world is" is the problem of descriptions and causes. This is the problem with which human beings can come to grips; this is the perspective of inductive reasoning; this is the perspective of *what* is. "That the world is" is the given, the perspective of what *is*. The logic and the language of descriptions and causes is quite inappropriate in this perspective, because the use of this language immediately shifts the focus of attention from the *something-nothing* question to the *this-not that* question, and yet it is the only language available. Explanations are appropriate in the latter question; they are grossly misleading when applied to the former. Yet if we recognize that the something-nothing question cannot be explained in terms of a logical or grammatical quirk of language, and cannot be reduced without residue to a question of the this-not that kind, we want, nevertheless, an explanation.

This awareness of the possibility of not being at all is the sense of contingency, which is distinct from mere logical contingency. At the human level we are acutely aware of it. When a chemical is destroyed, when a book is burnt, when an animal dies, we know that the changes are not from something to nothing, but from one chemical and energy state to another. The individual human being, however, is acutely aware, not of the possibility of being changed into another chemical and energy state, but of the possibility of not being at all. It is only at the human level that the awareness of the logical and ontological possibility of not being manifests itself. Once again we can recruit another cryptic saying of Wittgenstein's: "There is indeed the inexpressible, it *shows* itself; it is the mystical."

This dimension or aspect of existing things, which we call "existence", is the foundation of the use of the term "God". God is "what" makes the difference between something and nothing. This cannot be proved in a rational or non-existential way. Nor can it be said *how* God makes the difference. All that can be said is that the difference is the foundation for the use of the term "God". The process of verifying this, however, is another question.

Now if it is the case that God is what makes the difference between being this and not being at all, he will be present to or immanent in all existing things. Secondly, he will defy description, for all terms applied to him would be taken necessarily and misleadingly from the vocabulary of *this-not that* or descriptive language. However, some terms are less inappropriate than others, and these are the terms, applicable in one way or another, to all existing things, insofar as they are existing, which have been traditionally applied to God. This was the significance of the theory of analogy. It was a negative technique of speaking about God which acknowledged first of all that God could not really be talked about and secondly that, granted that men would continue to talk about him, some words were less inappropriate than others. Unfortunately the theory of analogy has been given exaggerated significance among the followers of Aquinas. As Gilson says:

His [Aquinas'] texts on the notion of analogy are relatively few, and in each case they are so restrained that we cannot but wonder why the notion has taken on such importance in the eyes of his commentators. Perhaps it is due to a secret longing to redeem from an all-too-apparent misery the knowledge of God which St. Thomas will concede us. Commentators have gradually come to the stage where they speak of analogy as an almost positive source of knowledge giving us a more or less confused insight into a quasi-quidditative being of God.[26]

Aquinas made it quite clear that we can know nothing about *what* God is. All we can do is assert *that* he is. Once this assertion has been made the incurable human propensity to continue to talk demands a process of discriminating among the qualities and descriptions of things in an attempt to say more about God in a less inappropriate way. Yet everything that was said in Aquinas' view was said relatively, negatively and analogically. In other words while what we say about God might be logically possible and ontologically valid, it must be descriptively vacuous. This is the one sense of the meaning of the description of the distinction between the immanence and the transcendence of God. In the realm of describing he is completely other. Hence God is not a thing, or another kind of thing. God is not part of the world, nor is he the totality of the world. Thus the traditional Christian view of God insists on this tension between his presence and his otherness. If we could not point to this tantalizing quality which we call the contingency of things, this tension would be merely contradictory.

If we persist, however, in talking about God, the kind of attributes we would regard as less inappropriate when applied to God are likely to be conditioned by our view of the world. If we regard the static, the unchanging, the immutable, as ideals, then this sort of quality is likely to be attributed to God. If, however, in a different cultural context, we regard the dynamic, the evolutionary, the developing, as ideals, this sort of quality is likely to be attributed to God.

In one way, what we say about God doesn't matter. A reply which would have done justice to the Delphic oracle illustrates this. A perturbed woman wrote to a Catholic question box: "Is God dead?" "God is!" was the reply. In a sense it is immaterial whether you say "God is dead" or "God is alive" for all that can be said is "God is". But in another way what we say about God does matter, for God can become an idol on to which we project a particular view of the world in such a way that this idol dominates our life and restricts it.

Now if a certain fullness and unrestricted and uninhibited quality of life is the essential condition for the verification of the assertion of the existence of God, the establishment of a vital relationship with God and the emergence of an awareness of God, a world view that is misguided and yet entertained in the name of God will not only engender doctrinaire atheism in others, it will also develop an ontological atheism in the very champions of this view.

It is important, moreover, in this context, not to create too great a dichotomy between *what* a thing is and *that* it is, between its describable qualities and its existence. At the higher levels of things where we have a more perfect manner of being, we can discern a certain convergence of the two planes or dimensions, and this may be an indication, though at best only a hint, of one of the defects of the position of recent theism. The example of the relationship between matter and light can give something of an illustration of the significance of this kind of convergence. When a physical object is at rest it has solidity and stability and appears to be quite fundamentally different from light. As it accelerates, however, it loses weight, until at the speed of light it is light. With movement, there is a convergence between the two states which appear utterly diverse. Perhaps there is an analogous convergence between man becoming increasingly personalized and the state of pure existence, which in one Christian tradition at least is what God is called.

The problem of verification remains, however, and we saw that a statement of the conditions for the verification of the assertion "God exists" is also essential for the ultimate meaning of the statement. The fact of contingency provides the occasion for the hypothesis "God exists" and also the initial basis for the meaning of the assertion. More solid bases are provided with a statement of the area of awareness in which one could expect the assertion to be verified and the conditions under which verification can be established.

What I am going to claim is that "God exists" is not self-evident, nor is it provable in the limited logical or rationalistic sense. It is provable or verifiable in the existential sense, that is, in terms of the total personal experience and awareness of the human being. Because it is not a publicly established fact, it must be called a hypothesis. However, it is most important to distinguish between this idea of God as a hypothesis and the *use* of God to explain gaps in our knowledge on the level of *this-not that*. In this case, God is not used as an explanation, because we appreciate beforehand that explanations of the difference between something and nothing would have to be made in mundane terms which would not be an explanation at all. This kind of explanation is impossible. "God exists" is a hypothesis because it has to be decisively verified in a person's life.

A slight digression is called for here. The aim is not to establish or verify a logically necessary truth. If "God exists" is true he is essentially existing. But this means establishing and verifying not a logical property of propositions about God, but a matter of fact. As John Hick points out in *Philosophy of Religion*:

The concept of a "necessary being" used in the main theological tradition (exemplified by both Anselm and Aquinas), is not concerned with logical necessity but rather with a kind of factual necessity which, in the case of God, is virtually equivalent to *aseity* or self-existence. For this reason, the idea of God's necessary being should not be equated with the view that "God exists" is a logically necessary truth.[27]

The ambition of the programme of verification, therefore, is the exclusion of rational doubt about what is claimed to be a matter of fact. This is not equivalent to the exclusion of the logical possibility of error or illusion. Unfortunately theists often state their case as if this were their ambition and thus provide grounds for the refutation of the whole theistic enterprise.

The general kind of verification which is applicable to the assertion "God exists" is called by John Hick eschatological verification.[28] It is the kind of verification that will take place at some future stage. He relates a parable to illustrate this kind of verification:

> Two men are travelling together along a road. One of them believes that it leads to a celestial city, the other that it leads nowhere; but since this is the only road there is, both must travel it. Neither has been this way before, and therefore neither is able to say what they will find around each next corner. During the journey they both meet with moments of refreshment and delight, and with moments of hardship and danger. All the time one of them thinks of his journey as a pilgrimage to the Celestial City and interprets the pleasant parts as encouragements and the obstacles as trials of his purpose and lessons in endurance, prepared by the king of that city and designed to make of him a worthy citizen of the place when at last he arrives there. The other, however, believes none of this and sees their journey as an unavoidable and aimless ramble. Since he has no choice in the matter, he enjoys the good and endures the bad. But for him there is no celestial city to be reached, no all-encompassing purpose ordaining their journey; only the road itself and the luck of the road in good weather and in bad.

One advantage of this parable is that it places emphasis on the general way in which statements about God can be verified. There are, however, disadvantages. It does not provide any initial basis for a meaningful statement of the hypothesis of the celestial city, unless it is that "roads lead somewhere", in which case the parable is loaded in favour of the believer. The parable would be more true to life if there were no road and the travellers were given the option of heading in a variety of directions or of not moving at all. This brings in the second disadvantage which is that in Hick's parable, there do not seem to be conditions for the verification of the assertion. Each of the travellers, no matter what the speed or quality of his journey, would ultimately and equally verify the assertion. A third and related disadvantage is that the travellers merely cover the distance. They are not involved in the making of the road into the future.

It would seem that there would have to be two phases in the process of verifying "God exists". Provided that a person fulfilled the conditions required for verification, and we can discuss these in a moment, there would be first of all a proximate and relative verification of the assertion and secondly an ultimate and absolute verification. In the former, a fulfillment, though not yet complete, of the conditions for verifying the hypothesis could lead to an increasing conviction as to the truth of the assertion. The difficulty lies in *communicating* both the conviction and the sort of experiences which give rise to it because these can be expressed only in terms of mundane experience, and, objectively, are always explainable in terms of mundane experiences. In the latter case, i.e. of ultimate and absolute verification of the assertion, "the face to face" situation after the "glass darkly" situation, if it does take place, presumably it will be possible through some *unique* experience to distinguish it clearly from individual experiences or from the totality of mundane experiences. The unfortunate aspect of this for us is that this eschatologically verified assertion cannot be communicated either because it has not yet occurred as a cosmic event or because the individuals who have had the opportunity so to verify the assertion have so far maintained a discreet silence!

One minor qualification which needs to be made and which suggests a tantalizing possibility is that it could be the case that it is precisely in a totality of human experience that the unique quality of the awareness of God and hence the verification of the assertion of his existence emerges. It is important to entertain the idea of the totality of experience. One of the defects of a great deal of Christian theism in the past has been that it has tended to advocate that a relationship with or an awareness of God be developed through specific or limited, that is, "religious" areas of activity and experience.

The final element in the programme of verifying the, initially, hypothetical statement "God exists", is the conditions under which the assertion can be verified. In the case of Christian theism, these conditions are stated by Christ, and presumably, are continued to be stated by the community which claims to continue the message of Christ, the church.

What emerges from the analysis of the logical disavowal of God is that it is still possible and necessary to talk about God. Whether we can say anything about God that has descriptive value is another matter. We can begin to see, however, that the crucial issue in the question of the reality of God and the significance of assertions about God is the choice and the statement of the conditions under which his existence is verified and by which a relationship is established with him.

The logical disavowal of God has been instructive. God is not something which can be proved by logical processes, or contacted by esoteric techniques of knowledge or behaviour. And yet to speak about God at all, there must be some grounds. If God is not a thing, if God is not all things, if God is not any or the totality of the describable qualities or relationships of things, how does talking about him differ from talking about nothing? Even if we refer to God in some way as the future, why do we not simply speak of the future and avoid complicating talk about the future with talk about God?

Analysis of our language and of our experience reveals a factor which we call existence, but which cannot be named, or described, but only asserted. It is of a different order from the categories of things and from the categories of being, and it is in this direction and in the logic of this factor that we must seek the grounds for talk about God. A case could be made for the claim that the five ways of Thomas Aquinas were intended to draw attention to this factor in language and experience; that they were intended to highlight the ontological contingency of created things in showing that they did not contain within the range of descriptions of these things why they should *exist* at all. This lacuna at the very edge of our logic, our language and our experience, a lacuna on which all three depend and yet which defies description, does not allow us to assert that God exists or to say anything about God. It simply provides the non-definition of an area which is a ground for talking about God, an area which cannot be reduced to, or at least has not yet been successfully reduced to a logical category or to a category of being.

This ground for talking about God is at once very real and also very intangible. It is real because it is the difference between existing and not existing at all, a set of alternatives which is manifested not by the observation of chemical, physical, or biological change, but by the specifically human awareness of the possibility of non-existence. It is very intangible because talk about existence has to resort to the essentially alien logic of descriptions, to the logic of that other set of alternatives—why this and not that—the logic which is the substance of our consciousness and which preoccupies our conscious lives.

Most of the theologies of the past have attempted to base talk about God somewhere in the logic of the second set of alternatives, that is, in the logic of why this and not that, only to find that other mundane explanations competed successfully with God for the title on an increasing number of occasions. Other theologies claiming to maintain the transcendence of God have repudiated completely the enterprise of providing any grounds for talking about God which are in any way related to the mundane. This type of theology creates an absolute dichotomy between God and the world and between the logic of theology and the logic of mundane affairs. This sort of theology is chronically exposed to the charge of meaninglessness and seems disqualified from any kind of significant dialogue with men in a secular age, for talk about God cannot rationally and prudently begin with either a blind lunge into the orbit of this kind of talk nor can it be related entirely to the future. Some recent eschatological theology has shifted the grounds for talk about God *entirely* to the future. However, this will not do. If anyone, including the man Jesus Christ, wants to use the word "God" he must indicate the grounds for the use of the term other than the future, for otherwise there would be no reason for using the word "God" apart from the word "future".

The question "Why do we exist at all?" provides the grounds—even though ontologically tenuous and descriptively vacuous—for developing a logic of "God". The next step in the development of theology is the setting out of the conditions under which assertions about God can be verified, otherwise talk about God can never break out of or go beyond the realm of logic as happened with the ontological argument of Anselm. As John Hick pointed out, like the logic of "molecule", the logic of "God" entails a statement of the conditions for the verification of statements about God. In the Christian tradition these conditions are set out in the language of love. Hence it is useful and valid to speak of God in terms of the future only in relation to the existential verification of assertions about God resulting from the correct performance of the experiment of love.

The five ways used by Aquinas are of no value unless taken in the context of and in association with the whole of the *Summa Theologica*. You cannot come to the end of Aquinas' statement of the five ways and say "Therefore God exists". Aquinas himself says "This all men speak of as God". The use of "therefore" in relation to God can come only in the future and on condition of the fulfilling of the demands of love. Yet even this will not allow us to say what God is. When Christians say that "God is love" they claim it is the best description of God: better than "God is the One", or "God is the True", or "God is the Good", precisely because it contains a functional rubric of how men can relate to him, become aware of him, and ultimately verify his existence. Hence the dogmatic assertions of the church about God do not constitute a body of arcane knowledge about the nature of God, but rather a language about how we relate to God and a variety of objectifications of the experience of the members of the church who have attempted to implement this rubrical language.

If we approach the problem of talk about God in this way it is possible to reconcile the complete otherness of God in terms of descriptive qualities with the immanence of God with whom we share one non-descriptive factor, namely, real existence. The kind of analysis which uncovers the logical and ontological problem of existence poses a problem which provides grounds or a significant basis for a God-hypothesis which can be verified on conditions set out in the Old Testament, but especially, by Christ in the New Testament.

The Cultural Disavowal of God

In *The Gay Science* Friedrich Nietzsche related an intriguing parable:

Have you heard of that madman who lit his lantern in bright daylight, ran into the marketplace and cried continuously: "I am looking for God! I am looking for God!" Since many happened to be gathered about who did not believe in God there arose a great laughter. "Has He gone astray?" one asked. "Has He lost his way like a child?" said another. "Or is He hiding? Is He afraid of us? Has He boarded some boat, perhaps emigrated?" Thus the cries and laughter went. The madman leaped into their midst and pierced them with his eyes. "What has become of God?" he cried, "I will tell you! We have murdered Him, you and I. All of us are murderers. But how did we do it? How were we able to drink up the ocean? Who gave us the sponge to wipe out the horizon? What did we do when we unchained this earth from its sun? Whereto is it moving now? Whither are we moving? Away from every sun? Are we not continuously falling? And backwards, sidewards, forward to all sides? Is there still an up and down? Are we not wandering aimlessly through an infinite void? Does not an empty space breathe upon us? Has it grown colder? Isn't night and always more night approaching? Must not lanterns be lighted in the forenoon? Do we as yet hear nothing of the gravediggers who are burying God? Do we as yet notice nothing of the divine decay? — Gods also decay! God is dead! God will remain dead! And we have killed Him! The most sacred and the most mighty that the world has hitherto possessed has bled to death from our knives — who will wipe this blood from us? With what waters can we be cleansed? What feasts of atonement, what sacred games will we have to invent? Is not the magnitude of the deed too much for us? Will we not ourselves have to turn into Gods merely to seem worthy of it? There never was a greater deed — and whoever is born after us because of this will belong to a higher age than all history has been thus far!" — Here the madman was silent and again looked at his audience which also was silent and looked at him strangely. Finally he threw down his lantern so that it broke into pieces and went out. "I have come too early," he said, "it is not yet the time for me. This terrible event is still under way and wandering — it has not yet penetrated to the ears of men. Lightning and thunder need time; the light of the stars needs time; deeds, even after they have been done, need time to be seen and heard. This deed is still further away from them than the most distant stars — and yet they themselves have done it!" It is further told that on the same day the madman forced his way into various churches and there had intoned his "Requiem aeternam deo". When led out and confronted he had nothing to say but this: "What is there still to these churches if they are not the vaults and monuments of God?"[29]

This parable, published in 1882, did not effect the death of God, it merely proclaimed it. As Albert Camus has pointed out: "Nietzsche did not form a project to kill God. He found him dead in the souls of his contemporaries." The parable of the madman has provided a vehicle for the distinctive expression of an experience of radical doubt about and even of the absence of God in contemporary sensibility.

Nietzsche's contribution coincides with the task of both poet and philosopher. His imagination reveals synthetic powers of unification whereby divergent themes are fused through concrete imagery. Ambiguous, complex, multi-significant meanings are merged into single compelling aphorisms, striking parables and overwhelming visions. Thus the "God" whose death Nietzsche proclaims is a symbolic vehicle through which the dissolution and destruction of a number of related viewpoints that have been important in the history of western man is proclaimed.[30]

Nietzsche has become the prophet of "man come of age". A condition of man's emancipation into complete autonomy is the abolition of a God who challenges his autonomy. The Christian God drew man's vision away from this world to some "other world"; from this "other world" God continually judged man's actions and subjugated him by fear; through the prerogative of "mystery" and the demand for the virtues of "pity", "weakness", and "docility", this God sapped man's will to power and destroyed human creativity. This God, in Nietzsche's vision, must not simply be denied or ignored. He must be destroyed and his destruction announced to the world as a proclamation of the release of the world from the power of a tyrant. He is not arguing that assertions about God are logically untenable or that they do not have experimental verification. His language is not the language of philosophy at all, but "the archaic language of ancient poetry, religion, ritual; the language of dramatic events and concrete happening that occurs within a grand context of numinous emotion".[31]

Nietzsche at the end of the last century was experiencing, rather in advance of his time, a transition from a religious-sacred sensibility to a secular-profane one, a transition characteristic of contemporary culture. But if man is to be completely free from the old sacred and religious outlook, the liberation must be effected by a decisive and final event.

Simply to ignore the sacred by using languages of logic and science which are oblivious to it is not sufficient. The "power" must be truly "broken" and this requires that the modern sensibility enter one last time into the domain of the sacred. God will not be coldly denied by a calculation of logic. Rather, man as culture-hero must "murder" the deity and thus exorcise his numinous power . . . Thus atheism uses myth to destroy myth. The culture hero has performed his supreme act: the murder of God that brings to man a frightful gift, unlimited freedom and unbounded creativity.[32]

Some elements of the parable are ambiguous. There is not really a sense of exultation and this is not simply because the hearers in the marketplace are silent and stare strangely. A certain sadness manifests itself in the passing of "the holiest and mightiest that the world has hitherto possessed". There is an all-pervading sense of fear and apprehension at the sudden loss of orientation, the experience of a cosmic vertigo, the chill breath of an empty space breathing on us. Though men will belong to a higher age as a consequence of the deed they will have to turn themselves into gods to be worthy of it. But when men become gods . . .

Long before the overthrow of the "tyrant" who kept them in

subjection there was considerable unrest and rumblings of discontent among the peasants. John Robinson summarizes the substance of and the reasons for the cultural disavowal of God in an essay entitled "Can a Truly Contemporary Person Not Be an Atheist?"[33] He invited the reader to expose himself to

> the three thrusts of modern atheism . . . the three motives which have impelled men, particularly over the past hundred years, to question the God of their upbringing . . . They may be represented by three summary statements: 1. God is intellectually superfluous. 2. God is emotionally dispensable. 3. God is morally intolerable.

Christian apologists literally *used* God in many attempts to make him respectable and acceptable. He was invoked as an explanation of otherwise inexplicable phenomena. He was invoked as an integrating factor in the Newtonian system of physics. Since the Renaissance, however, at an increasing pace, the areas of experience which God explained have been accounted for in mundane terms; time and again the inexplicable has given way to scientific accounts and the God-hypothesis in whatever form, as an explanation of why this and not that, has been thoroughly discredited. In the prevalent scientific culture of our age, any phenomenon can in principle be explained or accounted for in terms of other phenomena without an appeal to an extra-mundane principle.

> The sciences have cumulatively established the autonomy of the natural order. From the galaxies whose vastness numbs the mind to the unimaginably small events and entities of the sub-atomic universe, and throughout the endless complexities of our own world, which lies between these virtual infinities, nature can be studied without any reference to God. The universe investigated by the sciences proceeds exactly as though no God exists.[34]

Science has gone even further. Emile Durkheim and Karl Marx have claimed to have shown that religion and belief in God are explicable in terms of the inherent dynamics of society. Durkheim's sociological theory[35] claimed that the gods whom men worship are imaginary beings unconsciously fabricated by society as instruments whereby it exercises control over the thought and behaviour of the individual. For Marx, religion was an instrument of class exploitation in the hands of the capitalists. Both of these thought that all talk about God could be reduced without residue to sociological factors or instruments in a capitalist socio-economic system.

And yet the God of Abraham, Jacob, Isaac, and Christ was never and was never intended to be a *means* to our intellectual satisfaction nor an *explanation* to be used to solve our cosmological problems. God is not and cannot be the cornerstone to any system within the world of related categories. Nor is God some kind of psychological integrator or compensation for psychological inadequacy. Sigmund Freud in *The Future of an Illusion*[36] claimed that religious beliefs were "... illusions, fulfillments of the oldest, strongest and most insistent wishes of mankind". In a situation in which men were at the mercy of natural catastrophes, disease, violence, and death, the illusion of protecting gods and spirits was necessary for the maintenance of some semblance of security and psychological health. However, Freud maintained that in the contemporary world man should learn to rely no longer on illusion but upon scientifically authenticated knowledge. It cannot be denied that for many Christians their religion is a kind of substitute for religion and they *use* God as a psychological crutch for their own immaturity and inadequacy. One of Freud's ambitions was to bring about the emancipation of man from religious illusions.

> True, man will then find himself in a difficult situation. He will have to confess his utter helplessness and his insignificant part in the working of the universe; he will have to confess that he is no longer the centre of creation, no longer the object of the tender care of a benevolent providence. He will be in the same position as the child who has left the home where he was so warm and comfortable. But, after all, is it not the destiny of childishness to be overcome? Man cannot remain a child for ever; he must venture at last into the hostile world. This may be called "education to reality".

What Freud claims disposes completely of God only on the assumption that a relationship with God is contingent on and must necessarily be one of emotional dependence. It is possible that acceptance of reality, including the realities of suffering and death, without any consolation and in complete abandonment by God is a condition of establishing a relationship with and achieving a knowledge of God. It is possible, also, that the conditions of this relationship with and awareness of God, are changing over the ages. In a past age these could have been relatively stable and rather puerile—from our point of view—while now they are much more demanding and "adult". This concept of the shift in the grounds for a relationship with God is quite compatible with the biblical notion of God's manifesting himself in history and his being "defined" or "conceptualized", provisionally, in terms of the prevailing *values* of the age. The signs of the times are not just of apologetic value, they are the substance of our relationship with God and the idiom of the conceptualization of our awareness of him.

One of the preoccupations of contemporary theology has been to emancipate Christian talk about God from the dominion of outmoded images and definitions, which tend to distract man from the real locus and style of living required for a relationship with God. Thus John Robinson's exercise in theological iconoclasm, *Honest to God,* attempted to dispel the Christian attachment to an image of God, "God up there", or to a definition of God, "God out there", and to promote a programmatic account of God as "the depth of our being" or the area of "ultimate concern".

Baastian Van Iersel in his book *The Bible on the Living God*[37] gives a scholarly backing to the claims of Robinson. Van Iersel claims that the Bible never attempts a definition of God but offers a bewildering variety of images of God.

What strikes us about Israel is that we search in vain through her sacred books, the Old Testament, for something we can call a concept of God, an attempted definition of what or who God is. Representations of God are many because he is often spoken of figuratively, as a father, or a king, or a shepherd. But the Old Testament is full to overflowing of a deep and lively awareness of God. And this is why it is so valuable to read the Old Testament: by taking part in the experiences of Israel we share this awareness of God, thus developing the sense with which we are to experience God in our own lives and in the history of our own times and become aware of God as an ever-present reality.[38]

He maintains that images, concepts, and definitions of God can be induced, especially in the process of religious education, and in this lies its danger. On the other hand the "awareness" of God cannot be induced. It can only be acquired by experience. It is not elaborated by the intellect or formed by the imagination but comes "from the depths of man's whole self". When the Old Testament speaks about God he is spoken of concretely:

No one ever stands aloof from God to hold him up as an object of knowledge. People are too deeply involved personally for that. What is written in the Old Testament about God is never something outside experience; rather it proceeds from the actual and full reality of experience itself. So it is not God as he is in himself who is written about but the Lord who reveals himself in the wonders of nature and in history.[39]

This scriptural account of God allows us to appreciate some of the characteristics of "the logic of God". Anything less than the totality of history or the totality of the person involved in the flow of history is incapable of expressing or saying or describing God. God cannot be called "Being" because this is either a term which is so abstract as to be vacuous or includes the totality of things. In a sense God is history, though included in this is the dialectic between events and persons. The difficulty in talking about God today is acute because the language and the logic of our age are those of specialization, of atomization, of precision. The logic of God is the logic of totality—the totality of history, the totality of the person, and the totality of the human community.

Yet man has inevitably to attempt to conceptualize his awareness of God, even if this awareness is best expressed as an absence, or even as a death. The first important lesson of the Old Testament is that any conceptualization is inadequate, provisional, and temporary. To make it anything more is to run the risk of idolatry. The second important lesson is that God is a "Person" with whom we *relate* in and through the medium of history. If this relationship is to avoid being sub-human, we as persons cannot expect to *exploit* or *use* God for our intellectual or psychological satisfaction. The third important lesson is that the logic of "God" is functional. It operates as a call, as a promise, and as indication of the conditions under which the promise will be fulfilled.

Recent exegetical researches indicate that the words of Revelation in the Old Testament are not primarily words of statement or of information, nor are they mainly words of appeal or of personal self-communication by God, but they are words of promise. Their statement is announcement, their announcement is proclamation of what is to come, and therefore the abrogation of what is.[40]

Thus God reveals himself to Moses: "I will be who I will be."[41] Hence biblical theophanies are not so much disclosures of information about God as techniques for drawing attention to the future in which God will reveal himself. They are not so much calculated to engender adoration and reverence as to generate action within history to bring the future to realization and fulfilment.

The function of Israel was to witness and testify to God's presence in history. This is also the function of the New Israel, the Christian church. Its mandate is to testify to its own awareness of God, but not to *sell* God as an intellectual panacea or a psychological anodyne. And yet there are conditions, in the Christian era, which have to be satisfied before an awareness of God can develop. These conditions we will see are the same as for the verification of the assertion "God exists".

When Robinson suggests that today God is morally intolerable, he is expressing what has been, in the Western world at least, the greatest objection to the existence of a God who is good and loving. In an age when man has a greater capacity for exploitation and destruction than ever before, the problem of evil is all the more acute. The doctrinaire atheists seem to have more conclusive grounds than ever that the existence of evil counts decisively against the claim that there is a God of the kind the Christians claim. Yet there is a strange ambiguity in the expression of this objection. Modern man does not want to accept God as a hypothesis for any of the positive phenomena which confront him. Even if God's existence is acknowledged, man does not want him or need him as an *explanation*. However, when the problem of evil arises they demand (and Christians far too often attempt rather too desperately to meet this demand) that a rational vindication of God be given. In a way this arises as a consequence of a persisting tendency to think of God as part of a rational system in which his existence and his goodness have to be reconciled with the fact of evil. In a way it arises from thinking of God as part of the world and to some extent identified with it rather than as the one who communicates himself through it and in terms of it, the joy and the sorrow, the good and the evil, the pleasure and the pain. Yet a relationship with God is not established by mere acceptance of suffering. Christians in the past have often succumbed not only to the lure of offering rational explanations of suffering but also of capitulating to evil as an integral part of the scheme of things. This was understandable in the context of a world view which was predominantly static. Nevertheless Nietzsche was led to see in Christian compassion a severe temptation to indulge in human weakness and mediocrity. He suggests that the Christian God has died of his "pity" for mankind.

God and his followers experience a heightened ability to feel the pain of the world that is not overcome by a corresponding will to power. The God who must die, and the human sensibility that must die with it, is one that is driven by the agony of "pity" into the search for escape into religious heavens, metaphysical realms, "other worlds" that, because they are not this world, are "nothing".[42]

Evil, suffering, and death in the world are not merely the crucible of love, they are part of the substance of the challenge to the creative power of man, and to that extent provide the material for the creative enterprise of man which leads to, and which is an indispensable ingredient of, a partnership with God the Creator. As Gabriel Vahanian has said: "The cornerstone of this post-Christian age is not an attempt to fit evil into a coherent view of the universe, but to eliminate it from the universe".[43]

It is important not to speak of God's action in history, but rather of history as being the medium and the idiom of our relationship with God and the substance of our awareness of him. God is present in history, in every aspect of it, but just as he cannot be invoked as an explanation of the various changes in history, neither can he be blamed for the suffering, the pain, and the evil which is part of the fabric of history. Indeed, suffering, pain, and evil are also part of the medium and the idiom of his presence and of our relationship with him, while they continue to pose challenges to man to overcome them and eliminate them.

When the rhetoric of the cultural disavowal of God subsides, we are still left wondering whether this has been after all a disavowal of God, or rather of an age which appropriated God for its coat of arms. The passing of the mediaeval world and the mediaeval world view is much more recent than most suspect. The mediaeval world was aggressively theistic. The culture in which we now live has reached the critical point of the confluence of the many factors and influences radically different from and alien to the mediaeval vision. For the first time in human history man (in principle) commands it both in his ability to survey it and his capacity to control its future unfolding. Is a God who must not be used and who cannot be described compatible with and acceptable to man who claims autonomy to control and create his own future? It is not clear that this is the case. On the contrary, there are many indications in the creation account of the book of Genesis, in the New Testament, and in the cultural dynamic of Christian tradition, that man is meant to be co-creator with God, that man is God's creative agent, God's own image and likeness. To the extent that man assumes the responsibility of creative autonomy, to that extent he progressively describes and defines God and realizes in mundane terms, rather than in ecclesiastical icons, his image and likeness.

The Theological Disavowal of God

The "Death of God" movement in theology can be looked on as the final Christian capitulation to atheism and secularism or it can be regarded as a necessary phase in the secularization and purification of theology.

The aim of the movement, if it can be called a movement, is to face up to the challenge which contemporary sensibility poses to Christian faith. This challenge is summarized by Gabriel Vahanian: "The contemporary Christian's total religious dilemma: in order to be true to himself, he must face his—and our—culture's incapacity for the Christian God."[44] The dilemma seems to be that for the Christian to acknowledge God he must sacrifice any hope of being a man come of age, for as Thomas Altizer says: "If there is one clear portal to the twentieth century, it is a passage through the death of God, the collapse of any meaning or reality lying beyond the newly discovered radical immanence of modern man, an immanence dissolving even the memory or the shadow of transcendence." Conceding Nietzsche's, Blake's, and Hegel's protest against the Christian God, Altizer acknowledges that "It is God himself who is the transcendent enemy of the fullness and the passion of men's life in the world, and only through God's death can humanity be liberated from that repression which is the real ruler of history."[45]

This, of course, is the crucial point. Is it clear that God is himself the transcendent enemy of the totality of the human person? Or is it that the culture of a past age and a church too deeply influenced by it and too inexorably wedded to it proclaimed a God who appeared as a challenge to man? For Gabriel Vahanian in his book, *The Death of God*, God's death is a *cultural* fact, not an event. It means the loss of a transcendental realm as the context in which man understands himself and his world. Man's perspective is now immanent or horizontal and God is "wholly other". For Paul van Buren (*The Secular Meaning of the Gospel*), it is impossible to talk about God. Christians must give up the enterprise in the interests of clarity. Hence in his theology, the death of God is a linguistic death. He argues that the word "God" and its theological equivalents and derivatives are either meaningless or misleading. He claims, moreover, that the Christian message can be proclaimed and the Christian life pursued without the use of "God" or similar terms. The point of reference of his theology is Christ, but he eliminates from any account of the life of Christ anything incompatible with the secularist viewpoint. He seems to accept, at least implicitly, an ideology of immanence, that is, secular*ism.*

When we come to deal with William Hamilton and Thomas Altizer, we have to realize that we are dealing with theology which is literary or poetical in style and ethical in fundamental intention. Altizer especially uses a style that has been called prophetical, and while prophets are generally to be taken seriously they must not be taken too literally.

Thomas W. Ogletree[46] describes Hamilton's writings as having a "strikingly personal or confessional quality about them" and there is in his thought a clearly discernible process of evolution or, perhaps, even devolution. In *The New Essence of Christianity*[47] he seems to indicate that a new image or idea of God is called for:

> The God seen as a person, making the world, manipulating some people towards good, condemning other people to damnation — the objectified God, in other words — this is the God many have declared to be dead today. This is the God who must disappear, so that we may remake our thinking and our speaking about him.[48]

In the meantime Christian faith consists in prayer for the return of God. Indeed "we ought to conclude that the special Christian burden of our time is the situation of being without God".[49] Yet in this very situation, "believing in the time of the 'death of God' means that he is there when we do not want him, in ways we do not want him, and he is not there when we do want him".[50] Hence, in this view, God is really there, *somewhere,* somehow.

Later on, however, Hamilton speaks of *The New Essence of Christianity,* as a "last, rather lonely failure—a last attempt to live under the pressure of the Hound of Heaven, who hunts us and who is never here when we want him, but before whom we can stand in doubt and anxiety and in horror, before whose absence we can stand".[51] No longer is there a conviction that God will return, but the certainty that he is gone forever and the Christian is left with the task of "trying to see if it is possible to make it as a Christian without God". In an essay, "Thursday's Child", in *Radical Theology and the Death of God*[52] Hamilton describes the outlook of the American theologian:

> What does it mean to say that the theologian in America is a man without faith? Is he therefore a man without God? It would seem to follow. He

has his doctrine of God, several of them no doubt, and all correct. But that is surely not the point. He really doesn't believe in God, or that there is a God, or that God exists. It is not that he is fashionably against idols or opposed to God as a Being or as part of the world. It is God himself that he has trouble with . . . At the centre of his thoughts and meditations is a void, a disappearance, an absence.⁵³

For the Christian theologian then, the focal point of theology becomes not God, but Christ. The new Christian arena is not the church but the world. The Christian obligation is not to God, but to his neighbour in the world. The consequence is: "I do not see how preaching, worship, prayer, ordination, the sacraments can be taken seriously by the radical theologian."⁵⁴ Hamilton thus shares with van Buren the belief that God is so utterly beyond our comprehension that only Christ can be related to and spoken of.

In Altizer's concept of the "death of God" we come to the climax of the theological disavowal of God. It is the most radical and far-reaching of all. It took place ultimately, absolutely, and finally in the Incarnation of Christ. Thus for Altizer Christ is not simply the one the Christian theologian is capable of talking about, given the logical or ontological impossibility of talking about God. Christ is the agent of the death of God. He sees the present "cultural fact" of God's absence as an historical actualization in the consciousness of all men of an event which happened on Calvary when Christ cried, "My God, My God, why hast thou forsaken me!" Hence Altizer is not attempting to write a theology without God. Nor is he saying, like Nietzsche, that man must have the courage to kill God. He claims that God "emptied" himself, sacrificed himself to his creation in Christ.⁵⁵

The radical Christian proclaims that God has actually died in Christ, that this death is both a historical and a cosmic event, and, as such, it is a final and irrevocable event, which cannot be reversed by a subsequent religious or cosmic movement. True, a religious reversal of the death of God has indeed occurred in history, is present in the religious expressions of Christianity, and is now receding into the mist of an archaic, if not soon to be forgotten, past. But such a religious reversal cannot annul the event of the death of God; it cannot recover the living God of the old covenant, nor can it reverse or bring to an end the progressive descent of Spirit into flesh. Religious Christians may know a resurrected Lord of the Ascension, just as they may be bound to an almighty and distant Creator and Judge. Yet such a flight from the finality of the Incarnation cannot dissolve the event of the Incarnation itself even if it must finally impel the Christian to seek the presence and the reality of Christ in a world that is totally estranged from Christianity's established vision of the sacred.[56]

Unlike Teilhard de Chardin, who saw in the increasing complexification of matter the process whereby the inwardness of matter is revealed and the thrust towards increasing personalization realized, Altizer sees the development of contemporary consciousness as the process whereby Spirit is immersed in and sacrificed to flesh. The development of history is the inexorable emergence of the autonomy of this world, in spite of the tendency of Christians to refuse to accept the reality and the theological significance of the Incarnation. The Incarnate Word, as the central notion of the Christian faith,

> thrusts us in a direction which is directly opposed to that of oriental mysticism. Rather than promising the disclosure of the sacred in the negation of the profane, it dramatizes the movement of the sacred into the profane. Rather than orienting us to the recovery of an eternal, quiescent, and primordial totality, it directs us ever more deeply into process, change, activity, movement . . . it calls us to participate in the forward movement of history towards a final End in which the profane world in its profanity is affirmed and redeemed.[57]

Unfortunately, in Altizer's view, Christians, in spite of the Incarnation, have desperately sought to retain God as a living ultimate, and even to keep Christ resurrected and apart in another world. This constitutes "a Christian religious reversal of God's act in Christ".[58] The Christian acceptance of God's act would demand a complete surrender to the progressive immersion of God in Christ and Christ in secular history; the redemption of the world arises from the complete annihilation of God through Christ in and for the sake of the absolute secular autonomy of the world. Yet this has been something that has become psychologically possible in our time when the scientific revolution has provided the intellectual and technical instruments of this autonomy. Before the scientific age Christians always ran the risk of the religious reversal of God's act,

> for a faith that isolates the sacred events of Christ's passion from the profane actuality of human experience must inevitably enclose Christ within a distant and alien form and refuse his presence in the immediacy of our existence. Every Christian attempt to create an unbridgeable chasm between sacred history and human history gives witness to a refusal of the Incarnation and a betrayal of the forward-moving process of salvation.

We can discover a reversal of the kenotic movement of the Word in the very insistence of the religious Christian that faith has once and for all been given, that it is fully and finally present in the Scriptures, the liturgies, the creeds and the dogmas of the past, and can in no sense undergo a development or transformation that moves beyond its original expression to new and more universal forms. All such religious claims not only attempt to solidify and freeze the life and the possibility of the enlargement and evolution of faith, but ruthlessly set the believer against the presence of Christ in an increasingly profane history, thereby alienating the Christian from the actuality of his own time. The radical Christian calls upon his hearer to open himself to the fullness of our history, not with the illusory belief that our history is identical with the history that Jesus lived, but rather with the conviction that the death of God which has dawned so fully in our history is a movement into the total body of humanity of God's original death in Christ. Once we grasp the radical Christian truth that a radically profane history is the inevitable consummation of an actual movement of the sacred into the profane, then we can be liberated from every preincarnate form of Spirit, and accept our destiny as an occasion for the realization in the immediacy of experience of the self-emptying or self-annihilation of the transcendent and primordial God in the passion and death of Christ.[59]

The death of God, therefore, is an inevitable theological and cosmic consequence of the movement of God into the world, of the Spirit into the flesh, of the sacred into the profane. The actualization of the death of God in contemporary experience and the extension of this, through the secularizing processes, to all the nations of the world, is a decisive sign of the continuing and forward movement of the divine process. This divine process continues to negate its own expressions by moving ever more fully into the depths of the profane. The Christian, then, has "a faith that knows this process as a self-negating and kenotic movement, as both embodied and symbolically enacted in the passion of Christ" and "knows that it becomes manifest in the suffering and the darkness of a naked human experience, an experience banished from the garden of innocence, and emptied of the sustaining power of a transcendent ground or source." The Christian recognizes the spiritual emptiness of our time as "the historical actualization of the self-annihilation of God."[60] Hence,

Once the Christian has been liberated from all attachment to a celestial and transcendent Lord, and has died in Christ to the primordial reality of God, then he can say triumphantly: God is dead! Only the Christian can speak of the liberating word of the death of God because only the Christian has died in Christ to the transcendent realm of the sacred and can realize in his own participation in the forward-moving body of Christ the victory of the self-negation of Spirit.[61]

The opponents of Christianity must find it disconcerting that Christian apologists so often take what appears to be a most crucial objection to some fundamental aspect of Christian teaching, and claim that this, after all, is what Christianity really teaches. We have seen that Cox claims that secularization has its origin in the Bible. Now we find, in the face of the contemporary disavowal of God, the claim of Altizer that Christianity is pre-eminently not just the disavowal of God but the symbol and the agent of the cosmic enterprise of the self-emptying and the self-sacrifice of God to the world which he created. The difficulty is that we cannot tell whether Altizer wants this taken as a cosmic process or whether it is an exercise in theological hyperbole, a heuristic device in a fundamentally ethical enterprise. His concept and theological expression of the death of God vividly emphasize certain important features of the historical character of Christianity, the freedom and creative autonomy of man, and the secular implications of the Incarnation. These features are essential to the development of a contemporary Christian awareness and involvement and even indispensable for the reconciliation of being, at the same time, a Christian and a child of our age.

God is a problem for the Christian in our age. Van Buren disposed of the problem philosophically. Altizer goes a step further and disposes of the problem theologically. In a sense, Altizer is invulnerable, for he appears to write prophetically. Yet he cannot be completely impervious to and dispensed from the demands of logic. For Altizer to dispose of God theologically, he has to resurrect him logically. What is or who is the God who thus empties himself? No doubt we breathe a sigh of relief as God exits from the stage and the secular dimension is left to prevail unchallenged. But what does Altizer mean by God? In what sense does he use the term? If he means no more than to indicate the emancipation of man from the image of God, then he resorts to a rather spectacular theological denouement. However, we find, after the initial impact of the imagery, that the philosophical problem has reappeared. Then, of course, there is the problem of why we had to wait nearly two thousand years for the significance of Christ to emerge. Altizer appears committed to the proposition that almost immediately after the death of Christ his followers succumbed to the temptation to lapse back into the mystical orientation of a search for eternal and unchanging forms, and to freeze the meaning of the Incarnation in a past and decisive occurrence. While his theology is radically oriented to the future, that is, it is radically eschatological, it seems to be structured in a secularist ideology. He does not appear to allow for the possibility of the awareness of the transcendent in Christ's own account of himself, nor in the second coming of Christ, whatever that will involve. In pronouncing the death of God Altizer disqualifies us from any opportunity of eschatological verification of claims about God. We saw that some prediction about the circumstances of verifying a claim is part of the meaning of the claim. Now if Altizer does not offer some other basis for the use of the term "God", his whole theology runs the risk of being meaningless.

This brings us to a fundamental consideration in speaking about God and about the possibility of an awareness of God in contemporary experience. Almost invariably, the theologians of secularity have accepted the terms of contemporary culture and experience rather too easily. Contemporary culture is too often accepted as given and theology tailored to measure. Harvey Cox accepts the culture precipitated by the secular city as an indication of the Christian style for the twentieth century. Vahanian, Hamilton, and Altizer all seem implicitly to concede the values which dominate the culture of the technopolis of today. Perhaps they need to ask whether the contemporary Christian must work towards a radical change of this culture as a condition of the possibility of developing an awareness of God and the possibility of speaking about him.

If it is the case that man establishes a relationship with and an awareness of God only to the extent that he assumes the responsibility of creative autonomy in the world, obstacles to assuming this responsibility will inevitably prevent the development of a relationship with God. The radical theologians emphasize the need to be rid of the images of God and the ecclesiastical laws and values which are the stifling detritus of the past, in the interests of accepting the world as it is. They insist on man's being free of ecclesiastical restrictions so that he can enter into his secular heritage. They see clearly that God has been so closely identified with the restrictions of the past and the debilitating domination of the church that man must be rid of God, at least in some way and for some time, before he can become a creator in the image of God. But what they fail to see is that a great deal of contemporary post-Christian culture has taken over from God and the church the role of the Grand Inquisitor. They are radical theologians. They are not radical human beings. It would seem that men have to be radical human beings before they can once again develop a relationship with and an awareness of God.

We saw, previously, that there are, as a consequence of both the scientific and philosophical developments in this century, reductionist tendencies rampant in our culture. Knowledge, sensibility, and society tend to become fragmented and atomized. To the extent that consciousness, personal or social, becomes specialized and disintegrated, then there is the danger that the totality of the person will be threatened. There is the danger that the fullness of the person will be frustrated through an arbitrary disqualification from areas of experience and the possibility of communicating the totality of experience.

An even greater, though not unconnected danger, is posed in the economic basis of our culture. If the whole tenor of Western society demands that man be a consumer rather than a creator, if man, as a condition of belonging to society must compete, and be either exploiter or exploited, it is conceivable that the absence of God is not just a stage in the emancipation of man, but rather a pathological condition of man and society. In the Western world today man is almost invariably reduced to the role of consumer, when his God-given role is that of creator. If this is the case, then the task of the Christian is not the burial of God, but his resurrection through radical social, economic, and cultural reform; the task of the Christian is the development of the awareness of God through championing the totality of the experience of the human person against persisting reductionist tendencies and the integration of human society against the atomizing effect of competition, be this economic, racial, or national.[62]

The claim I want to make, therefore, is that whenever man is subjected to reductionist factors or influences, his capacity for awareness of God and his ability to speak about God are in jeopardy. Yet the factors which challenge the integrity of the person and human society are legion. Reductionist factors inhibiting experience can be the sophisticated ones of a logical, mathematical, or metaphysical world view. They can be the more practical ones of a scientific, technological, or industrial preoccupation. They can be the more emotional and potentially explosive ones of national, racial or ideological allegiance. The most destructive factor is the one which reduces man the creator to man the consumer. A fundamentally capitalist society does just this, as does a church which becomes a retailer of spiritual consumer goods at the price of loyalty, obedience, and docility to an image of God made in the likeness of those who exact the tribute. Marx was wrong when he claimed that capitalists used religion, i.e. God, as the opium of the people, as a compensation for lack of material goods. Today goods are consumed as the opium which suppresses the demand of God that man be a creator. The sense of alienation which pervades so much of the literature, the theatre, and the cinema today could arise, not so much from the experience of the absence of God as from man's inability, in the context of his culture, to become himself, and this is so, not because of the domination of God or church or the past, but because of some aspects of our culture which make man an individualistic god who consumes goods and himself as incense on the altar of his own satisfaction.

We need, now, to attempt a summary. With Karl Barth we can appreciate the positive value and the deep concern of the contemporary disavowal of God: "What men this side of the resurrection name 'God' is most characteristically not God . . . he is, in fact, 'no-God'. The cry of revolt against such a God is nearer the truth than is the sophistry with which men attempt to justify him."[63] And yet, again with Karl Barth, we have to acknowledge: "We ought to speak of God; we are human, however, and so cannot speak of God; we ought therefore to recognize both that we should speak of God and yet cannot, and by that very recognition give God the glory."[64] The source of the possibility of speaking about God is the sense of ontological contingency, the awareness, peculiar to man, that he hovers on the brink, not of becoming a corpse, but of nothingness. From this initial awareness a Christian will follow the logic of contingency. True to the tradition which has proclaimed God, he will know that God is not a thing among other things, nor the totality of things. True to the contemporary demand for human maturity he will not seek in God a psychological crutch nor a cosmic or intellectual integrating principle. He will seek God as a person, asking nothing and expecting nothing, aware that God is in one sense completely other and in another sense completely immanent. The contemporary Christian will be especially sensitive to the danger of the idolatry of attributing absolute value to any image or definition of God or any value proclaimed in the name of God. He will expect the arena and the dynamic flow of history to provide the context, the substance and idiom of his relationship with God, and will not expect, in ecclesiastical sanctuaries or ceremonies, privileged access to, nor a monopoly of, the deity. Indeed, he will expect that the world itself, the totality of things and the totality of the person, will provide the only definition in any way worthy of God, while recognizing that these are not God. His very assertion of the existence of God will have a relatively large element of the hypothetical in it. Not that this assertion of God will be proffered as an *explanation* of anything. Rather, the hypothetical will indicate that both the meaning and the reality of God will be contingent upon verification: proximately and relatively in the process of living, ultimately and absolutely in the eschatological situation, whatever that is. In the meantime, and especially today, the Christian, whatever his ecclesiastical status, will be noted for his reticence about God. He will be most unwilling to say anything that gives the impression of having just had morning tea with God, and he will be acutely aware of the danger that his claims about God can obstruct the development of another's relationship with God.

The central challenge of atheistic humanism today is the claim that the existence of God is a threat to the creative autonomy of man. The claim I want to make is that the Christian's contemporary experience has allowed him to see that it is precisely in and through assuming the responsibility of creative autonomy that man must relate to God, that it is only when all the vital connections are made that man connects with God.

What are the conditions for verifying assertions about God? What are the characteristics of "creative autonomy"? How do we discriminate between vital connections and disconnected lines? One of the characteristics of the theologies of secularity is that they focus very clearly on Christ the man. In varying ways and in varying degrees, the shift in emphasis is away from God to Christ. As the process of secularization spreads throughout the world, it is possible that only Christians will continue to talk about God and their talk will depend entirely, for the conditions of meaning and verification, on the life and person of Christ. They look to Christ for the life-style which will establish a relationship with God and provide the milieu in which assertions about God can be vindicated.

Theological Probes

One final observation is called for. The discussion of the problem of God over the past century or so has been conducted in highly individualistic terms. Logicians and theologians have sought either in linguistic analysis or in their reflection on a personal response to the secular world, indications of the reality of God. Perhaps this method of approach, and the signal bankruptcy of results, is a symptom of the general atomization of our culture. The awareness of God proclaimed in the Old Testament is an eminently social and corporate thing. This probably indicates that men do not relate to and become aware of God as individuals but socially and in community. The early church, indeed, conceived and expressed its awareness of God precisely as a community of persons, the Trinity.

Christ the Man of the Future

The Bible is not a theology for man, it is an anthropology for God.
Abraham Heschel

It isn't difficult to keep alive, friends—just don't *make* trouble—
or if you must make trouble, make the sort of trouble that's expected.
*Robert Bolt
A Man for All Seasons*

Throughout the history of Christianity the church has given a variety of answers to the question "What think ye of Christ?" As each age approached the phenomenon of Christ with images and associations conditioned by the outlook and the temperament of its own milieu, so there arose new and different attitudes to the mystery of Christ. This variety of attitudes is illustrated in the New Testament itself. Already the Hebrew, Hellenic, and oriental mystery outlooks effect differences in approach to and emphasis on the life of Christ and its personal and cosmic implications.

However, all the answers to Christ's own question assert a

vital and unique relationship with God, in such a way that Christ is the means par excellence by which God reveals himself to mankind, even if this answer amounts to the self-emptying, "kenotic", even deicidal revelation suggested by Thomas Altizer. The Christian tradition is unanimous in this, at least, that we must go, and rely on Christ for any hope of learning anything very significant about God, and to discover the conditions on which man can verify the reality of God and establish a relationship with him.

The failure of belief in God and the strident proclamation of the death of God in our time are due, in all probability, not merely to a philosophical or cultural breakdown, but to a failure, on the part of the church especially, to focus with accuracy and insight on the person and the significance of Christ. Indeed Maynard Kaufman suggests that "the failure of Christology implicitly preceded the so-called death of God, but that it became explicit only afterwards, and that the contemporary theological situation should therefore be positively affirmed as post-Christian. It is possible to be a post-Christian theist rather than a Christian atheist."[1] Kaufman sees in the death of God theology the most radical acculturation of Christianity in its history:

The perniciousness of the secular theology lies in the fact that it promulgates religiosity with its superfluous justification of the status quo ... The secular theologian, still informed by that truncated theology which says that God (or Something Ultimate) is active in history, views with indiscriminate seriousness whatever comes to pass. He is in bondage to the givenness and facticity of history.[2]

Though it is not true that the secular theologian is necessarily in bondage to the "givenness" of history—for an essential element in this type of theology is the emphasis on the creative task of the Christian—Kaufman's suggestion that the disavowal of God is due to the failure of Christology must be taken seriously. Yet the failure of Christology is not the failure of Christ, but the failure of the church which claims to continue his work and to proclaim his message.

The failure to pose the challenge of the phenomenon of Christ to the modern world has two relatively distinct sources or features.

On the one hand there has been the tendency to make Christ a man *of* our times, rather than a man *for* our times. On the other hand, there has been the tendency to assimilate Christ to God and frustrate the prime function of Christ as the mediator between God and man. But both of these features have a common source. Christ was made to cater to human need, whether this need was the satisfaction of the religious instinct, the craving for ontological or psychological security, the demand for an easy way to God, or the stimulus to and a model for authentic existence. All of these were attempts on the part of the Christian church to make Christ appeal to rather than challenge the modern world. The image of Christ was used by the church as a means either of ingratiating itself with the world in the case of many Protestant churches or of dominating the world in the case of the Catholic church, which tended to make Christ the founder of an oracular dynasty.

On the one hand Christ today becomes the victim of his own image and words, captured in the saccharine banality of phrases made almost incurably impotent by a whole age of parsonic intonation and pietistic application. The Christ of the Hollywood movies or of popular religious art is effectively disqualified from achieving any contemporary epiphany. He can function only as a curious psychological palliative, in rapidly diminishing demand as techniques of narcotherapy improve. Even in the fundamentalist tradition which refused to make any concessions to contemporary sensibility, Christ is reduced to a set of archaic verbal and imaginative conventions without relevance to a technological age.

On the other hand, in the Catholic tradition, the actions and the words of Christ serve not a dynamic, challenging function, but the conservative one of acting as the foundations, the beams, and the buttresses of the timeless scholastic edifice and the static ecclesiastical power structure.

Yet Christ was a revolutionary. He was not a man *of* his time. He was the man of the future. But the church, mandated by Christ to carry on his work, will not correct the image of Christ and give renewed impact to his words by theological speculation and apologetic endeavour. The pietistic myths and scholastic metaphysics which continue to enshroud Christ will be dispelled, and Christ's power to reveal God will be displayed, only if the church courageously assumes Christ's revolutionary mantle, by refusing to yearn for the past or to accept the present.

The revolution in knowledge in the nineteenth century caused acute embarrassment to Christian theologians. How could the Christ of the New Testament, with its devils and its miracles, be reconciled or made compatible with a culture radically scientific in outlook.

This situation provoked the distinction between the Jesus of history and the Christ of faith. The view which gained a great deal of support was that the historical Jesus had become so submerged in or transformed by the interpretative faith of the early church that the person and the events of his life could no longer be recognized. The biblical scholars, therefore, set about reconstructing the "real" Christ using the techniques of historical and literary criticism. The result of this enterprise was the Christ, not of history, but of liberal Protestantism and Catholic modernism. All transcendental elements were eliminated from this picture of Christ and Jesus was presented as a simple Galilean villager with no radically challenging message other than the fatherhood of God and the brotherhood of man. Some of the early exponents of liberal theology believed that Christianity was the highest form of religion, but later exponents regarded it as a manifestation among other possible manifestations of religious experience.

This attempt to meet the challenge of a scientific age and to explain faith in terms acceptable to it failed for a number of reasons. First of all, it was opposed to the whole Protestant tradition of faith and replaced the fundamental Protestant principle with that of human reason seeking faith through the method of historical criticism. Secondly, the simple category of "religious experience" invoked to explain apparently non-empirical phenomena was inadequate to account for the phenomenon which was Christianity. Thirdly, the disquieting events of the New Testament were not dealt with satisfactorily; they were eliminated too facilely. Finally, and most importantly, the historical quest itself failed. In spite of the sophisticated techniques of literary and historical criticism, the residue, after the process of filtering was completed, invariably and inevitably was not Jesus, but the first Christians' belief in Jesus and the interpretation of him that they offered to others.[3] As R. H. Fuller points out,

> It was the merit of the older liberals that they had been aware of the presence of this mythological element in the New Testament. But they had sought to meet the difficulty by eliminating the mythological outworks of the kerygma — virgin birth, empty tomb, literal ascension, etc. — and by subtly modernizing the rest — incarnation, atonement, Holy Spirit — into the timeless truths of religion and ethics. Thus they lost the sense of the New Testament as the proclamation of the unique eschatological act of God.[4]

Christ the Man of the Future

Albert Schweitzer's monumental *The Quest of the Historical Jesus* drew the curtain on this search with the concluding words: "There is nothing more negative than the result of the critical study of the Life of Jesus. The Jesus of Nazareth who came forward publicly as the Messiah . . . never existed."

The reaction, precipitated by World War I, which exorcised the optimistic view of human nature and the myth of inexorable human progress, took the form of dialectical theology. This theology rested on the assumptions of the crisis of man's fundamental condition and the complete otherness or transcendence of God. In this state of crisis man attempts to find security especially in religion, hence man must be rid of the search for and the claim to find God which is characteristically human and remain open to the saving word of God manifested in the New Testament. Reason can have only the very subsidiary role of ministering to faith. Thus Karl Barth asserted a *fides quaerens intellectum,* where reason must follow the blind leap of faith into the word of God gratuitously revealed to man, a revelation which refuses to yield to or to be judged by human categories and criteria. That man knows God is the result only of the miracle of God's redeeming action in Christ. This school of theology had extensive influence, but as John Macquarrie says,

> Its success has probably been partly due to the fact that by returning to a more dogmatic type of theology and by reinstating at its centre the idea of an absolute divine revelation, it has appealed to those traditionalists and obscurantist elements in the church who are only too glad to escape the philosophical problems which contemporary thought poses for the Christian religion.[5]

Macquarrie goes on to criticize Barth for his view that revelation is the exclusive source of theology and for the relatively negative role he accords to reason. He criticizes this school secondly for the arbitrary narrowing of the field of revelation to biblical revelation and thirdly for "the tendency to degrade man below the level of personality and responsibility".[6] The general tenor of this theological trend was to accept the Christ of the New Testament in a somewhat fundamentalist way, in spite of advance in human knowledge and the exigencies of contemporary sensibility. It reasserted elements in the New Testament eliminated by the liberals, but, in effect, identified the life of Christ with the apostolic kerygma.

The Christ of dialectical theology appeared to *defy* modern man. Rudolf Bultmann, on the other hand, saw Christ as a challenge to modern man. For him, the exegetical task was the fundamentally pastoral and apologetical task of posing this challenge in all its force, confronting man with an "existential" decision and summoning man to an authentic existence. The first phase in this task consisted in "demythologizing" the New Testament; the second phase consisted in reinterpreting it in contemporary thought patterns so that Christ's challenge would be communicated to men today. Bultmann accepted the inevitable conclusion of biblical research that the account of the life of Christ and its interpretation were structures in terms of the mythical (i.e. pre-scientific and pre-philosophical) world view of the New Testament writers. However, his aim, unlike that of the liberal Protestants, was not to eliminate the myths, but to interpret them. Nevertheless, Bultmann's own philosophical outlook —that of Martin Heidegger—led him to enunciate criteria for determining myths and principles for re-interpreting them which had a reductive or eliminating effect. For Bultmann, every statement must be interpreted existentially, for no statement concerns me at all unless it summons me to and is understood in an actual authentic decision; objective facts, which are simply "there", have no relevance for me. Consequently, New Testament proclamations of events, truths, and mysteries which are claimed to be universally valid and salutary, and which are claimed to have cosmic significance, must be regarded as myths and interpreted accordingly. The virgin birth, the miracles, the resurrection and the ascension of Christ must not be written off as irrelevant: though they are not to be taken literally, they must be interpreted and their significance for me today analysed and appreciated.

Scholarly analysis of the New Testament has shown, however, that though the element of summons to an existential decision is an important one, the life and the significance of Christ cannot be reduced to this alone. Indeed, it is difficult to see, in this kind of account of the life of Christ, why Christ needs to be a historical figure at all, for some of the monumental works of literature would be equally capable of providing the stimulus to the making of such a decision. While Bultmann's work did underline the importance of the need for a contemporary interpretation of the New Testament and emphasized the vital contact which Christ, through preaching, must make with contemporary man, at the same time the realization grew that the historical Christ could not be ignored. Moreover, theologians began to think much more seriously about what was meant by "historical"and to wonder if this concept had not suffered from the reductionist influence.

Indeed, the existentialist phase of recent theology did suffer from a reduction of human horizons to concentrate on the present existential situation of the individual. The pressure of the horizon of the future thus tended to be ignored. As J. B. Metz points out:

> This horizon characterizes the attempt of theology to surpass and go beyond the modern transcendental, personalistic and existential theology without disregarding its valuable insights . . . However, this theology faces two dangers. On the one hand, this anthropological theology tends to limit the faith by concentrating on the actual movement of the believer's personal decision. The *future* is then all but lost. On the other hand, this anthropological theology tends to become private and individualistic. It fails to bring into sufficient prominence the social and political dimensions of the believer's faith and responsibility.[7]

This all too brief and totally inadequate account of the two main lines of theological development in the Protestant thought of the twentieth century allows us at least to grasp the terms of the problem: that the Christ-event cannot be isolated from its significance for the contemporary situation, nor can it be merely reduced to it. The need to attempt a synthesis of these two aspects of the problem of Christ has led to the new quest for the historical Jesus. This new quest did not, like the old, attempt to separate the person and the words of Christ from the interpretation the New Testament gives to them. Though the two are distinguishable, in theory and sometimes in the practice of biblical scholarship, they are not separable as the object of theological study. As R. H. Fuller says:

> Neither the historico-critical approach nor the existential approach gives us the same contact with Jesus as does the kerygma. For the contact with Jesus which the kerygma gives us is neither merely "historisch" nor even merely existential; it is eschatological. Through the existential approach we can encounter Jesus and other historical figures only as unique figures, who offer us possibilities, among others, of self-understanding. In the kerygma, and only in the kerygma, we encounter One who was not only unique, like other historical figures, but once for all, One who confronts us with an eschatological, final, absolute claim, who offers the final, authentic self-understanding.[8]

The central difficulty is that the proclamation of the good news embodied in the New Testament writings has a conviction and a finality that we do not find in the words of Christ himself. Jesus proclaims that God is beginning to act in himself. The New Testament claims that God has decisively acted in Christ, though this action awaits a consummation. There is a greater degree of fulfillment in the kerygma than there is in the historical Jesus. There is a greater consciousness of the Messianic significance of the events of the life of Christ than there is in some of the sayings of Christ and this significance is often projected back onto the events and sayings of the historical Christ—to the extent that this can at present be gauged. But there is a peculiar feature of the New Testament kerygma. It has a quality of certitude and conviction which rests on a twofold foundation: the events of the life and death of Christ on the one hand and the future verification on the other.

The problem that arises for the Christian today is whether he must accept the quality of certitude and conviction about the divinity, the resurrection, and the cosmic significance of Christ which the New Testament and the early councils of the church exude, or whether this quality is one that grows under certain specified conditions. Under the heading "Inductive Faith" John Robinson says:

Doctrine is the definition of experience; the revelation discloses itself as the depth and meaning of the relationship. To ask men to believe in the doctrine or to accept the revelation before they see it for themselves as the definition of their experience and the depth of their relationship, is to ask what to this generation, with its schooling in an empirical approach to everything, seems increasingly hollow. In all this frontier-debate I have been made aware that about the one church in Britain whose public "image" is not a positive liability is the Society of Friends. And I believe this is because it appears to men to respect this order. I could not myself go with it in rejecting creeds and sacraments, liturgies and ordinations. I believe that these have their rightful place, and I have myself been duly exasperated by the woolliness of the Quakers at their worst! But I am convinced by the integrity which they seem to men to have. I have no evidence that they are in fact less hypocritical than the rest of us. But they do not present the impression that the results are prescribed. And I believe it to be a prerequisite of the search in our day that the ends should be genuinely open.[9]

To illuminate this problem further we can examine the more rigid and stable Catholic theological tradition with regard to the divinity of Christ. If we disregard the "modernist crisis" of the early part of this century we can make the generalization that the Catholic tradition has accepted the definition of Chalcedon unquestioningly throughout the whole period since the Council. However, one of the important reasons for this is that the Catholic tradition has maintained, relatively intact, the fundamental conceptual framework within which the Chalcedon definition was elaborated. Once that conceptual framework becomes unacceptable or outmoded, difficulties arise about the definition. Yet this is precisely what is happening at the moment.

There are two levels at which we can consider these difficulties; at the psychological level and then at the philosophical level. First of all, the psychological difficulties. These were very clearly expressed by the Bishop of Woolwich in *Honest to God*. If Christ was God—and most Catholics rightly or wrongly speak of Christ as if he were simply God—the Incarnation (the New Testament does not use the term) loses a great deal of its human value.

> For as long as God and man are thought of as two "beings", each with distinct natures, one from "the other side" and one from "this side", then it is impossible to create out of them more than a God-man, a divine visitant from "out there" who chooses in every respect to live like the natives. The supranaturalist view of the Incarnation can never really rid itself of the idea of the prince who appears in the guise of a beggar. However genuinely destitute a beggar he may be, he is a prince; and that in the end is what matters.[10]

Robinson uses another forceful analogy:

> If one had to present the doctrine of the person of Christ as a union of oil and water, then it made the best possible attempt to do so. Or rather it made the only possible attempt, which was to insist against all efforts to "confuse the substance" that there were two distinct natures and against all temptation to break the unity that there was but one indivisible person. It is not surprising, however, that in popular Christianity the oil and the water separated, and that one or the other came to the top. In fact popular supranaturalistic Christology has always been dominantly docetic. That is to say, Christ only appeared to be a man or looked like a man: "underneath" he was God.[11]

In its less crucial aspect, the problem is one of the approach that is used. The New Testament and the classical Christian dogmatic assertions about the nature and the role of Christ were made in a cultural context in which God—or gods—was a living reality, an accepted part of the scheme of things. The dynamics of the descent of God to earth from another world was a credible expression of the phenomenon of Christ in both the Jewish and Eastern cosmologies and in the world view of the Stoic and Neo-Platonic metaphysics. The description of the Christ-event in terms of descent, incarnation, death, resurrection, and ascension was both psychologically feasible and pedagogically appropriate. It is absolutely necessary to appreciate the full significance of the profoundly different outlook of the man of the secular age, and this in its positive and valid characteristics, before it is possible to appreciate the need for a fundamentally different approach to and hence relatively different understanding of Christ. In the past Christ was looked on as God because the mystery of Christ was approached from the direction and the point of view of God. Unfortunately most of the ecclesiastical "watchdogs of orthodoxy" have been trained and conditioned to see things from this point of view. As the mentality of the secular age spreads through the increasing standard of education they will be able to maintain their Olympian outlook only at the price of insulating the men of today from the question of Christ.

The second level at which we can consider the problem is the philosophical. The task of the theologian is to formulate an answer to "What think ye of Christ?" in propositional terms. At one extreme there is the simple answer that "Christ was God". At the other extreme is the answer of the liberals and the modernists which equates Christ's divinity with his perfect humanity. The definition of the Council of Chalcedon was calculated to guard against both of these extremes.

The central part of the text of Chalcedon is as follows:

Following then the Holy Fathers, we all with one voice teach that it should be confessed that our Lord Jesus Christ is one and the same Son, the Same perfect in godhead, the Same perfect in manhood, truly God and truly man, the Same of a rational soul and body; of one substance with the Father as touching his godhead, and the Same of one substance with us as touching his manhood, sin alone excepted; begotten of the Father before the ages, as touching his godhead, and, in the last days, the Same, for us and for our salvation, of Mary the Virgin, *theotokos,* as to his manhood; one and the same Christ, Son, Lord, Only-Begotten, made known in two natures without confusion, without change, without division, without separation, the difference of the natures, having in no wise been taken away by reason of the union, but rather the properties of each being preserved, and both concurring into the one *prosopon* and one *hypostasis* — not parted or divided into two *proposa*, but one and the same Son and Only-Begotten, the Divine Word, the Lord Jesus Christ . . .[12]

This statement of Chalcedon does not solve the problem of Christ. In terminology that is far removed from the rich and dynamic imagery of the New Testament, it states, rather, the terms of the problem which must not under any condition be eliminated as part of the solution. It is quite inadequate as a statement of Christ's mission to and his relevance for mankind, but it does define the context and the limiting features for any explanation of Christ's mission. Chalcedon aimed at safeguarding the unity of God, the manhood of Christ, the personal unity of Christ, and to forestall any theory which would attempt to explain Christ simply in terms of his manhood. However, the emphasis in the definition and the point of view from which it is made is the divine, the suprahistorical and the timeless, and this is what is disconcerting for us today.

In the first place, we do not know *what* the perfection of either manhood or Godhead consists in. Before it was realised that man is an evolving being it was possible to entertain the illusion that the essence of man was understood; this is not so now. Even the scholastics insisted that we do not know *what* God is, but only that he is. The point of view adopted is that of standing outside the human context in order to assert that Christ is like, even consubstantial with God, as if we knew what God was like and were applying divine criteria to examine the claims of would-be revealers of God. As Inge once wrote:

The controversy about the Divinity of Christ has been habitually conducted along the wrong lines. We assume that we know what the attributes of God are, and we collect them from any source rather than the revelation of God in Christ . . . But surely Christ came to earth to reveal to us not that he was like God, but that God was like himself.[13]

The philosophical categories in which the Chalcedon definition was stated served to preserve the theological gains of the two competing schools of Alexandria and Antioch and delineate the boundaries beyond which assessments and descriptions of Christ could not go without doing violence to the church's consciousness of Christ. Even though the definition is positive in logical and grammatical form, from the evangelical or apologetical point of view it must be regarded as a negative strategy, that of asserting what aspects of the person of Christ cannot be denied.

Hugh Montefiore in an essay "Towards a Christology for Today" sums up the value of the statement of Chalcedon:

> The New Testament gives us a few "stills" near the beginning of the church's developing Christology. As this Christology begins to develop, we see ontological definitions gaining ground. How did this happen? The Greek theologians took three basic biblical images, two of which had been used by Jesus himself, and they transformed these into philosophical concepts. The Logos was unable to bear the ontological weight which was put into it, and it tended to become a mere title of Christ. The Son of Man and the Son of God became the "vere homo" and the "vere deus" of orthodox Christology. While Harnack was right in claiming that the Hellenization of the gospel was a process of rationalization, he was wrong to suppose it was also a degenerative process of secularization. The definition of Chalcedon was the only way in which the fifth century fathers, in their day and with their conceptual apparatus, could have faithfully credalized the New Testament witness to Christ.[14]

One of the inadequacies of the philosophical apparatus which has had and continues to have an unfortunate effect is that of the concept of "person". The predominantly philosophical notion demands that Christ be not a human person at all, but a divine person with a human nature. Yet in the modern concept of person, if a human nature is not at the same time the structure and mode of behaviour of a human person, it can hardly be a human nature. If one's approach is from the side of God, the personal unity has to be established in the way that Chalcedon asserted it. If on the other hand, one's approach to Christ is from the side of man, he must be what he appeared to be, and what the early church held him to be— a human person.

If we approach Christ from the side of man, we accept first of all that he was a human person and that in and through the unique quality and style of his life he opened up new possibilities and horizons for human activity to the extent that he revealed in himself, in his own person, the substance of God. Jesus Christ broke through the limitations imposed upon us by the merely human condition. In some mysterious way or another he achieved mastery over death and became "the first fruits of those who have fallen asleep" (1 Cor. 15:20). He refused to accept the limitations of the human condition, was not content to accept a limited autonomy restricted within the boundaries of birth and death, but in and through a life of love for and complete commitment to others, developed an awareness of God, became "consubstantial" with God and thus triumphed over the grave. That this happened, of course, was due to the gratuitous gift of God and not to the inherent powers of human nature, though it is difficult to distinguish clearly or adequately between these two areas.

It is rather paradoxical that the technological age, the age in which man has achieved his greatest mastery over his environment, the age in which man most vociferously asserts his freedom, should be the age in which he most dogmatically denies the possibility of the total freedom to which Christ challenges him. The demand for freedom made by the secularists of the twentieth century is a very attenuated freedom and is ideologically disqualified from examining the claims, traditionally, though ambiguously, made by the church about Christ. As Helmut Thielicke points out:

Jesus Christ has been crucified again and again in the course of history. He has been amputated to fit the bed of Procrustes, the human notions of each age. He has been buried again and again in the grave of human thought-forms, to rise again each time. No sepulchre can hold him. Christ does not end in the cemeteries of philosophy.[15]

Thus when Bertrand Russell asserts "I believe that when I die I shall rot, and nothing of my ego will survive", or when Richard L. Rubenstein says "I believe that eschatology is a sickness with which man conceals from himself the tragic and ultimately hopeless character of his fate",[16] they are not stating a belief so much as the dogmatic imposition of limits on human possibilities; they are burying Christ and themselves, definitively, in the cemeteries of their philosophy. This is precisely the ideological mechanism which operated in the case of the liberal Protestants and in the remythologizing of Bultmann. Christ did not reveal God, Christ did not become consubstantial with the Father, Christ did not rise from the dead in any but the metaphorical sense, because, in the reductionist view, these phenomena are not possible. Yet this limitation on human possibilities is not arrived at nor based on the very principle of inductive verification which the secularist view appeals to as the great emancipating factor in contemporary sensibility.

Hence it is at this particular point that Christ, the Christ of history and the Christ of the kerygma, has relevance to and can have an impact on modern man. Surreptitiously, and hence insidiously, factors can operate on human consciousness, individual or collective, which frustrate the potential of man and prevent him from realizing in any credible way the image of God in which he was created. These factors erode the freedom of man and undermine his capacity to undertake the task of creative autonomy which the image of God entails. Thus for our age, Christ is the free man, free from all the limiting factors to which human beings so easily succumb, free for others and free for the future.

It is not my aim to establish that this concept of Christ the free man is the ultimate and absolute description of Christ. No doubt, like all the descriptions of Christ throughout history from the New Testament concept of Christ as the lamb of God through to the contemporary Hollywood vision of Christ as the all-American boy, the concept of Christ as the free man is a historically conditioned one. However, it does have the value of striking a balance between the existential appeal of Christ and the Christ of the dogmatic assertions of the New Testament and of the early church.

The failure of the search for the historical Christ does not disqualify us completely from knowing a great deal about the actual events of the life of Christ. As Joseph Bourke points out:

An obvious and striking weakness of form-criticism is that it grossly underestimates the capacity and intention of the New Testament writers to record historical facts about Jesus. They were indeed concerned to apply the meaning of what Jesus had said and done to their own contemporaries' post-Easter situation. Their memories of Jesus were, no doubt, selected and arranged, presented and interpreted upon this principle. But they were presented quite unequivocally as real memories, the authenticity of which could be vouched for by still living eye-witnesses.[17]

One of the obstacles to contact with and an appreciation of the person of Christ in the gospels is the doctrinal thought patterns in which Christians have been reared. These make it difficult to think of Christ as part of and involved in the milieu in which he lived. The discovery of the Dead Sea scrolls has helped overcome this, yet there is the danger that we think of Christ as performing a "redemptive" programme independently of the concrete details of Nazareth, Jerusalem, and Palestine two thousand years ago. If we overlook the specific contexts and interests in which Christ was involved, if we think of his life as a ritual, a sacrificial ritual executed in a way extrinsic to the content of his life, inevitably Christ will lose his significance for us. Not only do we have to get behind the interpretative account of the New Testament writers themselves, without ignoring this account, we have also to get behind or beyond the interpretative account to which we have been reared.

One of the central themes of the life of Christ is enunciated by Christ himself in John 8:31. "If you continue in my word, you are truly my disciples, and you will know the truth, and the truth will make you free." His own life was a progressive establishment and proclamation of his freedom. The prelude to his public life was a disavowal of personal concern and ambition. In the episode in the desert (Matt. 4:1-11) Christ rejected the three basic temptations to which men are subject and to which they so often surrender: to live by bread alone, to use power in their own interests, and to seek "the kingdoms of the world and the glory of them".

Throughout his life he showed himself to be free of the shackles that usually bind men, frustrate their rising above the limitations of their domestic or social or racial or ideological condition, and induce them to seek in this condition the safety, the security, and the consolation which Christ challenges us to forego. His reply to Joseph and Mary, "How is it that you sought me? Did you not know that I must be in my Father's house?" (Luke 2:49), was not a rebuke but an assertion of the broader horizon of his activity. When he apparently repudiated his kinsmen after being told that they were waiting for him, it was not the rejection of family ties but the extension of them to all men. His call to celibacy was not, by implication, a denigration of marriage, but the suggestion that a champion of the kingdom could be a more effective one if he could rise above the bonds of domestic life.

Christ refused to be constrained by the boundaries which are inevitably erected to contain the human person. He rose above and refused to recognize the racial boundaries between the Jews and the Samaritans. He had no qualms about talking to the Samaritan woman at Jacob's well (John 4:1-26). He used a Samaritan traveller to illustrate his injunction of love. Christ did not recognise and would not submit to social limitations and he associated and dined indiscriminately with scribes, Pharisees, publicans, and sinners. When exposed to the political trap of the Pharisees (Matt. 22: 15 ff.) Christ refused to acknowledge either that Caesar was God or that the God of the Jews was necessarily opposed to the presence of Caesar in the promised land.

In that context Christ was perfectly free to say what he thought should be said, to condemn what he regarded as reprehensible, to approve what he regarded as praiseworthy. He had nothing to lose by his honesty and his frankness. Unlike the foxes he had no place he could call his own and when executed on Calvary possessed only the seamless robe for which the soldiers cast lots. His heart was free from the many concerns, preoccupations, and affections which can occupy it.

> Do not lay up for yourselves treasures on earth, where moth and rust consume and where thieves break in and steal, but lay up for yourselves treasures in heaven, where neither moth nor rust consumes and where thieves do not break in and steal. For where your treasure is, there will be your heart also (Matt. 6: 19-21).

Christ even refused to accept the limitations of the category or stereotype of the holy man. His vision was not that of holiness in the formalistic and ritualistic sense which prevailed. He did not fast like the Baptist and the official holy men and when challenged he gave a mildly mocking and ironical reply. Sin did not pose any obstacles to him for he did not recognize it where other men saw it. Yet he could taunt his enemies with impunity to accuse him of sin.

However, Christ's freedom was not only negative in its scope as if it were merely a formal triumph over the limitations of the human condition. In its negative dimension it was a death to self, a denial of all the factors which turn the self in upon itself and imprison it there. The various manifestations of the negative dimension of Christ's freedom were merely preconditions for the realization of the positive dimension, his openness to, that is, his love for others.

The more sophisticated obstacles to the gift of self to others, the more insidious excuses for the refusal of the death to self which must come first provided the substance of Christ's protest in his public life, the topic of his conflict with the Pharisees and the reason for his own actual death on the Cross, without satisfaction, without consolation, without fulfillment.

In a way it is irrelevant whether the miracles of Christ actually occurred as they are described in the New Testament. We do not have any ontological or empirical justification for saying that they *could not* have occurred. However, the point is that whether taken metaphorically or literally, the accounts of the miracles establish Christ's independence of "the laws of nature" and his willingness to violate them in the interests of human persons. Christ brings this same "cavalier" approach to the religious laws of the Jews. He enunciates the principle "The Sabbath was made for man, not man for the Sabbath; so the Son of man is lord even of the Sabbath" (Mark 3:1 ff.). He forecasts the day when religious ceremonies will no longer constrain men: "But the hour is coming, and now is, when the true worshippers will worship the Father in spirit and truth, for such the Father seeks to worship him" (John 4:23). It was on this principle and in this cause that Christ was called upon to actualize the style of selflessness in his death on the cross. Yet even in his death, he repudiated any gratification or consolation. The ultimate freedom was freedom from the presence of or the support of God.

Hence in its negative dimension Christ's life was the complete repudiation of the human tendency to seek pleasure, gratification, consolation, escape, refuge, or security in an absolutizing of some aspect of the human condition, be it pleasure, power, ambition, a race, a nation, a church, a theology, or an ideology. In its positive dimension Christ's life was one of love for others. But it was not an abstract love without content or purpose, not a detached love without specific human relevance and significance. At the personal level it was directed to the creative satisfaction of real needs: bread for the hungry, sight for the blind, wine for an embarrassed wedding host, health for the leprous. At the social level it was directed to the reconciliation of all men. The charter of this ambition of reconciliation was the sermon on the mount; the symbol of it was the eucharistic ceremony of the last supper.

There is little in the life of Christ that can compel commitment. The events of the life of Christ taken individually or collectively cannot be made the principles or the theorems of an apodictic process which leads logically to the conclusion: you must be a follower of Christ or you must be a member of the church. Professor Donald MacKinnon of Cambridge has pointed out:

If you try to make faith invulnerable, if you try to make it the kind of absolute commitment that nothing will shake, then it binds. But if you look at it in a different way, it can liberate. The more I ponder the vulnerability of faith, the more I realise that this is a place at which those who are working in the sort of fields that I'm working in are not altogether inhabiting a different world from that inhabited by the scientist who stresses always the vulnerability of his hypotheses to refutation. Moreover you are doing justice to, you are perhaps paying the price for, one of the most precious elements in Christianity, that is the ordinariness of Christ, the Christ who comes so close to men that they do not notice him.[18]

It is possible to summarize the life of Christ, the free man, as one devoted to loving, creative, reconciliatory activity. These terms are interrelated, for the first implies the last two, though "creative" adds the idea of a responsible thrust into the future where the perfect community of men, Christ, and God will be realized. These three terms describe the style of Christ's life: they describe the way in which he revealed God, became consubstantial with the Father and ultimately achieved the perfection of freedom, the conquest of death through resurrection. The loving, creative, reconciliatory activity of Christ set down in human terms the conditions under which a relationship with God can be established, an awareness of God can develop and the reality of God can be verified. The word "love" is the only name that can in any way feasibly be substituted for "God", and yet not as a definition to be reverenced but as an exhortation to be fulfilled.

It is curious that so often the Christian church shifts the focus of loving, creative, and reconciliatory activity away from the very practical and material areas in which Christ exercised it. The central concern is shifted to salvation, to the spiritual life, to people's souls, on the principle and with the solemnly reiterated warning that man does not live by bread alone. This shift in focus or concern results either in an introverted exercise in psychological isometrics or in a form of spiritual domination which has a dehumanizing and de-Christianizing effect on both the dominated and the dominating.

Nicholas Berdyaev uncovers the quality in man to which Christ appeals, the quality of which he is the prototype and the "first fruits":

> In man there is a divine element, and grace itself, if it is not understood in a legal way and not associated with the idea of authority, is the disclosure of the divine element in man, it is the awakening of the divine in him . . . True and deep anthropology is the revelation of the Christology of man . . . What God expects from man is not servile submission, not obedience, not the fear of condemnation, but free creative acts. But this was hidden until the appointed time. The revelation which is concerned with this cannot be divine only; it must be a divine-human revelation in which man takes an active and creative part.[19]

The question that immediately arises is that it seems, at first sight, that the church, associated with the idea of authority, can only but restrict the freedom and the creative autonomy of man. This seems to be especially so in the imposition of a definition of the nature and significance of Christ which we find in the Council of Chalcedon. Part of the answer to this is that we have to understand something of the function of these definitions. In the first place, they serve the negative function of making sure that some aspect or dimension of Christ is not eliminated as a result of the application of historically limited or conditioned criteria. In this she guards against the myopia of commitment to ephemeral absolutes. If for example a theologian denies that Christ was or became consubstantial with the Father, or claims that Christ was a human person used by God merely as an instrument, and the justification for these theological views is that Christ *could not* have been divine or anything but a separate instrument of God, the church in relatively unspecific terms holds out against this arbitrary restriction upon what is possible. It is not so much a challenge to human freedom as the champion of it in the transhuman achievement of Christ.

In the second place, as Yves Congar points out, "Here is a fact not without profound significance: the formulas with the most dogmatic content and emphasis are often found in doxologies: the church confesses the plenitude of its faith in the praises offered in its worship."[20] Dogmatic formulas, whether found in the official pronouncements of the church or in its worship, are calculated overstatements. This offends the susceptibilities of men reared in the age of the careful and systematic differentiation of consciousness. Yet it can be justified for two reasons. The church has to champion, in propositional form, the broad expanse of human (and divine) possibilities revealed in the life of Christ, and secondly straddle, propositionally and symbolically—in the liturgy—the past, the present, and the future.

Hence all the statements of the consciousness of the church must have this eschatological element, a statement of the situation which will ultimately prevail, or of the situation which can ultimately be verified. The profound difficulty is that these statements relating to the future must be made in terms which we can understand only in the light of the events of the past and the present. Moreover, there are in these statements, either implicitly or explicitly, the conditions—namely a life modelled on the style of Christ's life—under which the statements can ultimately be verified. However, it must not be thought that the church has a privileged access to a specific descriptive knowledge of the future situation. Its function is to keep open the almost infinitely wide variety of human options. It cannot give an accurate description of these, but though it is constrained to use language that is mythical and metaphysical, this idiom allows it to hold out against, sometimes in an apparently obscurantist way, becoming entirely a child of its times. On the other hand, it does have a positive foundation for its stand. It does not hold out for the hopelessly vague range of options of what is logically possible for human beings. The foundation of its cause is what happened to Christ after and as a result of his complete death to self on the cross.

The usually unrecognized and unacknowledged factor in New Testament and ecclesiastical dogmatics about Christ and his significance is precisely the unfinished character of the story of Christ. Yet the "return of Christ", whatever this means, is central to the New Testament. A secularist says that Christ's bones remained in the tomb after his death because nothing else could have happened. The New Testament clearly testifies to the fact that something else did happen, but does not have it within its verbal capacity to communicate what did actually happen. Hence the church continues to proclaim an event that is more than the human condition allows for, in terms that are either grossly *of* the human condition or borrowed from some mythical condition.

In one sense the resurrection cannot be regarded as a completed and final event. It is part of the biblical story which points to the future fulfillment. As Carl E. Braatan points out:

> The arrows in the biblical conception of reality as history are always pointing towards the future. The tremendous emphasis on remembering the past is due precisely to the fact that it contains the promises which articulate our hopes in the future . . . biblical eschatology deals with what is central in human existence; man's hopes burst open his present, connect him with his past, drive him towards horizons of the not yet realized future.

Braatan contrasts the vision of Heidegger, "which shuts man up with a finitude whose core is anxiety and whose boundary is death", with the optimism of both Marxist and Christian visions of the future. He points out that the modern Marxist bases his optimism on his hopes for the future state of humanity and the world, though his repudiation of God is an excusable though misguided protest against "a divine hypostasis who obstructs the freedom and the future of man, and instead guarantees the prevailing forces in nature and society". However, for the modern Christian whose perspective is horizontal, the divine imperative stemming from Christ is precisely one of creative involvement and endeavour to bring about the future. In this perspective "the end of history is present prophetically in Jesus of Nazareth. In his resurrection the final end of universal history has been anticipated."[21]

One of the functions of the liturgy of the church is to state in symbol and ritual that there are more things in heaven and on earth than are dreamt of in any man's philosophy. We cannot simply be rid of myth, symbol, and ritual, just as we cannot be simply rid of metaphysics. Ritual has the capacity to express and evoke in a much more intuitive and at the same time much more comprehensive and fully human way. That is why the liturgy of the church has a much greater power to mediate and evoke a positive response to the challenge of Christ than do the predominantly discursive and philosophical statements of the church. As Berdyaev says:

> The most important thing is to grasp that in the process of objectification to which the historical and social life of man is liable Spirit is symbolized and not realized. The source of the symbolization is to be found in the fact that only prefigurations of the coming realization, signs of the other world (age?) are given. But symbolization loads men with chains when it is regarded as being already realization. In a deep sense of the word both worship and culture are symbolical, but in them a way towards realization is provided if that symbolism is not regarded as static, as though it were a final consummation.[22]

Yet it is here that the pitfalls occur. Do the dogmatic statements and the liturgical celebrations of the church mediate a positive response on the part of the Christian to Christ's challenge to accept responsibility, to accept the burden and the power of his freedom, or do they rather provide a refuge from them? Here the crucial question arises as to whether the creeds and the liturgy of the church dominate the human person or minister to his imitating Christ the free man. Do the creeds and the liturgy provide a haven for him from the "terror of history" or the "angst" of existence or do they provoke him to overcome them? Do the creeds and the liturgy provide a consoling substitute for freedom or do they encourage the Christian to assume the responsibility of creative autonomy in and for the world? Do they focus on the past or do they point to the future?

Unfortunately, in recent centuries the church has allowed the dogmatic and liturgical prefigurations to harden into and take on the appearance of "a final consummation". The hypothetical character of the creeds has been allowed to condense into static categories; the eschatological character of the symbolism of the church has taken on the appearance of an event already accomplished; the challenging quality of the liturgy has become obscured as the ceremonies of the church provided a refuge from the world for the spiritually and psychologically frail; the church itself, the symbol of the power of love to achieve total freedom, has come to exercise the power of authority and has taken on itself the burden of men's freedom in return for security at the price of humility, docility, and obedience.

Berdyaev, the prophet of authentic Christian freedom, penetrates to the core of the almost chronic malaise of the church in the secular age:

Throughout its history, Christianity seems to have been beset by the temptation to deny this liberty; nothing has been more difficult for Christians than to safeguard its integrity. So burdensome is the yoke of liberty to man that he even tried to rid himself of it within Christianity itself . . . Our Lord would not come down from the Cross as unbelievers called on him to do, because he craved for "the free gift of love, not the obsequious raptures of slaves before the might that has overwhelmed them" . . . A divine truth panoplied in power, triumphant over the world and conquering souls, would not be consonant with the freedom of man's spirit, and so the mystery of Golgotha is the mystery of liberty; the Son of God had to be crucified by the princes of this world in order that human freedom might be established and emphasized . . . There lies the whole secret of Christianity, and every time in history that man has tried to turn crucified Truth into coercive truth he has betrayed the fundamental principle of Christ.[23]

A symptom of the propensity to turn crucified truth into coercive truth is the traditional tendency to interpret Matthew 16:19 as a mandate to Peter and the apostles to exercise a supreme right of dominion, when the text itself—"I will give to you the keys of the kingdom of heaven, and whatever you bind on earth shall be bound in heaven, and whatever you loose on earth shall be loosed in heaven"—is a proclamation of the supreme freedom of the followers of Christ, the church. It is significant, of course, that only the binding power of the church is generally referred to, and this one-sided reference completely distorts the whole meaning and impact of Christ's words, as a charter for the creative autonomy of the church, an autonomy from all the limitations of history and the human condition to assume the loving responsibility for the world and to inherit ultimately what Christ inherited as a consequence of his triumph over the limitations of mortal existence.

The search for the historical Christ is in most senses a futile enterprise. The central Christian fact of today is not God or Christ, but the church. The impact that Christ makes on our age, the relevance that Christ has for our age, is not achieved fundamentally by making Christ available in terms that are descriptively compelling. Christ is made present to our age in the sociological phenomenon which is the church. Christ is today what the church is today. If Christ has little relevance and no impact, it is because the church has no relevance and no impact. This is not to say that the church must not constantly refer to the Christ of the New Testament and continue to adjust its consciousness of Christ to ensure its authenticity. But it is to acknowledge two important facts: Christ lived two thousand years ago and secondly, Christ asserted over and over again, in various ways, "As the Father has sent me, I also send you", "He who hears you hears me."

If the church in any age concedes victory to the Pharisees, if it allows the money changers back into the temple, if it permits its mind and its heart to be where its treasure of prestige, power, and privilege is, all the theological ingenuity of its greatest thinkers will not make Christ present to the world of today. Only a church which can credibly embody Christ's law of death to self and display a Christlike openness to all men and to the future can hope to manifest Christ in all his impact and relevance. A church which is a haven of all too human security, a church which is the victim of ideological myopia, a church which is in thrall to national, racial, financial, or social considerations, no matter how casuistically disguised, can only ever display to the world a Christ who is an anachronism.

The Morality of the Noosphere

> The currents and eddies of right and wrong, which you find such plain sailing, I can't navigate. I'm no voyager.
>
> *Robert Bolt*
> *A Man for All Seasons*

> Owe no one anything, except to love one another; for he who loves his neighbour has fulfilled the law.
>
> *Epistle to the Romans*

It is impossible to accede to a fundamentally new environment without experiencing the inner terrors of a metamorphosis. The child is terrified when it opens its eyes for the first time. Similarly, for our mind to adjust itself to lines and horizons enlarged beyond measure, it must renounce the comfort of familiar narrowness. It must create a new equilibrium for everything that had formerly been so neatly arranged in its small inner world. It is dazzled when it emerges from its dark prison, awed to find itself suddenly at the top of a tower, and it suffers from giddiness and disorientation. The whole psychology of modern disquiet is linked with the sudden confrontation with space-time.[1]

Teilhard de Chardin has just arrived at the peak of the upward spiral which is the whole process of evolution, at the point where man is capable of turning round and looking downwards to take in the whole pattern, with its unity of structure, its unity of mechanism, and its unity of movement. Man is the culmination of this evolutionary spiral. But though man has been on the face of the earth for thousands of years, he has now reached a new phase in his own evolution. Man is now conscious of the process of evolution; is conscious of the mechanism of "groping" and "invention" which has given rise to the process and is now aware, for the first time, that he must control the direction and the quality of his own evolution in the future.

Yet, standing as he does at the uppermost point of this spiral, "something clashes, for there is no natural place—no genetic place—for human thought in the landscape".[2] There is no unconscious genetic plan for the future direction or the future shape of human evolution. Teilhard continues:

> Hence we were not saying enough when we said that evolution, by becoming conscious of itself in the depth of ourselves, only needs to look at itself in the mirror to perceive itself in all its depths and to decipher itself. In addition it becomes free to dispose of itself — it can give itself or refuse itself. Not only 'do we read in our slightest acts the secret of its proceedings; but for an elementary part *we hold it in our hands,* responsible for its past to its future.[3]

This conscious responsibility for the process of evolution is what causes the contemporary vertigo in man, as he finds himself at the top of the tower, confronted with space-time! It is only now that man is finally casting off the last moorings which held him to the Neolithic age. So far, the evolution of the human race, its biological, its economic, social, political, and cultural evolution, has been the result of forces which had been unconscious and uncharted. But, beginning with the Renaissance, the human race has become increasingly conscious of these forces, has become better able to describe and to analyse them and ultimately to control them.

Man is faced with a frightening responsibility: responsibility for a future for which he has no blueprints. In undertaking it he can only simulate the genetic mechanism of "groping" and "invention". But he must not be hindered in this task by dedication to or domination by "hidden" norms and laws, taboos or oracular prohibitions. In acknowledging and accepting that there has been a fundamental shift in the structure and function of human responsibility from a conformist to an inventive and creative responsibility, man has to evolve a morality which can adequately minister to and facilitate it.

Evolution in the biosphere was spontaneous; evolution in the noosphere will from now on be under the control of man. But

> we shall never bend our backs to the task that has been allotted us of pushing noogenesis onward except on condition that the effort demanded of us has a chance of succeeding and of taking us as far as possible. An animal may rush headlong down a blind alley or towards a precipice. Man will never take a step in a direction he knows to be blocked. There lies precisely the ill that causes our disquiet. Having got so far, what are the minimum requirements to be fulfilled before we can say that the road ahead of us is *open*? There is only one, but it is everything. It is that we should be assured the space and the chances to fulfil ourselves, that is to say, to progress till we arrive (directly or indirectly, individually or collectively) at the utmost limits of ourselves.[4]

Arend van Leeuwen also sees the characteristic of our time as the end of the Neolithic age, as a phase in which the Western civilization "liberates itself—and with itself all other civilizations—from provincialism and self-perpetuation and comes to grips with the question of the future of mankind".[5] More specifically he sees the Christian church faced with the same kind of task, only this time a much more serious and difficult task, that Augustine faced, that of discerning the signs of the times in the light of the gospel.

Van Leeuwen suggests:

> This the church can only do — as Augustine did in his own day — with the intellectual and philosophical equipment which the twentieth century affords and with the historical and scientific knowledge now placed at her disposal. That means that the best theological approach to history must inevitably be a "Christian philosophy of history" which is "contemporary" in the sense of being highly provisional and relative.[6]

How well equipped is the moral theology of the Catholic church to cope with the problem of entering the phase of history ahead of us? The stresses of the shift in consciousness and outlook are most crucial and disturbing precisely in the area of moral theology. The development of historical and critical awareness has already subjected the traditional codes and systems of morality to abrasive and even destructive criticism. This would seem to be inevitable because the traditional systems were based on the demand for a conformist integrity rather than on the need for creative responsibility. And yet, in the first stage of this criticism, the only alternative appears to be an individualistic moral anarchy.

Earlier in this book it was suggested that relationship with God and even a developing awareness of God depended, not on finding an area of life—a "religious" area—left over when all the vital connections had been made, but on the very making of all the vital connections in life. A Christian depends on Christ to enunciate the conditions under which statements about God can be made meaningful and ultimately verifiable. An analysis of the life and the significance of Christ reveals that he was not a law-maker so much as a law-breaker. Christ's life was not one that can be slavishly imitated, nor did Christ offer his followers clearly defined prescriptions and injunctions. Unfortunately Christians projected back onto Christ the role of legislator and this has prevented them from seeing Christ as the one who broke free from the only too human legalistic syndrome to assume the God-given role of creative responsibility for others.

At best, meditation on the life of Christ must evoke a total or existential response. His life and his challenge cannot be reduced to glib formulations which will form the basic principles and theorems of a Euclidean moral system. And yet it is possible to capture in the three words "loving", "creative", and "reconciliatory" something of the essence of the life-style of Christ. They can thus be used as signature terms of a Christian approach to life, and the foundation of a Christian morality. However, none of these terms allows for stability, security, finality, and comfort. Each embodies in it an intimation of dynamic tension and this is where each of them challenges sin, which, in some of its aspects at least, is the inherent propensity of man to seek refuge in or settle for ultimates and absolutes that are less than God himself and even less than man himself.

Christian morality has already been subjected to the process of secularization. It is in the sphere of moral theology that this process can be seen to be, if not a specifically Christian thing, then at least of great service to the Christian cause. There is always the danger that the church will avoid worldly responsibility by proclaiming its sometimes idolatrous reverence before absolute laws which it believes to have been decreed by God in the Bible, or revealed in the unchanging order of things in the world. There is always the danger that Christians will take refuge from the task to which Christ calls them in indubitable moral panaceas to which they can always appeal and from which they can obtain the consolations of the sense of righteousness. The process of secularization is inexorably dissolving the absolutes and discrediting the panaceas.

However, this process has not by any means come to fulfillment. Many Catholics still bring unwanted children into the world so that they can continue to enjoy the euphoria of hierarchical approval in spite of the fact that they know that this will disqualify their giving their children the educational opportunities which are today so necessary. Other Catholics allow tension and alienation to develop in the home because of a refusal to make love with their marriage partner, in the interests of a "good" conscience. The church allows Catholics married to divorcees to continue to carry a debilitating burden of guilt throughout their lives unless they are willing to renounce their deep responsibilities to the domestic society which results. A great deal of individualistic, conformist, sex-preoccupied, and ecclesial centred morality of Catholics is a source of suffering to some Catholics themselves, a scandal to genuine humanists, a cause of division with other Christians, a source of profound moral insensitivity in areas of social and international concern, and an obstacle to a vital relationship with God.

The first step in understanding the extent of the need for secularization in Christian morality and the changes that are necessary before Christians can elaborate a theology for creative autonomy in the world is to examine the structure and functions of the traditional moral theology. In this analysis I will concentrate on the Catholic structure, but many of the defects of this system are represented in analogous ways in the moral outlook of the other churches. As John Robinson points out:

The supreme example of this way of thinking is, of course, the corpus of Roman Catholic moral theology, and it is magnificent in its monolithic consistency. But it is a way of thinking that pervades, even in more muddled form, the whole of the church's ethical thinking, Catholic and Protestant, official and unofficial.[7]

The traditional system of Catholic moral theology was geometrical in structural design and philosophical in content. Scripture provided the texts which were applied usually apologetically to justify, almost extrinsically, the conclusions reached by the process of reasoning. In this system the virtue of charity was given pride of place as a category among the two other theological virtues of faith and hope, but once dealt with in this way it no longer exerted a dynamic and central effect on the moral issues that were considered.

Thus in dealing with the moral virtues of prudence, justice, fortitude, and temperance, the specifically Christian moral principle of altruistic love, on the model of Christ's love, was extrinsic to the bulk of the ethical structure. Though recognized as of supreme importance as a category of virtue it was not effectively acknowledged as an ever relevant and dynamic principle. The relevant and dynamic principles were philosophical. They were the principles of natural law built into or manifested in the natures of things.

This structure resulted first of all in a negative morality. The laws of nature must not be violated. It became possible to map out the boundaries of what was morally permissible and within this area or inside these boundaries a person could claim to be a Christian, and even a good Christian, without any credible reference to or implementation of Christ's positive directive to love. One of the ambitions of the so-called "new morality" in Christianity is to restore to its central position the one criterion of being a Christian: that of love. It is much more difficult to be a Christian in this situation, for the directive to love applies always and in every situation. In a negative Christian morality, provided a person does not violate any of the boundaries of the so-called Christian moral legal code, he can feel assured that he is an authentic follower of Christ.

Actually the handbooks of moral theology and the courses generally given of Catholic moral theology did an injustice to the classical system. Taken comprehensively this system did not or should not have resulted in a negative bias or orientation. Moral theology was divided into three sections: the lowest and the relatively negative aspect, moral theology, then ascetical theology, and finally mystical theology. The last two sections are of the utmost importance to the whole enterprise for they embody the positive phases of the law of love and also the empirical examination of the consequences and implications in the lives and the writings of the mystics. It is only in the last phase that the emphasis on the complete purification of the Christian life from reliance on or resort to consolations of any kind is fully established. In this phase, the all-consuming importance of altruistic love emerges and, as a necessary element in the realization of this perfect love, death to reliance on the awareness of God. The theology of the classical mystical writers was in fact the first death-of-God theology. In the writings of John of the Cross, Teresa of Avila, and Henry of Susa we find a creative responsibility for man increasing in direct proportion to the decline of a reliance on God and the consolations which this kind of reliance can afford.

The first fundamental defect, therefore, of Catholic moral theology, as generally understood and applied, was that the law of love was not its dynamic principle. The second fundamental defect was in the philosophical principles which took its place. These were taken to be derived from the nature of things, from the nature of man, from the nature of society, the use of money, the use of sex, the nature of the institution of marriage, and so on. From the vantage point of history and as a consequence of the findings of psychology and cultural anthropology we can now see that many of the "immutable" philosophical principles which were brought to bear were themselves the products of and generated by a particular historical and cultural situation.

The relevance of these philosophical principles to a structure of Christian moral theology was based on the assumption of the existence of a natural order leading to God the author of nature which the supernatural order elevates and complements. The substance of the ethical system was thus provided by the natural law and the function of the order of revelation or grace was to elevate and sometimes correct this order. The complementary or corrective directives, the directives which "elevated" the natural order, were found in the Bible. This view presumes that the Bible contains moral directives from God in propositional form, a presumption that is scarcely tenable today, and relies on a theory of natural law which subjects man to nature.

The problem of "natural law" is one which is periodically relegated to the limbo of pseudo-problems and which just as frequently reappears for serious academic analysis and consideration. In an article entitled "Natural Law and Its History",[8] Joseph Arntz, O.P., traced the various conceptions of natural law which have obtained since it first appeared among the Greek philosophers. The Greeks distinguished between "phusei dikaion", what is "by nature", "by itself", and "nomooi dikaion", what is by force of law. This distinction contained no declaration about an unchangeable nature. However, Arntz claims, the Greek world view contained a feature which tended to eliminate the distinction, for they assumed that the world was a cosmos, an ordered and harmonious whole.

The Morality of the Noosphere

By assuming an immanent Logos in nature and in man, the Stoics cancelled out the difference between nature and reason in principle. For the Stoic thinker, to act according to reason and to act according to nature are identical. And since the law is the product of reason, law and nature are united, and henceforth we can talk of "natural law."[9]

As the cosmic order is unchangeable, natural law is unchangeable.

When Christianity left the Jewish context for the broader cultural context of the Hellenic culture, the Christian moral teaching began to use the Stoic idiom and adopted, though not altogether consciously and deliberately, the philosophical tradition of Stoic natural law.

In the writing of Aquinas there are the ingredients of the traditional theory but his treatment in Ia-IIae 90-108 has elements, and a system of checks and balances, usually overlooked by the systematizers who followed him and invoked his authority. For Aquinas, law is an ordinance of reason; law is also an analogous term. To ignore the analogous character of this term is to run the risk of legalism. Aquinas' concept of "eternal law" is not identical with a static, external order in the nature of things. It is identical with God's Being (conceived as pure existence, which is infinitely dynamic and open-textured compared with the conceptions of God as the One, the True, the Good, etc.), his Providence, and his government of the world. God governs the world according to the nature of things, and participation in eternal law is expressed in two ways: firstly, irrational things participate in eternal law in so far as they are directed by their nature; secondly, rational beings participate in eternal law by and according to their reason. The final element which is essential to the concept of natural law as understood by Aquinas is that the nature of things can be asserted only in the factual judgment. In the pre-scientific age the basis for making this judgment was a teleological estimate of the function of a thing. But, as we will see, the epistemological basis established by Aquinas was an important development the significance of which was generally overlooked.

If any of these checks and balances in the theory of natural law are ignored, either of two moral systems results: (a) a rationalistic morality which attempts to construct a purely deductive science of morality, in which conclusions are arrived at by logical processes from given premises, and, on the assumption of the correspondence of thought and being, presumed to represent the natural order; (b) a morality based on physical teleology, which regards man's physical nature as normative. This is the morality invoked in most medical and sexual moral arguments. It invariably considers various organs and physiological features in isolation from the human and social composite in the name of the natural law. This represents a reversion to the Stoic conception, for in this view the emphasis falls on nature. In Aquinas' view the emphasis falls on man and his knowledge and freedom.

It is both paradoxical and unfortunate that the architects and exponents of the great system of Catholic moral theology piously regarded themselves as devoted exponents of Thomistic thought. Nearly all the examples of Catholic moral theology of the manuals are intoxicating combinations of these two deviations from the moral theology of Aquinas. By combining natural law rationalism and physicalism they effectively foreclosed on both man's knowledge and his freedom. What the physicalists overlooked or perhaps never suspected is that nature does not seek the integrity of the organ, but always provides for the integrity of the organism.

The question that must be asked is this: is nature, including man in all that we know of him, the *master* of the art of living, or is it merely the *matter* of the art of living? The so-called natural law theorists have claimed that nature is the master of the art of living, so that ultimately it dominates man to the extent that he must obey the rules which an investigation of nature, if properly conducted, reveals. And yet it can be argued that man is revealed as a master of sub-rational nature and of himself; that man is a creator and his nature as a creator demands that he act accordingly.

It should be obvious that a shift from a static concept of the world and man to an evolutionary concept of the world and man is partly, though not entirely, responsible for this difference in viewpoint. Even if a person acknowledged fully the evolutionary structure of reality, he could still demand that man take a passive role in investigating the nature of things as they unfold. Yet the point in history at which we now find ourselves seems to demand that man no longer accede to the drift of things but bring them under deliberate and conscious control.

However, and this is of the utmost importance, if man does subscribe to the belief that nature is the matter of his art, does this not concede him the merely gratuitous disposition of the components of reality? Does this not lead inevitably to antinomianism? No artist is completely free from the demands of the medium he uses.

A painter, a sculptor, a composer, or a poet must achieve mastery in his field according to the structure and the potentialities of the material he is working with. He cannot simply disregard the nature of the material or the instruments he is using. But on the other hand he must not be dominated by them either. His claim to be an artist rests on his ability to capitalize on and rise above the limitations imposed by the material. To the extent that he capitulates to these limitations and uses them as an excuse for his shortcomings, to that extent he is a failure as an artist.

The question that is raised here is just how the church or moral theologians go about determining the nature of things. The fundamental objection to the natural law procedure in moral theology was not that it assumed that nature was in some way normative, but in the way moral theologians determined the nature of things. For the most part, these crucial decisions were made as the result of deductive reasoning or by teleological insight into the purpose of things. There was very little scope for an inductive approach. Consequently, the most important reform that has yet to be implemented in Christian moral theology is that of using a strictly scientific approach to determining the nature of things.

When the defenders of the Catholic view of the immorality of contraception speak of its evil effects for the partners, the family, and society, the judgment that there are evil effects is not based on exhaustive empirical observation, but on the simple a priori process of pronouncing that there *must be* evil effects because the church is already committed to the view that contraception is evil. When Pope Paul criticized an Italian parliamentary divorce bill, he claimed that the absence of divorce in a state is a moral and social advantage and a sign of a superior civilization.[10] Is this judgment based on a scientific comparison of various states and civilizations or is it based on the assumption that because the Catholic church regards divorce as evil, this must be the case?

It seemed, when the special commission on birth control was convened by the Pope, that a new era had dawned for Catholic moral theology. Among the members of the commission, along with the theologians and philosophers, were demographers, sociologists, biologists, psychologists, gynaecologists, psychiatrists, and so on. There were grounds for thinking that the complex issues involved would not be solved by deductive and speculative techniques carried out in isolation from the actualities of domestic life and the real effects of domestic issues on human persons. However, it seems that these scientists were called in to provide scientific backing for the "traditional" and official view. It was not envisaged that they would contribute substantially to the elaboration of a conclusion different from the official view. In spite of a majority decision in favour of a change in the Catholic view, it remained the same as it was before.

Unfortunately there has been a profound ambiguity about the object of moral decisions. Christ's command is to love one another. This entails seeking what is good for the other. The initial problem is the method of determining what is good for the other. Is this decided by an inductive procedure or by some other procedure? At first sight, in a scientific age, the answer would seem to be that what is good for people should be determined by scientific means, that is, by the use of methods of observation and analysis employed in the various scientific disciplines of psychology, sociology, and so on. However, there persists in the church a mental block to this way of answering questions about the nature of things and about what is good for people. The block manifests itself in the claim that the official or hierarchical pronouncements of the church assert what is really good for the person or for society. The ultimate appeal is to a supra-phenomenal good, a spiritual good, which is beyond the resources and the scope of the various sciences to comprehend or illuminate. This good can be appreciated, so it is claimed, and adequately understood only by those with the hierarchical power or who are sufficiently developed spiritually. Hence, the official teaching on birth control and divorce is rendered invulnerable. Even if all the resources of all the sciences reached the conclusion that contraception was good for people, some moral theologians would reply that even so contraception would be against the spiritual good of people and would not be really good for them at all. It is significant that this kind of distinction does not appear in the New Testament. Christ did insist that man does not live by bread alone, but he did not decide that it would be good for the spiritual lives of the multitude if they went without bread in the desert. "Good" certainly is an analogous term, but the clear-cut dichotomy between the good of persons which can be determined by inductive means and the "real" good in the spiritual order, which is determined by privileged insight, can be sustained only on the assumption of the validity of an ontocratic world view. It is this ontocratic world view that the process of secularization is gradually eroding.

Nevertheless, there is a sense in which what is good for persons transcends the conclusions of a particular science. The person, and the good of the person, cannot be adequately accounted for or described in the configurations of any one science and as the techniques and conclusions of the various sciences are not yet interconnected and continuous, science cannot be relied on completely for the definitive decision as to what is good for a person. The integrating principle must be, in the last analysis, a sensitivity for and a connatural intuition of what constitutes the integral good of the human person. The important point is that though the methods of the various sciences concerned with man are not continuous, nevertheless the substance of the knowledge on which the intuition is based must be provided by systematic and laborious observation and analysis, that is, inductively. While an estimate of what is good for a person cannot be made independently of scientific observation, it must not be dominated by it either, because the human person cannot be simply analysed into or reduced to the data which are the idiom of scientific method. Moreover, science is capable of telling us what human beings are, in their psychological, economic, or sociological aspects. Science does not tell us, however, what human beings can become. The realm of the ideal or of the imaginative must also enter in.

The traditional moral theology has been dominated by principles which have been to a large extent generated unconsciously by past socio-cultural situations. Science enunciates principles arrived at by induction from the observation of socio-cultural situations as they are at the moment. The combined task of moral theology and science as man stands on the threshold of the noosphere is to suggest "models" by which men can achieve the greater integral good of persons and the more effective realization of the community of persons in the future.

The debate over Christian morality which has raged over recent years has been conducted along lines which could lead only to a confusion of the question and a false polarization of the issues. The debate has appeared to be one between the advocates of absolute and objective principles of morality on the one hand and situationists or contextualists on the other. In the first place, any attempt to categorize usually does an injustice to the theologian concerned, for as Gustafson points out: "Christian ethics can and does begin from at least four points, and no matter which one is primary for a particular theologian, he moves towards the other three as he extends his moral discourse within a Christian frame of reference."[11] In the second place, each of the theologians intent on a renewal in moral theology seeks to make Christ's law of love the dynamic source of Christian morality; each is opposed to the substitution for this law of love of some other philosophical or sociological law which can at best be only penultimate. What has often happened in the past is that a moral principle, which in a particular historical or cultural context embodied the law of love, gradually, as the context changed, came to frustrate it. A clear example of this is the law against usury: in a subsistence economy which prevailed in a feudal culture, the prohibition of usury ensured and embodied the law of charity. In a different type of economy which depends on the extension of credit, the law of social and personal charity demands the abolition of the prohibition. Consequently, theologians today often state that love is the only obligation or the only absolute norm. They are vehemently opposed by the champions of absolute moral laws and then the debate becomes lost in a morass of casuistry as to whether the laws given as examples are really moral absolutes at all. Yet it seems that the debate should be about the epistemological question of how we decide what is good for persons. Do we rely on a metaphysical insight, do we leave it to the existential response of the person in his unique moral context or can the matter be illuminated, even if not entirely, by an inductive approach?

In an article in *New Blackfriars*[12] James Tunstead Burtchaell criticizes Joseph Fletcher[13] for the reduction of the dimensions of the moral problem to that of the intention of the agent. He points out that the traditional morality has maintained that any human action involves four distinguishable ethical factors: (*a*) the motive of the agent; (*b*) the intrinsic nature of the act; (*c*) its foreseen effects; (*d*) the modifying circumstances.

Despite its name, situation ethics does not revolve on situation at all. Fletcher moves about — messily at times, it seems — from motive to consequences to situation. But the crucial factor in the method is the motive. The system really should be called intention ethics. What is novel about it is the claim that any action, in any situation, with any consequences, is good if it is an action of love, and evil if an action of nonlove. Love, urges Fletcher, is the only norm, the only measure. All ethical judgement must therefore revolve about purpose. It is essentially indifferent what forms a man's behaviour takes, provided this behaviour be the outward expression of inward caring.[14]

In spite of the centrality of the theme of love and the careful insistence that this love is "agape" and not "eros" or "philia", one begins to suspect, sometimes, that the real source of this kind of moral theology is not a desire for developing a morality of concern for others but a desire to dispel the pall of guilt that enshrouds the old morality. A great deal of the so-called new morality is preoccupied with the problem of subjective guilt, even though this question is not explicitly stated. The question is a valid and urgent one, but preoccupation with it can lead to the kind of solution which reduces morality to the intention to love to the detriment of actual concern for the concrete good of the object of the love. However, it should be pointed out that Burtchaell is probably less than just to Fletcher's point of view. Fletcher does require that the person making the moral judgment assess carefully the extrinsic factors relevant to the situation. His writing certainly stresses over and over again that love alone is always good, and that "the intrinsic theory of value traps its holders into the untenable position of making absolute prohibitions of certain acts, regardless of circumstances".[15] Burtchaell is correct only in so far as his criticism is directed at the emphasis in Fletcher's writing, for Fletcher does recognize[16] the four traditional factors at stake in every situation, viz. the end, the means, the motive, and the consequences.

A Christian who has sex relations with a woman who is not his wife cannot settle for a moral decision which is based on an introspection of his own attitude towards the woman as to whether this attitude is one of love or one of exploitation. In the last analysis this would not be Christian love at all, but an exhibition of moral narcissism, for his concern is primarily with his own moral justification. This path leads just as surely to the "other-worldly" morality which is one of the defects of the traditional morality. An essential element in the moral enterprise is finding out what is actually good for the other person. No matter what the intention of the Christian towards the woman, his having relations with her outside marriage will have psychological and social consequences for her and for him, which will be good or bad independently of the propriety of his motives. The important change that has to come, however, in the enunciation of objective moral norms, is that they be made as a result of inductive study and not be made by theologians in ivory towers. The fact that this kind of information is not generally available does not invalidate the principle, it simply underlines the urgency of the task.

What is required, therefore, in Christian morality today is an objective element which will be provided by the social sciences. This is not to say that the norms that will be established as a consequence of scientific investigation will be absolute and final. At best, as with any scientific conclusions, they will be provisional. That this must be so is due not just to the nature of scientific method but also to the evolutionary character of human society, and the creative role man will have to play in determining the future. But more of this later on.

Some further observations need to be made about the moral theology which settles for love as the only law. In one sense, it is a species of "angelism". It ignores the effects that things and actions have on the person himself no matter what his basic and prevailing attitude or motives. There is a dialectical interaction of person and actions, or of person and things. Purposes certainly shape deeds, but deeds also ultimately shape purposes. As Burtchaell says:

Single actions are not expressive of our total character nor utterly decisive in our life. But over a period of time certain characteristic trends and traits appear, personality patterns emerge, an overall direction of our affairs is felt and observed. In a certain sense it is right to speak of a duality here — not a severance between intention and deed, but a dialectic between this fundamental option (let us say, our fundamental selfishness or selflessness) and the complex of individual actions. What I do and what I am are constantly interacting upon one another. My character discloses itself in what I do, yet can be shaped and modified by changes in what I do. My life works from the inside out and also from the outside in.[17]

It is probable that the advocates of love as the only absolute are capitulating to the same fundamental human weakness that they often deplore in the proponents of the old morality, though for different reasons. The old or traditional morality sought to establish incorrigible moral moorings either in metaphysical propositions—in the case of Catholic morality—or in biblical injunctions literally interpreted—in the case of Protestant theology. The precipitation of the moral principles or the criteria for selecting the specific biblical injunctions resulted from the unconscious factors of the particular cultural situation in which they occurred. Yet each sought clear-cut principles for Christian behaviour which would provide a sense of moral security and also the basis for passing judgment on others.

This second function of clear-cut moral principles, that of providing criteria for judging the behaviour of others, has played a usually unacknowledged but very important part in the development of moral theology and also in the genesis of many of the difficulties facing Christian morality today. As Albert Mirgeler points out in *The Mutations of Western Christianity*,[18] the Celtic monks who converted Northern Europe established a kind of monastic theocracy over the people they converted, a rule which extended from the political and economic dimensions right down to that of the individual conscience. In this context private confession grew in importance, together with a corresponding systematization of morality, sin, and guilt. The development of scholasticism provided the theoretical tools for this process of systematization and intensified the process. The combined tradition of private confession, a scholastic system of morality, and ecclesiastical supervision has persisted to this day. In a less organized way, the same propensity to supervise morality and seek clear criteria of acceptability has profoundly influenced the Puritan tradition. And yet this whole enterprise of moral supervision is in clear violation of Christ's injunction to his followers to renounce the urge to judge others: "Judge not and you shall not be judged."

Now the appeal to love as the only absolute is indeed a healthy reaction against the all too un-Christian tendency to pass judgment from the eminence of facile moral absolutes. It is also an admirable attempt to release Christian morality from the restrictions of the limited cultural situations which have so profoundly influenced it. But the appeal to love as an absolute still concedes that there is a credible absolute on which we can rely and in which we can seek refuge. Like any other absolute, it can be used as a substitute for responsibility and undermine the creative endeavour to which man is called. It allows the person to retreat into the sanctuary of his personal moral euphoria generated by the complacency of his impeccable motives. This sort of morality dispels the pall of guilt and disbands inquisitions, *but it does not change the world!*

What is called for is what Bonhoeffer called a "worldly morality". The morality of love suggested by Fletcher is not really a worldly morality for it is quite prepared to leave the world as it is provided the individual feels justified. If a poor man steals, or if a girl wanders indiscriminately from bed to bed, or if a man is emotionally incapable of the stable relationship which is marriage, or if people under pressure of circumstances "drop out" or resort to alcohol or to drugs, it is not sufficient to develop a morality which will merely reassure them of the mercy of God. What is also required is a morality which while absolving them from guilt, will assert that what they are doing is wrong and harmful and which will demand a change in the conditions which caused the evil in the first place.

This brings us to another fundamental defect in the traditional morality: its perspective is limited, for the most part, to the individual horizon. This in its turn is a consequence of the church being regarded and regarding itself as a retailer of spiritual consumer goods. Christianity has over the past hundred years become acculturated to the prevailing individualistic values of the Western world. In return for the assurance of eternal salvation individuals paid the price of fidelity to the dogmatic, moral, and liturgical injunctions of their church. As this was in the historical context of the isolation of the church from the substance of life—the world of politics and economics—morality became an eminently personal and individualistic thing. Hence even today, in the Western world, a Christian would regard a night in bed with a woman to whom he was not married with deep moral seriousness, but he would be morally impervious to spending thousands of dollars on a material status symbol, a new home or a new and more expensive car, while millions starve in other parts of the world. The powerful resources of the Catholic church are mobilized to counter any legislative moves to liberalize contraception or divorce, but these same resources are strangely lethargic when there is question of racial equality, the morality of a war involving national prestige, economic aid to developing countries, and the development of the world community. It is indeed an indictment of the church generally that, as F. C. Happold says, "It has not been the Christian church but the scientists and the humanists who have led the advance in the march towards toleration and free enquiry and towards social justice and a better life for the common man."[19] It is a symptom of the introverted preoccupation and otherworldly or vertical perspective of Christian morality that the Christian missionaries and the colonists of the traditionally Christian nations of the West seemed incapable of effecting the transformation of the developing countries of the world but only their economic and cultural exploitation.

The individualistic character of the traditional morality is highlighted in the role the symbolism of the cross played in the asceticism of the church. Mortification and penance were widely advocated and practised in imitation of Christ's sufferings, but they were detached from the whole purpose of Christ's passion and death, viz. its value for others. Discipline was an important element in the life of the church but it was of a Spartan, not a Christian, kind; it was concerned with the development of spiritual muscle and the personal storing up of treasure that rusteth not. Imitation of the cross ran the danger of becoming a parody of the cross, that is, an exercise in self-concern and self-interest. Mortification, penance, and discipline are of value precisely and only to the extent that they symbolize and make possible an altruistic concern for others. The abstinence from meat on Friday and the substitution for it of lobster mornay is an elaborate moral farce. The abstinence from both meat and lobster on Friday and the gift of the cost of these to the poor is an authentic imitation of Christ's cross.

The fundamental weakness of much of the new morality promoted under the heading of situationist or existentialist ethics is that it is also radically individualistic. As Burtchaell says:

It shares the old idea that morality has to do with guilt or innocence, with responsibility (=answerability). It thus ignores that much of the evil we do is not due to our evil intentions and purposes, but to the evil values that our cultural milieu foists upon us. A situation ethic should recognize more clearly that our situation is to a large degree evil, and that our worry should be to defend ourselves against the false values accepted in our society. Ethics cannot afford to be individualistic, when so much of the lovelessness in individuals is inherited from a bad society. The Christian's duty is so often to fight free from his situation, though he may be destroyed in the process. Like Christ.[20]

Perhaps the most important condition for the development of an authentic Christian morality capable of coping with and orientated towards the future is the eradication of the myth of guilt from the area of morality. The sense of guilt has acted as a sanction for the preservation of the moral, social, and cultural status quo. It has emasculated creative responsibility in the past and continues to do so today. The myth of guilt exerts its conservative power because it is instilled on the assumption that evil brings its own punishment and is inculcated as an integral part of a morality which is basically a respect for taboos. Louis Monden[21] emphasizes the importance of the distinction between the feeling of guilt and the awareness of guilt. The first arises as a consequence of sub-moral indoctrination and psychological conditioning, of misguided domestic or formal education and of traumatic experiences. It has nothing to do with mature moral responsibility and a rational recognition and acknowledgment of guilt. Yet it operates, and is used, to reinforce "traditional" values and attitudes. The point is that the feeling or the sense of guilt has little to do with the immutable nature of things. It rests ultimately upon the level of instinct.

The law which directs this instinctive ethics comes not from within but from without, from the pressure of reality, and especially of society, which by means of prohibitions and "taboos", builds a dam against the impulses of individual instinctivity . . . Guilt and sin of this kind consist in the material transgression of some prohibition or taboo . . . Contrition for sin too is, on this level, not an awareness of one's wickedness and a desire for amendment, i.e. for becoming one's good self again, but simply the instinctive urge to escape the consequences of the transgression. On this level contrition looks mostly for formula, rites of reconciliation and magic gestures by means of which the angered powers are placated.[22]

A great deal of the cohesion and of the impregnability of the structure of Catholic morality has depended on the inculcation of rigid moral injunctions at the instinctive level. This insures a considerable amount of immutability. Though some may temporarily reject the Catholic faith, if they have been reared in a Catholic family and in a Catholic school, the sense or the feeling of guilt will effect the eventual return of a great many of these "lost sheep".

The problem which arises for many Catholics who decide that they have the moral obligation to resort to contraception is how to cope with the feeling of guilt which inevitably accompanies its use. A woman might decide, on very rational grounds, that she is morally obliged to contravene the papal prohibition of contraceptives. Provided that no crises occur to upset the balance of life, everything may go well. But if some tragedy occurs, the sense of guilt can then become an important factor, and cause a great deal of emotional stress and harm. The effects of moral indoctrination and emotional conditioning cannot be eliminated by a balanced and responsible assessment of the moral options and an authentic moral decision. These effects operate through the sense of guilt to inhibit and frustrate the kind of freedom to which Christ calls us, and the sense of responsibility for the society and the world in which we live. Rather than carry the burden of the sense of guilt, which seems, for the present, to be an inevitable concomitant of any attempt to effect change in the Catholic church, many settle for the sense of security and tranquillity which a compliance with the taboos affords. It does not strike them as odd, of course, that they feel no sense of guilt about the moral demands which are thus neglected. But then many of these demands, the standard and the quality of the education of the children, the care required for their emotional and psychological development, the importance of a tranquil domestic situation, have not been part of the taboo system in which they were so meticulously trained. The Vatican Council was very explicit in this regard: "Man's dignity demands that he act according to a knowing and free choice. Such a choice is personally motivated and prompted from within. It does not result from blind internal impulse nor from mere external pressure."[23]

The myth of the sense of guilt is part of a more fundamental myth, the belief that there is an intrinsic connection between an observance of the order of things on the one hand and happiness on the other. This belief results in what has been called "the teleological suspension of the ethical". People seek happiness, and the secret of happiness, so it is claimed, is to observe the laws of nature. Apart from the difficulty involved in deciding what happiness consists in, and apart from the disconcerting fact that people who observe the "proper order of things" do not appear to be significantly happier than those who do not, this belief is becoming increasingly difficult to practise in a world in which the order is imposed by man himself. The ethics of "eudemonistic hedonism" may have been a viable system in a pre-industrial, rural culture. It is, however, both inadequate and incredible in the secular city. An ethics intrinsically tied to the achievement of happiness cannot, moreover, call itself Christian because its basic assumption is incompatible with the facts of Christ's life. As the perfect man he undoubtedly would have observed the order of things. Yet the end of his life was turmoil, an agony of psychological and moral anguish in Gethsemane and a profound sense of having been abandoned by God on Calvary. Was this happiness?

Christ was in conflict with his environment because he was unwilling to accept it. He wanted to change it. This led to friction with his brethren at Nazareth who rejected him, with his fellow Jews who repudiated him, and with his religious superiors who crucified him. Christ's life certainly did not end in the classic circumstances dear to the popular hagiographers: at peace with the world, reconciled with the church and in the odour of sanctity. He died an intransigent—Pilate would have said a sullenly intransigent—revolutionary; a revolutionary of love, it is true, but a revolutionary nevertheless. Unfortunately, in one sense, we know the rest of the story with Christ, and this detracts from the moral of the story.

Revolutionaries of lesser status, even if they are the advocates of the love Christ championed against the desiccating effects of ecclesiastical legalism, are judged and their happiness assessed in reference to the norms spawned by that legalism. Their inner turmoil is displayed, the conclusions are drawn and the myth persists. This is not meant to imply that man must renounce happiness as a surrender to a situation which as a Christian he should not tolerate. It is not meant to advocate a new kind of Manicheeism which regards anything in this life as evil or imperfect. The Christian attitude should be one of balance between an acceptance of what is good and an enjoyment of it on the one hand and a yearning for something better for which he must strive on the other hand. The seeking of happiness in this life, the sharing in the joys and the pleasures of this life are important ingredients in being human. But joy, happiness, contentment, and peace of mind do not indicate or guarantee Christian moral probity; they could easily be symptoms of bovine complacency and these symptoms are quite compatible with either the strict observance of the order of things or the violation of the order of things.

The whole enterprise of looking for an order which will provide clear ethical guides for action is in jeopardy as the human race moves more completely into the world of second creation, man's creation. In the world of first creation it was appropriate to seek guidance from the structure of nature and from the structure of man himself. But today the total environment of man is man-made, or at least man-controlled. Without exaggerating the control that man has actually established over his environment in the comprehensive sense, it can be asserted that the prevailing Christian morality is the outmoded one of first creation. The traditional Christian morality is quite inadequate for the age of second creation. Man has, in principle, the power to control the composition of genes and the structure of chromosomes. He can multiply the cells of the cerebral cortex. In a word, he can change and direct the biological and hence psychological and spiritual evolution of the human species. He has it within his capacity to change, through the use of drugs and surgery, the very personality of a human being. Man can devise and implement plans for new and better patterns of domestic and community life in which both personal and social values can be more fully realized. It is possible effectively to emancipate women from the burden of the period of gestation, to develop embryos in scientifically controlled laboratory conditions, and to supervise the quality of the human race by control of the genetic composition of the offspring. Aldous Huxley's *Brave New World* is no longer science fiction; it describes today's scientific endeavour and tomorrow's moral problems.

Fundamental to the task of theological renewal is the need for the church to achieve a cultural acclimatization. The church and Christian culture generally has never really felt at home in the age of the industrial revolution. It has continued to be an essentially rural church in an alien urban and technological environment. Its heart is still in Arcadia. This is not to say that the church has not accepted and even capitulated to some of the attitudes and values of the industrial age, for example, the tendency to relegate man to the role of consumer. But the church has never really accepted the role of man the maker of artifacts, man the creator, man the manipulator and the transformer of his own environment and his own self. The church has remained romantically attached to nature as man inherited it from God.

The fundamental repugnance to the use of artificial means in the control of life is not merely the result of an ideological block; it is also a manifestation of a much deeper cultural alienation; it is a symptom of what is felt to be the obscenity of the obliteration of grass, trees, soil, skins, and flesh by concrete, steel, synthetics, and plastics. The official church has no repugnance for the elaborate and tasteless intricacies of the rhythm method of avoiding conception, for this is "natural". But it does have deep misgivings about the use of plastic, or rubber, or drugs to achieve the same effect because these are "artificial".

The birth control issue indicates the profound ideological and cultural incapacity of the church to cope with the moral problems of the noosphere. Until it is prepared to accept man in the capacity of creator, elaborator of artifacts, and master of his future destiny, the church will simply complicate and obstruct the task of undertaking Christian responsibility in the world of the future.

And yet, in spite of its persisting sense of living in an alien environment, the church has stood for the primacy of the person in the industrial and technological age. In the great social encyclicals from *Rerum Novarum* of Leo XIII to *Progressio Populorum* of Paul VI, and in the social allocutions of Pius XII, the official church has championed the rights of the individual person against the tendency to relegate him to a factor in production in laissez-faire capitalism or to a unit in the proletarian revolution of early communism.

Yet the papal insistence on the rights of the individual has been of ambiguous merit. The insistence has been directed against the incursions into the area of personal rights on the part of economic and political power, it has not championed the rights of the person against the destructive effects of a suffocating ecclesiastical power.

The Vatican Council endorsed what Cardinal Urbani described as "the progressive enrichment of the concept of the primacy of the human person". However, the early phases of this process of the enrichment of the concept of the person took place at the initiative of the philosophers of the Enlightenment outside and even in conflict with the official church. Until recently the Catholic church especially used the language of human nature rather than the language of human persons in its moral discourse. If you use the language of nature you emphasize what men have in common and subject them to universal laws. If, however, you use the language of person you must emphasize what is unique to each man, his irreplaceable and irreducible quality which sets him above, though it does not make him entirely independent of, laws deriving from what men have in common.

One of the recent trends in the enrichment of the concept of the primacy of the person is what can be called the philosophy or the theology of personal being. This trend, beginning with Kierkegaard and reaching a climax in *I and Thou* of Martin Buber, provided a corrective for the individualism of many existentialist philosophies and a warning against the tendency, in a technological age, to treat persons as things, or as means to impersonal and even sub-personal ends. For Buber, the "I" emerges and finds realization and identity only in relationship with the "thou". "I-it" relationships can be expressed discursively and even legalistically, but "I-thou" or personal relationships involving the whole being of the persons involved cannot be discursively described nor legislated for. While Buber did not provide any formal structure for the establishment or maintenance of these personal relationships—in part his work was a protest against such formal structures—he did highlight the unique personal and Christian quality of them and warn against the tendency to reduce either of the partners in the relationship or the relationship itself to the status of an object.

An adequate qualitative appreciation of the uniqueness of the person and of personal moral decisions which bring the person into being entails a realization of the inadequacy of stringent moral absolutes intransigently applied, and of the moral insensitivity that results from crude applications of this kind. A negative deterministic view concedes only a negative function to conscience, that of applying laws to the particular situation, and fails to recognize the positive and inventive function of conscience of seeking ever new and more effective ways of realizing and embodying the Christian law of love. In fact, traditional morality is statically rather than dynamically structured. It was developed in a cultural context with a vertical perspective, but as modern life assumes, more and more, a changing, evolutionary quality, the vertical structure simply crumbles and disintegrates.

However, the traditional morality did not always act as a grid on which moral integrity was crucified. There was, in fact, considerable flexibility between the immutable moral absolutes and the human situations to which they were applied. That the rigidity of the system rarely resulted in moral monstrosities was due to the science of casuistry. This was as much the science of finding excuses for applying the principles and the art of effecting the triumph of common sense and Christian charity over the principles as anything else. But as the historical and cultural context to which the principles were applied became further and further removed from the context which gave rise to them and lent them credibility, the pyrotechnics of the casuists became increasingly implausible and ludicrous. The inventiveness exerted by Catholic theologians to allow the use of contraceptive pills within the framework of the "natural law" and papal prohibition scheme of things is the latest and probably the last great virtuoso performance of sustained scholastic casuistry. It gave rise to the conviction that a radical restructuring of the whole corpus of moral theology was called for. Yet there is a certain nostalgia associated with the passing of this type of casuistry somewhat like the nostalgia felt in witnessing the final performance of the last great travelling circus, with its lion-tamers, its contortionists, and its acrobats.

Fundamental to the process of renewal in moral theology must be a conception of a moral decision as contributing towards life as the practice of an art rather than as the application of a recipe. If it is conceded that the human person is unique, then it must also be conceded that the development of personality must involve a quality of uniqueness in moral decisions. In the past the Christian theories of morality offered their adherents formulae for living, prescriptions to be applied to the various life-situations which were likely to arise. Yet this approach ignores the dimension of the artistic in life, that is, in the very living of a specifically human and Christian life.

A young artist must be made familiar with the fundamental techniques of his art; he must be trained to reproduce accurately the works of the masters. But if his facility and talent never go beyond this stage, if he does not bring to his canvas a creative intuition of his own, a unique insight and expression displayed in an individual style, he is not and never will be an artist. Indeed, the very mechanics of a moral decision demand this quality of art. Even if there existed principles for the correct application of the eternal moral laws or absolutes, there would still be the problem of the order of priorities among competing moral imperatives. Difficult moral decisions do not revolve around the unilateral application of a principle to a particular case. They arise when there is the demand to establish a dynamic balance among a number of values that ought to be maintained or when there is a limited choice among a number of evils that ought to be eliminated. Moral indignation or condemnation, whether practised by ecclesiastical officials or Christian social opinion, often takes on a specious validity only because attention is drawn to one among a number of moral factors which are in fact operative. The virtue of prudence and the influence of the Holy Spirit did have their place in the old scheme of things, but somehow the rigidity of the system curtailed their modifying influence to that of academic recognition; it did not allow them to percolate to the level of practical and concrete decisions. A prudent decision tended to be defined as one which conformed exactly to the demands of the law.

One peculiar consequence of the rather legalistic moral pattern of thinking was that a multiplication of evil circumstances could only result in a unilateral accumulation of evil. Hence from the point of view of Catholic sexual morality, intercourse among unmarried teenagers is wrong; the use of contraceptives is wrong. If these teenagers use contraceptives, they would, in the unilateral assessment of the morality of the situation, be compounding the evil of their illicit relations. Yet if the moral act were regarded as the art of establishing a dynamic balance among the various relevant factors, the use of contraceptives—even if regarded as morally wrong—by unmarried teenagers would surely ensure the avoidance of an unwanted child. However, most Christians would be very loath to take the line with teenagers: if you must be promiscuous, you have an obligation to use contraceptives, for you must not run the risk of the gross injustice of bringing an unwanted child into the world.

The moral inhibitions displayed in a case like this reveal another serious defect in the structure and application of Catholic moral theology. It was not concerned primarily with human persons but with abstract ideals. The ideals meant to embody the love of human persons and ensure their welfare ultimately became more important than the persons; they must be preserved at the cost of human persons. This was very obvious in the past when crusades were fought, and men were burnt at the stake in the interests of abstract truth; it is evident in the teleology which still dominates the official thinking about birth control and in any instance where absolute norms compete with the concrete good of persons. In the question of abortion, and in the intransigent stand the Catholic church has taken on this issue in recent years, it appears, nevertheless, as the inflexible champion of the rights of the human person, expecially of the innocent and the harmless. However, this stand is ambiguous and inconsistent, and one can suspect that it is not so much a sign of an overriding concern for the good of persons as another manifestation of a propensity for absolutes and a preoccupation with gynaecological morality. When the death of one person is caused directly to save the life of another person, the mother in the case of abortion, the church objects. Yet when the death of many people, some of them innocent, is caused directly to ensure the freedom, the security or the lives of other people in the case of war, the church does not object. At the international level another system of morality operates from the one applied at the individual level. In the abortion debate there is the problem, first of all, as to what constitutes a human person. Is an undifferentiated mass of cells a human person who has rights equal to a living human person? Even if it is acknowledged that the foetus at whatever stage is a human person, can the proposition "You shall not kill this person" be a moral absolute which will always be wrong no matter what the circumstances? The point I want to make is that answer in the affirmative rests on the assumption that moral decisions are of unilateral application. It gains plausibility from the fiction that "circumstances" are always of less significance individually or cumulatively than the central moral feature. But this is not always the case. Sometimes the crucial question can be asked in a way which allows the central question to be relegated to the category of circumstance, and this variety of options about how the question can be asked simply illustrates that the moral decision, in the last analysis, cannot be merely the implementation of a recipe but must be the practice of an art.[24] No facile enumeration of absolutes can save the human person from the agony and the responsibility of a moral decision.

Of course, the unstated factor in a great deal of discussion about the nature and the structure of Christian morality is what would happen if people were allowed to use responsibility. The spectre of the uneducated sweaty masses incapable of the art of making moral judgments is raised. This is a problem. But it is a problem different from the nature and structure of Christian morality. It is the problem of education in moral responsibility and/or social and legal controls. Until the two are recognized as two separate problems people will tend to be kept in thrall to invalid moral absolutes and the church will continue to neglect the task of the sophisticated moral education which our age demands.

The analogy between the training of a painter and the education to Christian morality has its shortcomings. But it does emphasize a neglected aspect of Christian morality and underlines the immense task facing the church. At the moment there is room in moral structure or attitude for neither moral improvization nor experiment. When the future did not appear to be likely to be any different from the present and when man did not seem to have any particular responsibility for its direction, that is, when the world did not have a developed historical and critical consciousness, scope for improvization and experiment would have seemed a preposterous attempt to dissolve the whole fabric of Christian morality. Today the church is faced with the alternatives of acknowledging the fact of the future and assuming its rightful place in it, or of persisting in the myth of monolithic absolute moral norms. If it chooses the second, it will renounce its right to exert a Christian influence on determining its course; it will confront many serious Christians with the very difficult task of exerting a Christian influence regardless of and in spite of the church and demand that these Christians carry the extra burden of alienation from the body of the church in which they believe. Unfortunately, in some important areas where experimentation is called for, the only response of the official church so far has been one of moral indignation.

In the Catholic tradition it is almost impossible to imagine what form moral improvization and experimentation could take. Perhaps the very suggestion conjures up thoughts of wicked scientists experimenting with human brains! Or perhaps it evokes memories of the Nazi experiments with people in horror camps. However, the kind of preparation for and penetration into the future which would be involved would be based on and undertaken in the interests of personal good and personal rights. Moral experimentation is called for in those areas of morality where prevailing values and social pressures seem to limit both personal and community good. We can begin to suggest that it could be concerned with new forms of personal relationships and community patterns. However, it is also important to emphasize that experiments of this kind would have to proceed carefully and tentatively. One of the limitations on any change in behaviour patterns is the ties the person or the group have with the past and with other groups in society. Any changes in behaviour pattern cannot be conducted in isolation from the effects upon or the pressures exerted by other groups in the community.

In the past the horizons of the application of the virtue of charity have been rather limited. Christian charity tended to concern itself with the alleviation of want and distress at the individual level. The various charitable organizations provided hospitals, homes, welfare centres for the sick, the aged, and the outcast. They attempted to deal with mental, psychological, emotional, and spiritual distress, abandoned wives and children, drug addiction, alcoholism, and the rest. So far, the tremendous will to do good which has manifested itself in charitable work in the Christian church has been directed towards the symptoms of the ills of society. What seems to be called for now is that the Christian church assume the role of a leaven in society to work to change the structures which produce the ills. Christians have railed in the past about the evils of society but these condemnations have expressed the belief that the evils resulted from society's neglect to acknowledge the "other world" for which the church stood, rather than from defects in the very structure and function of society itself and the values and attitudes which this structure embodied. Rather than deplore impotently the neglect of "spiritual" or "supernatural" values in society—which often meant a failure to recognize and defer to ecclesiastical power and prestige—the church has to work creatively for new structures of society, both at the national and the international level, which will facilitate the reconciliation of men hopefully symbolized in the Christian eucharist.

However, the reconciliation of men is not brought about by glib recognition of supra-historical values nor by the facile performance of religious ceremonial. It is effected by the slow and difficult process of seeking through trial and error, that is, inductively, how economic hardship and inequality are eliminated, how emotional immaturity and psychological disturbance are overcome, how personal, domestic, class, and racial conflicts can be exorcized, and how the political consensus at all levels can best be achieved. These tasks cannot be accomplished by pious exhortation to adopt a priori social and cultural forms which are the theoretical detritus of a past and forgotten age.

This ambition of effecting the reconciliation of men extends over the whole range of the human spectrum, from the reconciliation of an individual with himself through to the reconciliation of nation with nation. The Christian brings to this enterprise a twofold conviction that the task can be accomplished only with a Christ-like love in the hearts of men, and that devotion to this task establishes a vital relationship with God who reveals himself as love. But neither of these convictions can absolve him from the difficult task of constant reassessment of the practical ideals in which this love is realized and a tireless search for the means to achieve them. As slums, poverty, dissent, and conflict spread in the world, and as long as they last, Christians cannot afford to allow the urgency or the nature of the challenge to be obscured either by smug nationalistic loyalties or by a rigid system of moral absolutes.

There is, however, a serious obstacle to this enterprise. To illustrate this obstacle: recently I listened to a sermon asking American Catholics to give financial support to the Society for the Propagation of the Faith. The preacher assumed and appealed to a set of moral attitudes which can only be described as an investment morality. The "charity" the preacher wanted to mobilize was the fundamental consumer variety of a generosity which was a good investment: give a little to the missionaries in the developing countries of the world because it will pay off in the long run; you will *get* a greater reward in heaven, you will *get* the grace of a happy death; it will keep the developing nations of Africa, Asia, and Latin America at peace and hence, in the long term, save us the taxes that we have to pay for wars like the one we are fighting in Vietnam. If only Catholics had given more generously to the missions in Vietnam ten or fifteen years ago, America would not have had to be involved in Vietnam today. The dedicated consumer knows and accepts that he has to pay a price for a worthwhile commodity or for comprehensive insurance. It is just a question of convincing him that the dividend is worth the principal expended. Magic wants to get; mysticism wants to give. Unfortunately a great deal of the legendary Catholic generosity can be reduced to the former, for too often it is exploited by an irresistible appeal to Catholic tribal instincts and a deeply ingrained consumer ethos which has been ecumenically assimilated from the Puritan tradition.

The central concern of moral renewal in the Christian churches and of the so-called new morality has been to eliminate from Christianity pagan attitudes and values masquerading in the guise of moralistic rhetoric about absolute ethical norms. The whole movement seems to have been hindered by basic tactical mistakes. Some of the early exponents of the new morality attacked the sensitive area of extramarital relations and gave the impression that the whole enterprise was a manoeuvre to liberalize sexual promiscuity and open the way to moral anarchy. Thus Arnold Lunn and Garth Lean in their book *The New Morality* indignantly condemn the whole enterprise with appeals to chauvinism and extravagant analogies based on the degradation of the later Roman emperors without, however, displaying even a rudimentary understanding of the central moral concern of John Robinson, Douglas Rhymes, Stanley Evans, Mervyn Stockwood, and the rest.

In its positive thrust, the movement for renewal in Christian morality wants to reassert in all its rigour the difficult and Christian command to love. It wants to focus on the positive quality of this command and show how it penetrates to every phase and every situation of our lives. It wants to claim that the new morality is, in the last analysis, a much more difficult morality than the old, which, in its popular form at least, allowed selfishness, racial discrimination, national pride, class and economic wars, international exploitation, and moral insensitivity in politics and business to go unchallenged; the emphasis tended to be that once the price of being on the Christian gravy-train had been paid by subscription to the sexual taboos, with which an absolutist morality could feasibly cope, the other moral issues were of secondary and rather ephemeral importance. The renewal in morality wanted to drive out the complacency, the hypocrisy or the just plain yearning for security which the Christian negative absolutes appeared to engender.

The drive for renewal in Christian morality has certainly resulted in the eradication of some traditional Christian ideological shrines, not because it represents an iconoclastic aversion to shrines but because Christians tend to use them as sanctuaries from responsible action in the world. Certainly it is a phase of and is profoundly influenced by the process of secularization. It aims to eliminate that other world to which we can appeal for the inscrutable and immutable laws which were said to govern our behaviour and in which we can "do good" for other people. Secularization results in the levelling of the hierarchy of entities, the telescoping of ontological strata and the horizontalizing of perspective, moral responsibility, and creative and reconciliatory effort. We can see why this is desirable. Christians in America and Australia constantly pray for peace in Vietnam. What is the thinking behind these prayers? Do they expect the prayers to operate like spiritual ICBM's which will effect the "real good", the "spiritual good" of the people of Vietnam in spite of and as a compensation for the bullets, the bombs, the napalm, and the social disintegration? When Christians pray in this way do they then regard themselves as excused from further effort in the cause of peace? Or does Christian prayer for peace provoke them to an introspection of their own national and racial assumptions? Does it stimulate them to undertake the arduous task of reading the history of the conflict, of pursuing the intricacies of foreign policy, of analysing and assessing the value of the political rhetoric to reach a responsible decision? Does it provoke them to stand for and work for the political implementation of a conviction responsibly arrived at? On the answer to these questions depends the real value of prayers for peace and the moral value of prayer in general.

A number of observations are now called for concerning the foregoing analysis of the "traditional" Catholic morality. In the first place, it has been something of a caricature to illustrate the features which still need to be changed. In the second place, the process of "the deflation of absolutes" has been going on for quite some time now. As John Reed points out:

For many decades now, natural-law discourse has been conducted, in the teachings of the popes at least, and by the moral theologians, not in terms of absolute, immutable essences or natures, but in terms of order, finality, and relationships in the dynamic operations of life, and the problem has been situated in the determination of the varying applications of a relatively small number of basic principles in a constantly changing environment, rather than in the supposition of a complete and detailed compilation of "laws" already fixed and permanent.[25]

The Morality of the Noosphere

In the third place, each of the claims about defects in the structure of the traditional morality could be refuted by an appeal to one of the great theologians or to the necessary distinctions and qualifications in the small print or the footnotes in the manuals of moral theology. And yet this would not be refuting claims about Catholic morality as it is structured and operates in the everyday life of the church, in the official statements, in the pulpit, in the confessional and in the prevailing beliefs and attitudes of most Catholics.

I have tried to avoid using the language of the current debate in neither advocating nor repudiating an absolutist morality, a contextualist morality, a situationist morality, or an existentialist morality. To resort to labels in the context of this debate is to be committed to elaborate explanations of what is not meant. If we are conscious of the defects of the traditional Catholic morality, it is possible to see how these defects can be remedied without becoming caught in the morass of a terminological debate about the existence or otherwise of moral absolutes. This also limits the terms of reference of the discussion to what constitutes Christian morality and avoids the pitfall of attempting to extend the validity of Christian morality to the whole of the human race. In this view, clear statements of what is right and wrong would function in the same way as metaphysical or mythical systems: they must minister to the creative responsibility of the person; they must not dominate and restrict it.

Any process of renewal in moral theology must, therefore, take the following factors as central in Christian moral discourse:

a) The uniqueness and value of the person making the moral decision. This is what could be called the basic philosophical datum or insight of what is best in contemporary secular experience.

b) The uniqueness, value, and freedom of the person or persons likely to be affected by the moral decision. The development of an appreciation of and concern for human rights is a project which is based on a common humanity independently of religious affiliations. It is the corollary of the uniqueness of the subject of the moral act. It is this notion of person and the rights of the person which John XXIII's *Pacem in Terris* relies on and appeals to. This also is a philosophical ingredient of a Christian morality. In this phase, the relationship between persons is predominantly negative: the recognition of the limits to the means taken to achieve one's own uniqueness posed by the uniqueness of other persons and the obligation of non-interference and non-violation which this gives rise to.

c) The positive obligations to love the other person, on the model of Christ's love, describes the theological dimension of Christian morality. This goes beyond the merely negative coexistence between persons willing to recognize each other's uniqueness and freedom which is the minimal non-Christian position. It provides the central creative dynamism of Christian morality, specifies the way in which the moral agent achieves fulfillment, namely, and paradoxically, by death to self, and indicates the condition on which a relationship with God is established. Nevertheless this love has to be disciplined, directed, and given form by two important factors: the recognition of the inviolable freedom of the other to whom the gift of self is made, and the objective assessment, appropriately determined, of what is actually good for the other. The acceptance of the freedom of the other person as an ineluctable datum saves the creative dynamism of Christian love from becoming a consuming or suffocating moral imperialism.

d) As already indicated, the object of this love, the good of the other person, must be determined by the proper means, that is, by an inductive process that is not simply limited by the findings of empirical observation and analysis, but which must, nevertheless, be based on them. This ingredient in the moral decision rescues love from the subjectivity of personal idealism, on the one hand, and from the fecklessly assimilated tribal values on the other hand.

A way of summing up, and as it were of capsulizing Christian morality, is to describe it as *loving, creative,* and *reconciliatory* activity in this world. This is not to claim that this describes Christians as distinct from anyone else, nor to claim that only Christians actually practise this morality. The latter two terms, in this order, make explicit what is implicitly—in the existential rather than in the logical sense—contained in the first. The three terms seem capable of capturing the essence and the purpose of the life of Christ, and enunciate the conditions on which a relationship with God can be established and talk about God can be rendered, in principle, significant and ultimately verifiable.

Reconciliatory activity must not be thought of as necessarily and inevitably demanding that a Christian assume the role of mediator and pacifier. It must not be presumed that reconciliatory activity in the world entails that political problems, economic injustices, and social inequalities be minimized or simply accepted with resigned equanimity. The human, secular, and Christian task is to seek political structures and economic and social organizations which more and more effectively minister to and embody the reconciliation of men. The Christian style will be to work for these changes in ways that are inventively peaceful and non-violent. But political and social structures which are tyrannical and economic organization which enshrines and perpetuates injustice and suffering can demand that the Christian, as a Christian, as a last resort, use violence to bring about a new political, social, and economic order capable of fostering the reconciliation of men. An absolute refusal to be a party to the overthrow of a political, economic, and social elite which holds a country in thrall and which perpetuates suffering and injustice; to be content to remain on the periphery of the political and social movements working for equality, a just distribution of wealth, and a better way of life; to be satisfied with piously exhorting to Christian patience and the avoidance of violence, can be to shirk, especially in the developing countries, the very creative task of making structurally possible the reconciliation of men in which a relationship with God must be established.

I have suggested that history is the medium of our communion with God. In ordinary conversation it is possible for two people to talk, to use the vocabulary and the idiom of conventional conversation, and still not establish any kind of vital relationship, that is, still fail to communicate. A certain attitude of mind, a certain sensitivity and an openness are necessary before conversation mediates a mutual revelation of persons. Indeed, sometimes conversation can result in the exacerbation of antagonism. And so the idiom of history provides us with the medium through which and in which we communicate with God. Christ in his life-style teaches us the conditions which will lead to the mutual relationship and revelation of God and the persons involved in this medium.

The word "love" speaks of the fundamental motive, attitude, and outlook the person must have. The word "creative" speaks of the direction this motive should take and rescues love from an impotent contemplation of or benevolence towards the other. The word "reconciliatory" speaks of the tangible ideal towards which this creative love must work. However, for these qualities of the life-style of Christ to be anything more than vague exhortations, for Christ himself to be anything more than a shadowy historical figure, the church—the community of Christians—must represent activity that is credibly loving, develop policies that are truly creative, that is, orientated towards the future, and display ambitions that are authentically concerned with the reconciliation of all men. Stated this way, the Christian enterprise appears to be a rather optimistically facile thing. Yet when this threefold ambition collides with the reality of personal selfishness and the obduracy which is ideological commitment in some form or another, the dedicated Christian will not be too far removed from his personal crucifixion.

The document of the Vatican Council on the Church in the Modern World[26] understandably emphasizes the Christian law of love among men. What makes it different from most other official documents of the Catholic church is the emphasis it gives to the creative role of man, and to the function of Christians and of the church to seek the very tangible goal of the reconciliation of all men.

Concerning the creative role of men it says:

The conviction grows not only that humanity can and should increasingly consolidate its control over creation, but even more, that it devolves on humanity to establish a political, social and economic order which will to an even better extent serve man and help individuals as well as groups to affirm and develop the dignity proper to them. (p. 206.)
For man, created in God's image, received a mandate to subject to himself the earth and all that it contains and to govern the world with justice and holiness . . . This mandate concerns even the most ordinary everyday activities. (p. 232.)
Christ is now at work in the hearts of men through the energy of His Spirit. He arouses not only a desire for the age to come, but by that very fact, He animates, purifies, and strengthens those noble longings too by which the human family strives to make its life more human and to render the whole earth submissive to its goal. (p. 236.)

The synonymous themes of "reconciliation" and "brotherhood" recur again and again throughout the document:

This Sacred Synod . . . offers to mankind the honest assistance of the church in fostering that brotherhood of all men which corresponds to this destiny of theirs. Inspired by no earthly ambition, the church seeks but a solitary goal: to carry forward the work of Christ himself under the lead of the befriending Spirit. (p. 201.)
While rejecting atheism, root and branch, the church sincerely professes that all men, believers and unbelievers alike, ought to work for the rightful betterment of this world in which all alike live. (p. 219.)
One of the salient features of the modern world is the growing interdependence of men one on the other, a development largely promoted

by modern technical advances. Nevertheless, brotherly dialogue among men does not reach its perfection on the level of technical progress, but on the deeper level of interpersonal relationships. These demand a mutual respect for the full spiritual dignity of the person. (p. 222.)

Respect and love ought to be extended also to those who think and act differently than we do in social, political, and religious matters, too. In fact, the more deeply we come to understand their ways of thinking through such courtesy and love, the more easily will we be able to enter into dialogue with them. (p. 227.)

To those, therefore, who believe in divine love, He gives assurance that the way of love lies open to all men and that the effort to establish a universal brotherhood is not a hopeless one. He cautions them at the same time that this love is not something to be reserved for important matters, but must be pursued chiefly in the ordinary circumstances of life. (p. 236.)

Indeed it is suggested that sin itself can be reduced to whatever interferes with or violates the brotherhood of men:

For when the order of values is jumbled, and bad is mixed with the good, individuals and groups pay heed solely to their own interests, and not to those of others. Thus it happens that the world ceases to be a place of true brotherhood. (p. 235.)

Most importantly, the church sees itself as the sacrament, that is, the sign and the agent, of unity and reconciliation among men: "By virtue of her mission to shed on the whole world the radiance of the gospel message, and to unify under one Spirit all men of whatever nation, race or culture, the church stands forth as a sign of that brotherliness which allows honest dialogue and invigorates it." (p. 306.) Moreover, the church is confident that this secular ambition of the community of all men is its immediate task and essentially related to the ultimate consummation of the earth and humanity even though we do not know "how all things will be transformed". (p. 237.) In seeking this ultimate ambition, however, the members of the church can have a variety of roles with a difference in emphasis on the symbolizing of the ambition of the brotherhood of men or on the creative role of working towards it:

Now the gifts of the Spirit are diverse. He calls some to give clear witness to the desire for a heavenly home and keep that desire green among the human family. He summons others to dedicate themselves to the earthly service of men and to make ready the material of the celestial realm by this ministry of theirs. Yet he frees all of them so that by putting aside love of self and bringing all earthly resources into the service of human life they can devote themselves to that future when humanity will become an offering accepted by God. (p. 236.)

It is possible, using these three terms, to provide a dynamic structure for a secular Christian morality, especially when we consider the words which are antithetically related to them. The antithesis of loving activity is exploitative activity, the antithesis of creative activity is destructive activity, and the antithesis of reconciliation is alienation. Exploitation, destruction, and alienation are existentially related in the same mode of explication and the same sequence of consequences as are love, creation, and reconciliation. All sin can be reduced to terms of exploitation, whether this be the exploitation of inanimate nature, the self or the other person. Each act of exploitation results in destruction of unity, whether this be personal or social, and alienation. When sin is considered in terms of exploitation, rather than in terms of violation of laws, Christian morality breaks out of the narrow confines of personal behaviour and relationships into the broader context of all the aspects of the modern world, political, social, economic, and cultural. It embraces that broad expanse of human activity which, in the past, was regarded as morally neutral because the Bible provided no explicit directives concerning it or because it proved intractable to the simplistic clarifications of the natural law system. Moreover, it leaves open and constantly imposes the task of investigating, by inductive techniques, what sort of behaviour is actually loving or exploitative. It becomes possible to include inanimate nature within the ambience of Christian morality and find in it the possibility of a creative reciprocity between the person and nature.

Traditional morality recognizes degrees of moral worth between the two poles of love and exploitation; it distinguishes between venial and mortal sin. Hence it is necessary to fill out the vocabulary of this strategy for a morality which is dynamically structured with three other terms, which are not related to the two extremes of love and exploitation as a medium which represents either a happy balance or a morally neutral alternative. These three terms represent the diminution of the excess of exploitation, destruction, and alienation, and hence are more closely related to them than to love, creation, and reconciliation. The terms I suggest to represent the state of mind or attitude traditionally described by venial sin are indifference, consumption, and competition. Indifference to other persons, simple coexistence with them, is a mode of behaviour distinct from that which is loving or exploitative, but which is not, from the Christian point of view, morally insignificant. Sometimes it is imposed on the person as a course of action because of the antipathy of the other, but it cannot be justified, in the Christian view, as a freely adopted attitude to the other person. It manifests itself in competition among persons and an attitude to life and things which is typical of the consumer to which a fundamentally capitalist culture, in both its economic and spiritual dimensions, panders.

It is possible thus to set out schematically the basic vocabulary of a Christian morality which is dynamically structured:

love	indifference	exploitation
creation	consumption	destruction
reconciliation	competition	alienation

What is initially revealing and disturbing about this diagram is that the second column appears to describe the basic characteristics of Western culture today. If it is the case that a relationship with God and the development of an awareness of God depend on the fulfillment of the conditions represented by Christ and indicated in the first column, then any significant cultural repudiation of these conditions will also entail a disavowal of God in and by that culture. It is, of course, a simplification that cannot be pushed too far or too hard. Nevertheless, it provides sufficient grounds to make us wonder, as I suggested earlier, whether this cultural context calls for radical theologians or rather for radical human beings. The palpable absence of God may not be the consequence of man's industrial and technological power, but rather the consequence of how that power is being used. The radical task facing the Christian, therefore, is not a return to the past, nor an attempt to explain theologically the absence of God; it is to work for fundamental changes in the culture which demands that human beings compete with each other, that they be consumers, and which consequently generates, at best, indifference among men and at worst, conflict and violence. What is disconcerting is that often the champions of "man come of age", and of the secular power and autonomy of man, are the ones who despair of man's capacity to bring about any significant change in the political, economic, or social structure which forms the context of the secularist boast, and regard any suggestion of radical change as naive. This indicates, of course, that man has not yet come of age.

He has merely reached the stage of critical consciousness and technological precociousness where human maturity is a recognizable option.

But to return to the structure of Christian morality: one feature which has so far been ignored in this analysis is the traditional role of authority in the church in relation to morality. It was suggested that one of the reasons for the rigid structure of Catholic morality in the past was the need to have readily available criteria for membership, and clear-cut norms for judging, in the application of canon law and in the confessional, the behaviour of the members of the church. In the novel, *Voss*, Patrick White says of one of the characters: "Mrs. Bonner, however, was creating groups of statuary. This was her strength, to coax out of flesh the marble that is hidden in it." This has also been the strength of the classical systems of Christian morality and of the supervisory authority of the church, to coax from the flesh the marble of inflexible norms. The task ahead, however, is that of coaxing the flesh of authentic moral responsibility from the marble of rigid ideological, religious, and cultural postures.

The Catholic church is prepared in principle for this task. In the document on the Church in the Modern World, Vatican II stated that the church

> Opens up to man at the same time the meaning of his own existence, that is, the innermost truth about himself . . . the church can anchor the dignity of human nature against all tides of opinion, for example, those which undervalue the human body or idolize it. By no human law can the personal dignity and liberty of man be so aptly safeguarded as by the gospel of Christ . . . For this gospel announces and proclaims the freedom of the sons of God, and repudiates all the bondage which ultimately results from sin. The gospel has a sacred reverence for the dignity of conscience and its freedom of choice, constantly advises that all human talents be employed in God's service and men's, and, finally, commends all to the charity of all. (p. 240.)

Thus the Catholic church has officially repudiated the Grand Inquisitor's rebuke to Christ: "You have come to bring love to man, but we have seen that man cannot bear the liberty of love, we have safely put him back under the yoke of the law, and we shall not tolerate your throwing him into any more adventures."[27]

But while this may be so officially and in principle, the Catholic church has a long way to go before it can dispel centuries-old attitudes and habits of thought so that it can become, credibly, the champion of the dignity of conscience and the liberty of love. Even in the post-Vatican II age it too often appears to want to impose the yoke of the law. What then are its functions in relation to moral decisions? The next chapter will focus on this problem. For the time being it will be sufficient to suggest that it is the matrix of the free and loving response of the Christian to the tasks encountered in his secular life. As a community which transcends—to some extent—race, nation, and specific culture, it can provide correctives against a person's succumbing to the limitations of his cultural environment. It must stand for the integrity and the dignity of the human person, for the possibility of the total experience of the human person, for the ultimate ambition of the reconciliation of all men, and for the primacy of love which, as Paul Tillich said, "can never become fanatical in a fight for the absolute, or cynical under the impact of the relative".[28]

The Secular Function of the Church

The Church is the Church only when it exists for others.
Dietrich Bonhoeffer

Christians cannot yearn for anything more ardently than to serve the men of the modern world ever more generously and effectively.
Vatican II

In the accelerating process of secularization the church has been increasingly relegated to the periphery of life. At the time of Pope Boniface VIII the church dominated Western society in all its dimensions. To use Belloc's phrase, "The Church was Europe, Europe was the Church." The gradual process of emancipation of the political, economic, cultural, and social spheres from ecclesiastical domination left the church without a domain except that of the specifically religious life, the realm of the supernatural, the order of grace. While a certain ontocratic outlook on life persisted, the domain of man's spiritual life appeared to be a relatively substantial one. The church became a retailer of spiritual consumer goods and legislated for the area of private morality in the lives of its adherents. In this area it has, to some extent accidentally, been the champion of certain human values, of some aspects of human freedom, and hence of the totality of the human person.

However, now that the eroding current of secularization has substantially undermined the ontocratic world view which persisted even after the effective emancipation of the world from ecclesiastical domination, it seems, to many, that the days of the church are numbered. Certainly, in many of the traditionally Christian countries, it still retains a great deal of influence over the minds and hearts of men, and because of this it is still an economic and political power to be reckoned with. It still has many members, it still has vast amounts of real estate, bricks and mortar and institutions, hence it is still possible to pursue an ecclesiastical career, and by becoming involved in the ages-old game of ecclesiastical administration, nurture the illusion that one is helping to develop something that is a living and vital thing. Essential to the persistence of this elaborate ecclesiastical fiction is the process of Christian education, as it is called, which often indoctrinates and emotionally conditions its adherents at an early age, and thus ensures the continuation of the demand for spiritual consumer goods in the future. Yet with the education explosion, it seems that this process of inverted circularity is taking place with a constantly diminishing radius.

The fundamental difficulty is that the church has been, to too many, a spiritual consumer organization. It has not been the champion of the creative and the altruistic. Marx's criticism of the church of the nineteenth century was more valid than most Christians are willing to acknowledge. It was not just that the church was used as an opiate to facilitate the economic exploitation of the dispossessed and the underprivileged. The church had been profoundly conditioned by the capitalist consumer ethic and distracted from its own authentic creator ethic. The church became the retailer of tailor-made truths, moral recipes for ingratiating oneself with God, and liturgical ceremonies capable of generating a fund of gold coupons in heaven. The price the customers were required to pay was that of obedience, docility, and loyalty. Consequently, the influence the church wielded was not a stimulating, adventurous influence. It tended to be almost always a restraining, conservative influence. It was not credibly the pilgrim and the champion of the future, but the rather strident prophet of the past.

Increasingly, the irrelevance of the church is having a formidable impact on the consciousness of Christians. Paradoxically, the Vatican Council, by opening windows onto the world and relaxing the centralized bureaucratic discipline of the Catholic church, has been a catalyst for the development of this consciousness among Catholics. The use of the vernacular in the liturgy has highlighted the elaborate meaninglessness of a great deal of it; the emancipation of the laity within the church has led them to question the value of activity in the church; the project of renewal in theology has provoked serious questioning about the worth of the enterprise. By opening the window onto the world, Pope John has shown that the world is more important than the church, that the needs of the world are greater, and that if there is a great fund of creative energy and goodwill in the church it should be expended on the world.

It could be that the Vatican Council was a rather startling and unpredictable act of institutional self-effacement. Through it the Catholic church gave up, in principle, the power it could have continued to exercise by its rigid discipline and organization. History may look back on this event as a dramatic self-inflicted institutional death. Indeed the Catholic church may be taking seriously Christ's observation that unless a grain of wheat dies it cannot generate new life. In the process of this structural and cultural death, a great deal of dissolution will take place and is, in fact, taking place. A great number who appeared to be fervent Catholics will fall away as the spiritual, emotional, and psychological props are removed. There will be fewer priests and religious as the prestige of these states of life declines rapidly. But all of this is a necessary precondition for the new life which will inevitably emerge. The flood of solemn warnings, official misgivings, and frantic salvaging activities merely provide a rather unpleasant funeral dirge for the interment of the church of the era of Constantine.

The crucial question then is what could conceivably be the function of the church in a secular age? If it is not to have the role it occupied in the Constantinian era, if it is not to occupy the periphery of life, or to be an uncertain tenant of the gaps until these are filled by specialists in the expansion of science, and if it is not to be expert in and retailer of supernatural commodities, what is its role?

The general thrust of contemporary theology has been to bring the church back to the creative centre of life where it will be relevant to the political, social, economic, and cultural spheres. But its presence will not be a dominating factor; it will be a leavening factor. One of the fundamental political assumptions of modern society is that the church must not become involved in politics. This is an assumption usually accepted by Christians and non-Christians alike. The assumption was generated because in the age immediately following the Reformation religious disputes were fought in the political arena and too often political weapons were used to settle them. The assumption was accepted because most modern incursions of the churches into politics have been to further the institutional interests of the churches themselves. In modern history, ecclesiastical influence in politics has almost invariably been exerted to insure the sectional interest of the church in terms of protection of ecclesiastical privilege, the securing of finance for church schools, the maintenance of political and social forces most likely to be sympathetic to the church, and the obstruction of political and social forces most likely to be unsympathetic to the church even though these might happen to be for the economic good of the masses.

It is essential for the church to exert an influence on life, and not merely through Christians acting individually. However, the three essential conditions under which this influence can be exerted are: that the influence be a leavening and not a dominating one; that its influence be a non-party one; and that it be exercised in the interests of human persons and society and not in the institutional interests of the church. In all probability, at least in the foreseeable future, the church will have to renounce even justifiable occasions for intervening in its own interests, to insure the development of an image that is credibly altruistic. As the Vatican Council pointed out: "Indeed, she [the Church] stands ready to renounce the exercise of certain legitimately acquired rights if it becomes clear that their use raises doubts about the sincerity of her witness or that new conditions of life demand some other arrangement."[1]

It is paradoxical that, until now, the organization which has preached self-sacrificing love on the model of Christ at the individual level, has been most unwilling to embody this at the collective level. This unwillingness manifests itself in the preoccupation in the church before the Vatican Council with its own health and institutional preservation through financial deals, educational facilities, and protective legislation. The practical and all-consuming endeavours to invest in a strong church left almost no role for the Holy Ghost and almost no time for the world.

In the social encyclicals *Mater et Magistra, Pacem in Terris,* and *Progressio Populorum,* John XXIII and Paul VI gave the lead to the Catholic world in focussing more intently on the problems of this world as the condition of any relationship with God. It is possible, moreover, to trace, in the development of Catholic social teaching over the past hundred years, a gradual elimination of the dualism, of the "otherworldliness", which tended to alienate the church from the creative forces in Western culture and relegate it to the periphery of society. Increasingly the popes, and especially Pope Paul VI, have been concerned with the problems of war, international tensions, and poverty. However, in many parts of the Catholic world this concern has not been reciprocated. Far too often the secular mission and function of the church is regarded, still, as a relatively unimportant adjunct to the "spiritual" and usually self-centred aims of the church. In spite of the urgent appeals of John XXIII and Paul VI a great deal of Catholic energy and activity remains otherworldly and introverted. Part, at least, of the reason for this is that there has not yet developed, in the church, a theological consciousness and perspective capable of integrating the unique mission of the church with the pressing problems of our age.

When the church takes up its true prophetic role in the world of politics, that is, in the world of human relationships, it will do so as salt in a wound, as leaven in dough, as the conscience of society in the interests of the integrity of the person, of the reconciliation of men, and especially as the champion of the poor and the oppressed. As Pope John said in his opening address to the Council: "Confronted by the under-developed countries, the Church presents herself as she is and wants to be: the Church of all men, and in particular the Church of the poor."

Unfortunately, the church in many countries thinks it cannot afford to be the effective champion of the poor—it stands to lose too much. It must be their champion not merely at the level of pious theological rhetoric: nor can it effectively be their champion if it limits its recommendations to charity at the personal level. At times, the church will have to hazard all, to stir the consciences of men to effect social and economic reform. Indeed, at times, and especially in the developing countries of the world, it might be called upon to support and work with the one political and economic ideology which appears capable, through its revolutionary dynamic and mass appeal, of effecting the emancipation of the poor. It is distressing that quite often the church does not seem to have profound misgivings about supporting the atheistic materialists of the right who unscrupulously exploit the poor and the under-privileged, but opposes, with almost fanatical dedication, the atheistic materialists of the left whose ideological ambition is the emancipation of the exploited masses of the world.

No doubt the principalities and the powers will deplore and oppose the return of the church to the political arena. No doubt the church will often suffer financially and in terms of membership. However, in the twentieth-century world, the real challenge to the church is not the advance of science, not the experienced absence of God, not the accelerating secularization. The real challenge to the church is its response to the problems of war, poverty, hunger, and racial discrimination. Will it respond by solemn pronouncements or will it empty itself of its wealth, privilege, and prestige as a stimulus to the conscience of the West?

We can begin to see, therefore, that the process of secularization does not dissolve the essential structure and function of the church. It allows us to see it more clearly in the light of the secular age. It allows us to see the church not as something which persists outside the world, or in spite of the world, or against the world. We come to see the church as very much within, very much a service to and very much a function of the world.

Perhaps it is important here to ask what is the primary focus of concern of Christian theology. In the not too recent past this question would have sounded rather absurd, yet when faced with the cultural, logical, and theological disavowal of God, to base a theology on the existence, nature, and attributes of God is to commit it to a tangle of problems from which it is unlikely to emerge. The failure, moreover, of the recent monumental search for the historical Jesus makes Christ also a rather unpromising starting point for theology in a secular age.

Professor John Macquarrie suggests beginning with *man*. "If man is, as Christianity asserts, a creature of God and dependent on him, then this should show itself in a study of man. It should be possible to see man as fragmentary and incomplete in himself, so that we are pointed out to God."[2] The difficulty with this is that it suffers from the kind of assumption of gaps which the theory of God has suffered from. As the gaps are filled, then claims about God are successively discredited. Secondly, it does not allow for the possibility that the very creative attempt to overcome these inadequacies might be a necessary condition for establishing a relationship with and for developing an awareness of God.

It seems that the focal point of Christian theology is not God, or Christ, or man, but the church. The church is an existing, living and tangible sociological phenomenon. The task of theology is to examine scientifically its structure, its dynamic principles and its consciousness, from within the community which is the church. The disadvantages of the traditional Protestant preoccupation with the kerygma are, first of all, the problem of the historical Jesus, and secondly the selection of criteria for re-mythologizing the kerygma in contemporary terms. Unless the persisting consciousness of the church as the community continuing Christ has its own built-in capacity to do this, the criteria would have to be extrinsic to the kerygma.

In the Catholic tradition, the church persists throughout the ages and has the mandate to judge and select the various expressions of the Christian message. However, in the Catholic church, the selectivity function has been institutionally restricted to the power structure of the church and popes and bishops have tended to exercise it almost exclusively as feudal oracles. As a consequence, the Catholic church has not shown the readiness to come to grips with the problem of the need for a contemporary expression of the Christian message as have Protestant theologians. However, the Vatican Council showed definite signs of acknowledging the need for the total consciousness or awareness of the church to manifest itself. In the document on the Church in the Modern World we find:

She [the Church] must rely on those who live in the world, are versed in different institutions and specialties, and grasp their innermost significance in the eyes of both believers and unbelievers. With the help of the Holy Spirit, it is the task of the entire People of God, especially pastors and theologians, to hear, distinguish, and interpret the many voices of our age, and to judge them in the light of the divine Word. In this way, revealed truth can always be more deeply penetrated, better understood, and set forth to greater advantage.[3]

The church then is a living community with its symbols, its ceremonies, its peculiar culture, and to some extent its peculiar language. It has its own consciousness of Christ, whom it proclaims and continues in space and time, and through Christ, its consciousness of God. But this consciousness must be an eminently contemporary thing, moulded in and through contemporary experience and expressed in contemporary idiom.

The Vatican Council spoke often of the church as a "sacrament". Thus the document on the Liturgy speaks of the church as the "sacrament of unity" (p. 147), and the document on the Church in the Modern World speaks of it as the "universal sacrament of salvation" (p. 247). The word "sacrament" is useful because it has a twofold significance. In using it the church claims to be a symbol and a sign of unity and salvation and also an agent in effecting these. In other words, she is not just a sign to the world, but also an agent in the world, working towards the goals she symbolizes. One of these goals is "the salvation" of the world. However, "salvation" in the biblical use of the term is not a commodity or an event over and above and independent of the events of this world and this life. The biblical use of the term[4] focusses initially on salvation from temporal evils, hunger, poverty, suffering, slavery, and natural and human catastrophe, and secondly, through concern for and an attempt to overcome these, on salvation from eternal death.

We can begin to see that the church today sees itself less as the champion of abstract metaphysical and otherworldly truth and more as the champion of existential truth, of the integrity and totality of the personal and community life of man. It is the herald of the essential conditions for this totality of life: that man be loving and reconciliatory through "the creative imitation of Christ's existence for others".[5] It carries in the language of its liturgy the name of "God" and proclaims the conditions under which this name has meaning and is verified. It is the symbol of the one worldly quality that best speaks of God: love. It is, therefore, the sign and the agent of the reconciliation of man with man, of man with nature and of all creation with God, which reconciliation will be achieved, not by a yearning for and an impotent attempt to embody some other world or the past, but in the future.

This emphasis on the symbol and agent character of the church and its concern for unity among men and their salvation clearly describes the task of the church in the modern world. The task is a very real and concrete one which can be programmed in very mundane terms. It rescues the church from its otherworldliness.

It redeems it from the category of impotent symbol. In its ceremonies, that is, in its liturgy, it symbolizes, proclaims, and celebrates what has already been accomplished in Christ and through the ages, but it also looks to the future and reminds us of the fact of the incompleteness of the task. The liturgy like the church itself is for the world and related to the world.

And yet, in practice, this is not the case. Even after the Vatican Council, the church is not credibly involved in, concerned about, or really relevant to the world. Ecclesiasticism is still in the ascendancy, even though in a somewhat modified and modernized form.

It is possible to detect two serious obstacles to the church's taking seriously and literally its proclaimed role in the modern world, which are reasons why many people who want to be Christians find so much that continues to pass as the activity of the church frustratingly irrelevant. These two obstacles are the resistance of the liturgy and of the hierarchy to the process of renewal in the church.

At first sight it will appear preposterous to claim that the liturgy of the church has resisted the process of renewal and is proving an obstacle to the church's accepting its proper secular role in the modern world. The document on the liturgy was regarded as one of the triumphs of Vatican II and the process of liturgical reform has been one of the most radical and rapid in the history of the church. The difficulty, however, lies in the general approach and attitude to liturgy. In the first place there is still the tendency to use the sacraments in a magical way. They still tend to be used as instruments for the retailing of graces, they still tend to be regarded as having cosmic, otherworldly effects, and this results in a failure to develop and capitalize on their sociological significance and psychological impact. This attitude is a function and an extension of the tendency to use God as an intellectual or psychological crutch. "Magic wants to get, mysticism wants to give—immortal and antagonistic attitudes which turn up under one disguise or another in every age of thought."[6] The reformed liturgy is still too much an opportunity to "get" in a fuller and more meaningful way. The urgent need is that it become more a sign of and a stimulus to the *giving* of self to the world.

In the second place, the difficulty is more fundamental. In an article entitled "Putting the Liturgy in Its Place",[7] Daniel Callahan claims that the document on the liturgy in the Vatican Council is at fault in stressing that "liturgical celebration. . . is a sacred action surpassing all others. No other action of the Church can match its claim to efficacy, nor equal the degree of it." In another place the document says: "the liturgy is the summit toward which the activity of the Church is directed; at the same time it is the fountain from which all her power flows." Callahan claims: "The primacy of place accorded to the liturgy is one of the most important hidden sources of the Church's failure to carry out its Christian work and witness in the world." This primacy of place, he says, is the cause of the persistence of the self-centred preoccupation of the church, even after Vatican II, and its failure to embody, at the collective level, the altruistic concern for others which it is its duty to proclaim. The over-emphasis on the importance of the liturgy makes it possible for the church to continue to devote enormous sums of money to house it, to continue to be involved in real estate and bricks and mortar, and to allow liturgical conventions, literature, and legislation to proliferate when this concern for rubrical trivia can be a distraction from and even a substitute for the pressing issues of our age.

There is here a problem, and it will probably be some time before the church solves it. As Callahan goes on to point out, the contemporary church has been trying to say two things simultaneously:

> It has been saying, on the one hand, that Christ is pre-eminently present to the Christian community during Mass, during the celebration of the Eucharistic liturgy. But it has also been saying, on the other hand, that Christ is present in the world as well—that he is present in our neighbour, in society, in the world.

The renewal of the liturgy of the church will be inadequate as long as the liturgy is a distraction from Christian tasks in the world and fails to stimulate Christians to assume creative responsibility for these tasks. As John Robinson observed in *Honest to God*:

> The test of worship is how far it makes us *more sensitive* to "the beyond in our midst", to the Christ in the hungry, the homeless and the prisoner. Only if we are more likely to recognize him there after attending an act of worship is that worship Christian rather than a piece of religiosity in Christian dress. That is what is implied in Jesus' saying that "the sabbath was made for man, not man for the sabbath". The whole of our religious observance and church-going must be prepared to submit to this test . . . the function of worship is . . . to focus, sharpen and deepen our response to the world and other people.[8]

Daniel Callahan concludes the article referred to above by suggesting four steps to insure that the liturgy will effectively symbolize the role of the church as the sacrament of the salvation of the world and to incite Christians to work for this. The first is that we cease placing the liturgy at the centre of our lives and insist on the prime importance of love of neighbour. The New Testament insists that the loving know God; it doesn't insist that the worshipping know God. Indeed, one cannot but be surprised by the spontaneous, gratuitous, and informal ceremony of love which was the last supper after the solemn, devised, and intricate technicalities which have been the staple of the liturgical revival. The second step that Callahan suggests is "that we break the link between liturgy and property—a link which keeps the money changers permanently in the temple", by reversing the Church's present financial priorities. "We should instead say that one must support the worthy cause of the world and, if any money is left over, it should go toward support of the Church." The third step is that liturgical worship should arise from Christian involvement in meeting a real secular need. Hence, Christian communities should not be established primarily for liturgical needs. As Callahan points out, "the most interesting thing about many of the 'underground' liturgical experimentations is not that they are experimenting with the liturgy but that they so often, in practice, subordinate liturgy to some other Christian work in progress". The fourth step is

that if the liturgy is to cease having so many affinities to an obsessional neurosis, it must rid itself of the awe and solemnity which still surrounds it. It must cease to suggest that Christ is to be found in the liturgy in a way superior to other ways of finding Christ. It must cease to suggest that it provides a magical short-cut way to Christ, transcending the profane, hard, usually frustrating discoveries of Christ in the world.

One reservation I would have about Callahan's suggestions is that the liturgy of the church, while providing a stimulus to altruistic responsibility in the world, must not become completely absorbed into or identified with specific mundane issues, nor must it express itself exclusively in the idiom of the day. In the first place, as an eschatological symbol, the liturgy must attempt to transcend the contingencies of the present. Now it cannot do this by appealing to some other world, nor, obviously, can it use language and symbols taken from the future. It has to resort to the paradoxical technique of transcending the present and representing the future through reference to the past. Hence the liturgy must, in its structure, idiom, and concerns, avoid succumbing entirely to what is topical and of immediate significance. The traditional motifs in the liturgy, the exodus, the new Pasch, the ancient doctrinal formulae, do not represent instances of the repetition of and return to a primitive archetype, but techniques of avoiding the facticity of the present to focus our attention on the future. The liturgy must, therefore, be a constantly changing dynamic balance between an expression of the mundane needs and concerns of the moment and a representation of the future in terms of the past.

In the second place, the liturgy is a symbol of the reconciliation and the community of all men. To the extent that it is a ceremony of involvement in specific political issues, then it could fail as a symbol of the ultimate community of men; it could easily become the partisan ceremony of one political option among others claiming equal worth and validity and thus a divisive force. The liturgy must embody and provoke effective concern for contemporary issues such as war, poverty, and race relations. But it must not become identified with a particular solution to these problems, so that its capacity to represent, credibly, the eschatological and catholic community of men is essentially compromised. Consequently, although Callahan's point about finance spent on church buildings while temples of the Holy Spirit suffer hunger is well taken, there is a way in which church buildings can stand for another age, the future. Unfortunately, these buildings still primarily represent the past. They do not credibly represent or summon us to the future. However, this capacity to symbolize the "pressure of the future" depends on the whole morale, perspective, and dynamism of the members of the church. The credible symbolic value of the liturgy and the church buildings will change only when the psychology of the members and of the leaders of the church changes.

The second serious obstacle to the church's undertaking effectively its secular role in the modern world is the failure of the process of renewal to have very much effect on the role of the pope and the bishops in the church. In an era when radical change is required in the church, development is inhibited within the still comparatively static framework of a hierarchical power structure. At the diocesan level and at the international level the bishops and the pope still retain the right to supervise and pass judgment on all developments in the church, and while advocating the need for development and renewal do not see this supervisory role as itself requiring renewal.

It is necessary to examine the possibilities for renewal and secularization in this area of the society which is the church for two reasons. The first is that there is the danger that a heavy-handed use of hierarchical supervision in the contemporary life of the church will result in the disillusionment of many and their contracting out if they think that this interpretation of the function of the hierarchy is essential to the Catholic church. If however they can see that there is a feasible and scripturally valid alternative, they are provided with a goal to achieve. If, on the other hand, the present role of pope and bishops in the Catholic church is, as tends to be presumed at present, the one fixed point in a changing church, then the rate of intelligent defections from the church is likely to increase and there will be very little development and renewal in the church itself. The second reason is that in examining the role of the pope and bishops in the church today we can look more deeply into the secular function of the church itself.

There are two aspects of the problem of the role of the pope and bishops in the church of the future. The first aspect is making sure that the problem is approached from the right direction. In the past, and we find this verified in canon law, the process of defining functions and roles in the church took the wrong direction, a chronic disorder inherited from the sacral age in which the church was the world. In this age, which canonically still prevails, the genus was defined with reference to, and in terms of, the specific difference, instead of the other way round. Hence bishops were defined in terms of pope, priests in terms of bishops, laity in terms of priests, non-Christians in terms of Christians, and the world in terms of the church. The implicit assumption of this procedure was that the fullness of the church was in the pope and/or the bishops and that ecclesiastical reality was gradually diluted as it descended the hierarchical ladder. The laity was left in the passive role of being what the clergy was not, and had ecclesiastical significance only to the extent that they received a mandate from, or shared in the work of, the clergy.

The method to be followed, therefore, in approaching this problem, is to begin with the world and define the church in relation to it; then define the role of the laity as the body of the church and the role of the clergy and hierarchy in terms of the laity.

The Secular Function of the Church

The second aspect of the problem is how the question is asked, for this can be as important as giving the correct answer. In the recent past, the question has been: how can the pope and the bishops exercise authority in a way that is compatible with contemporary sensibility? The answer has been that they must exercise it, not in the feudal manner, but as a service. This answer, however, is inadequate and simply glosses over the fundamental incompatibility of the notions of authority and service. I want to claim that the appropriate question is not "How will the authority of pope and bishops be exercised in the church of the future?" but "What is the role of the pope and the bishops in the church of the future?"

If we ask the question in the first way, we implicitly accept that the central function of the pope and bishops is that of exercising authority and we content ourselves with attempting to reconcile this with the modality of service. Yves Congar in *Power and Poverty in the Church*[9] gives an inventory of the vocabulary of the New Testament terms used to describe the role of the apostles. A number of conclusions can be drawn from this inventory. First of all, there is authority in the church, the authority of Christ, but this authority is that of the whole church. Secondly, words such as "arche", meaning power, "exousia" meaning authority or power, and "epitage", that is, authority to command, are almost never used to refer to the function or the role of the apostles. The word "hierarchy", as applied to the successors of the apostles, is not used of the apostles themselves in the New Testament.

Indeed, as John L. McKenzie shows in *Authority in the Church*, on a number of important occasions, such as the Last Supper, the journey to Capernaum, and in his reply to the request of the mother of the sons of Zebedee, Christ went out of his way to distinguish the role of the apostles, not just from the way it is exercised by political rulers, but from the exercise of authority as such. "The conclusion to be drawn . . . is not that Jesus left no instructions on how the Church should be governed, but that he commissioned the Church to find new forms for an entirely new idea of human association—a community of love."[10]

The power and authority of the church is the power and authority of Christ and this is the power and authority of love. It is not sufficient to say that this power is similar to political power except that it is exercised in a loving way. The power itself is that of love.

In a way it may be helpful to distinguish between the *exercise* of authority in society by the political power and the *expression* of the authority of love by the pope and the bishops. The pope and bishops do not exercise the authority, which is the love of Christ; they should express it. Now there is a sense in which pope and bishops do exercise executive authority, but this is interpreted not in sacred terms but in strictly functional terms. At the institutional level, which is the lowest level of the community life of the church, practical decisions have to be made in the interests of organization and efficiency. However, the making of these decisions, which bind under the obligation of avoiding institutional disarray, is peripheral to the essential role of pope and bishops.

To clarify this claim we need to seek a more positive conception, keeping in mind Christ's insistence on the uniqueness of this role of the pope and bishops in relation to the church. In predicting this role a number of guidelines need to be relied upon. The first of these is a sense of the history of authority and its exercise in the church, an awareness of the variety of the modes of the exercise of the papal and episcopal functions. In the recent past these functions have been invested with a sacredness and an absolute character which seemed to intensify as the challenge to the church's influence over the secular sphere increased. A knowledge that the popes and bishops have fulfilled a variety of roles in the church according to the variety of cultural circumstances in which the church found herself facilitates the process of secularization of the hierarchy. Just as the process of secularization effected the emancipation of the world from ecclesiastical control, so too, in its final phase, it will emancipate the church from the domination of pope and bishops. This does not, of course, mean the elimination of pope and bishops from the church. What it does mean is the emergence of a conception of their role unencumbered by a view which is heavily sacred and magical, and reflecting more authentically both the ambition that Christ expressed when he washed the feet of the apostles and the valid insights of contemporary experience. The emergence of a renewed conception of the role of pope and bishops in the church does not, moreover, imply a condemnation and repudiation of the role they played in the past. It simply acknowledges that the power of vital adaption of the church allows it, in its many aspects, to assume forms appropriate to a particular age.

In pursuing a description of the papal and episcopal roles in a church which takes seriously its secular function, we have to begin with the world and, as it were, work inwards. This is the method, suggested above, which is more in accord with the logical process of definition. In a period in modern Western history which saw the emancipation of the secular spheres from ecclesiastical domination, there developed a polarity between the church and the world. The church saw itself as set over against the world and to a large extent in competition with it. The use of the word "world" in the New Testament and in Christian history has been ambiguous. However, the fundamental contrast which emerges in the New Testament is between the world redeemed by love and the world which continues to resist the redeeming power of love. The contrast is not between the church as God's "world" and the profane world which somehow or another competes with the ecclesiastical "world". There is one world, one creation which God loved in the beginning and for which he manifested his love by sending his only-begotten son. The world in which we live and move and which we are is God's world. It is the substance of our contact with him, it is the medium in which he manifests himself, it is the stuff of our relationship with him and it provides the sole idiom of our necessarily ambiguous and totally inadequate way of talking about him. The Holy Ghost, in spite of the fact that "all is seared with trade; bleared, smeared with toil; and wears man's smudge and shares man's smell" continues to brood over the world. The function of the church is to testify to this, to be a symbol of it and an agent of the creative and redeeming power of love. The whole being of the church is, therefore, that of a *sacrament* of God's action in the world.

Therefore, the Council focuses its attention on the world of men, the whole human family along with the sum of those realities in the midst of which that family lives. It gazes upon that world which is the theatre of man's history, and carries the marks of his energies, his tragedies, and his triumphs; that world which the Christian sees as created and sustained by its Maker's love, fallen indeed into the bondage of sin, yet emancipated now by Christ.[11]

The church is the symbol of the emancipation of the world, in principle, by Christ. It is the agent, among many other agents, of the emancipation of the world in fact. The Vatican Council dispelled the illusion of antipathy between the church and the world. In doing so it stressed, either implicitly or explicitly, some important characteristics of the church:

a) It is fundamentally a *community,* which, though visible, does not rely intrinsically on specific organizational and institutional forms. This community is one whose principle of cohesion is not coercion or necessity, but love.

b) It is a *pilgrim community.* In bringing out this quality of the church the Council emphasized that the church is an evolving entity in an evolving world. This is one of the most fundamental changes in the culture and the conceptual framework of the church. Instead of regarding itself as a timeless organization impervious to the vagaries of history, it now regards itself as immersed in history and painfully trudging its way through it.

c) It is an *eschatological community* in the focus and direction of its concerns. The church is no longer the champion of the hidden dimension or stratum of being, that is of the supernatural or the spiritual realm, claiming access to privileged knowledge of these. Nor is it the champion of the past. It is the sacrament not of another space, but of another age, not the past, but the future, the second coming of Christ!

d) It is a *diaspora community,* that is, a scattered community assuming once again the function of a leaven in the world which Christ predicted and which the early church practised. In the post-Constantinian age it will be stripped of all political, social, and economic privileges. (Another way in which the church can be described is as a "kenotic community", i.e. one which empties itself of all self-interest.[12]) Its ambition will be to be of service to the world. In this role it will become much more radical in its outlook and activity. While the church stood for the past, it was synonymous with conservatism. While the church possessed political, economic, or social privileges it was in thrall to the forces which had a vested interest in the status quo. But when the church effectively repudiates worldly power, privilege, and prestige, then it will be in a position to act as a goad towards the future and credibly pass as the champion of the human person and the reality of the human community.

e) It is a *secularized community* in the sense that the church claims to be an expert only in its own origin, mission, and consciousness. It is not an expert on the world, and this renunciation of oracular power is part of its descent from an unworldly eminence to become immersed in and concerned about mundane affairs. Its perspective is no longer vertical but horizontal. In the horizontal plane it humbly works to discover and also to create the world redeemed, beginning with a faith, drawn by a hope, and inspired by love.

f) It is an *integral community*. This concept of integralness or wholeness has many directions and dimensions. The church stands, first of all, for the totality of life and experience, and hence it has been a champion against the modernist tendency to repudiate the past, the secularist tendency to reduce the richness and scope of the experience of the present, and the nihilist tendency to limit the possibilities of the future. Though the explicit means by which the church has espoused this cause have sometimes been unfortunate and outmoded, this has not detracted from the fact that the church did champion these human values. In the second place, the Vatican Council established a much more complete idea of the church. The church is not the hierarchy. When "the church speaks" it is not the pope and/or the bishop. The church is the whole community of men who are followers of Christ, and the word "church" can be used only when it is predicated of an action of the entire community.

g) It is a community with Christ at the head. In an outstanding speech in the second session of the Council, Maximos IV of Antioch insisted, against the prevailing custom in the Catholic church, that the pope should not be called the head of the church. This title belonged to Christ alone. The pope is merely the head of the college of bishops who provide a service to the community of which they are a part.[13] The implications of this change of emphasis have yet to be embodied in the practice of the Catholic church, for pope and bishops still continue to act as heads of the church and arrogate to themselves the rather exclusive use of the term "church".

h) It is a community which lives inductively. The appreciation of this is dawning very slowly, but it is a corollary of the Council's description of the church as a pilgrim community. In the way it understands and speaks about itself, in the way it understands and speaks about Christ and God, in the way it understands and speaks about the reality and the implications of the law of love, the church depends on the dynamic interaction between its past experiences and formulations and the unfolding of history currently before it in which it learns more of God's designs revealed in his creation. The church has a legacy and to this it must be true. But an integral part of this legacy is the promise of and a hope in the future. Hence conceptions of the past have to be constantly rearranged in the light of the discoveries of the present and entertained provisionally to leave room for the future. The church has always to avoid the danger of allowing itself to settle for the past or succumb to the present. It must be the credible symbol of Christ who is alpha and omega.

The point of this sketchy account of the characteristics of the post-Vatican II church is to illustrate how the old conception of the role of the pope and the bishops in the church is now no longer feasible. In the church in the age of Constantine the hierarchical structure, the static conceptions, and the relatively passive role of most members of the church made the dominating role of the pope and the bishops not only feasible, but even necessary. However, radical changes in the church's assessment and awareness of itself make an equally radical reassessment of the role of the successors of the apostles an urgent demand.

It is possible to illustrate further the urgency of this need by considering three problems which relate to the assertions of the "magisterium" of the Catholic church. When we look at these problems we can appreciate, in a general way, the sort of changes which need to be made to relieve some of the intolerable tensions which have arisen and persist in the Catholic church. Even the very term "magisterium" helps generate these problems for as John L. McKenzie points out,[14] this office or function of schoolmaster, the teaching office, is not the specific office of the apostles in the New Testament. This teaching function "is subsidiary to the office of proclaiming the gospel, and, in fact, teaching seems to mean the specialized work of explaining the Gospel in Old Testament terms". Moreover, "The gospel is not a doctrine, by which I mean it is not a body of knowledge . . . The gospel is the proclamation of a person and an event, and a call to a personal response to the person and the event."[15]

Now concerning the assertions of the magisterium of the church we can ask the following crucial questions:

a) What is the relationship between assertions about the same topic?

b) How are the assertions arrived at?

c) What is the relationship between these assertions and the individual conscience?

One of the difficulties facing the pope on the question of birth control is that of reconciling any modification of the Catholic position with the statements of his predecessors. This is not merely the problem of face-saving. It is a symptom of the deeper problem mentioned in Chapter 1, of a shift from a conception of the church in static terms to a conception of the church in dynamic terms. As the Catholic church faces the problem of doctrinal renewal this difficulty will recur. Already the task of speaking of the presence of Christ in the Eucharist in contemporary terms has encountered the difficulty of the formulations of Trent. How can an evolutionary, personalist, and political language about Christ be reconciled with the language of Chalcedon? How can death-of-God theology be reconciled with the explicit Trinitarian categories of Nicaea?

At the moment the persisting tendency is to demand logical or verbal consistency and ask "What did Trent say?" or "What did Chalcedon say?" However, developments in our understanding of the nature and function of language make these the wrong questions to ask. The linguistic kind of compatibility or reconciliation is impossible. Wittgenstein and Heidegger have shown that language is a medium—rather than a means—of communication; it is a living, evolving thing which depends so much on the total cultural context for its significance and impact. To attempt to hold up a formula, elaborated in a very different historical and cultural context, as a test of orthodoxy in the present does an injustice to the church which formulated it and hopelessly constrains the church of today which is dominated by it. Certainly it is possible to continue to demand assent to truths enshrined in unchanging formulae but only at the price of rather externalized acknowledgment of these assertions which lack existential meaning and impact, and at the risk of allowing the values and insights enshrined in them to become impotent doctrinal symbols.

The appropriate question to ask, therefore, is not "What did Trent say?", but "What did Trent mean?" "What was Trent getting at?" It is peculiar that the Catholic church which allows for the need to interpret the Bible has not yet really allowed for the need to interpret the documents of the magisterium. As Gregory Baum points out: "We have as yet no hermeneutical principles for the interpretation of the ecclesiastical magisterium."[16]

Nevertheless, a better understanding of what the assertions of the magisterium were getting at in the past would not necessarily release the church from the dominion of the past and open it to the realities of the present and the possibilities of the future. What is also needed is a fundamental acceptance of development. A better understanding of the assertions of the past could leave intact the demand for historical consistency, in attitude and policy. What is called for, however, is what we can describe as psychological consistency. This kind of consistency would demand that the church, in a contemporary context, avail itself of its vast historical experience, but in the light of this and new data, make a response which may be quite different from earlier responses.

A fundamental question, therefore, is whether the church is a repository for timeless truths which it can reformulate in different ways in different ages, or whether the church itself is a living truth and symbol, a community which will conceptualize its experience and awareness of itself in different ways, in different historical situations. In the latter conception, the community is more central and important than the assertions which in different ages it makes about itself. The tendency in the past, a tendency which today persists in the power structure of the church, was to make the "timeless truths" central and regard the church as occupying the rather subsidiary role of guarding these.

One of the most revolutionary documents of the Vatican Council was concerned with Revelation. In this document the church rescued itself, in principle at least, from the rigid formulae which were inhibiting its dynamic. It dealt first of all with the notion of revelation itself. In recent theology, revelation has been described as a set of propositions, or as an experience, or as an event. The Vatican Council attempted a synthesis of these three elements, but in doing so shifted the emphasis in the Catholic conception away from revelation as a set of propositions towards revelation as an event which is experienced and then conceptualized in propositions or assertions. Thus: "To see Jesus is to see his Father. . . Jesus perfected revelation by fulfilling it through his whole work of making himself present and manifesting himself: through his words and deeds, his signs and wonders, but especially through his death and glorious resurrection."[17] Commenting on this Karl Rahner says:

> At its origin, revelation is not the communication of a number of propositions . . . . but an historical dialogue between God and man, in which something happens, and in which the communication is related to an event, to an action of God. Moreover, Christ as the living medium between God and the world . . . is the object of an experience which is more simple, more comprehensive, more modest and yet richer than the individual formulae through which one can exploit this experience in a basically illimited progressive manner.[18]

The chronological order, therefore, is the event, the experience, the response, and the conceptualization of the response. However, the expression or conceptualization of the response to the event is necessarily limited and conditioned for it depends on, and is expressed in, the conceptual patterns of the age in which the response occurs.

The Vatican Council's description of tradition is equally dynamic. In the eighth paragraph of the document on revelation it elaborates an idea of tradition which is quite revolutionary: "So the church, in her teaching, life and worship, perpetuates and hands on to all generations all that she believes." In other words, tradition is the *total* life of the church in its developing awareness and in its vital responses. The document goes on to say:

> This tradition which comes from the apostles develops in the church with the help of the Holy Spirit. For there is a growth in the understanding of the realities and the words which have been handed down. This happens through the contemplation and study made by believers . . . through the intimate understanding of spiritual things they experience and through the preaching of those who have received through episcopal succession the sure gift of truth. For as the centuries succeed one another, the church constantly moves forward toward the fullness of divine truth until the words of God reach their complete fulfillment in her.[19]

Three important elements in or aspects of tradition as a vital process emerge from this text. It is a developing process, it results from a dialectic between the community which is the church and the experience of history, and, most importantly, it depends on all the members of this community. This last aspect is brought out more clearly in a passage in the document on the Church in the Modern World. This has been quoted above (p. 222), but it is of such significance that it will bear repeating. Speaking of the "living exchange" between the church and the diverse cultures of people which leads to the "adaptation" and "accommodation" of the gospel, the document says:

> To promote such an exchange, the church requires special help, particularly in our day, when things are changing very rapidly and the ways of thinking are exceedingly various. She must rely on those who live in the world, are versed in different institutions and specialties, and grasp their innermost significance in the eyes of both believers and unbelievers. With the help of the Holy Spirit, it is the task of the entire People of God, especially pastors and theologians, to hear, distinguish, and interpret the many voices of our

age, and to judge them in the light of the divine Word. In this way, revealed truth can always be more deeply penetrated, better understood, and set forth to greater advantage.[20]

From these texts we can see that the church, in principle, acknowledges that changes in formulation are inevitable because propositions are necessarily inadequate and provisional. Contemporary experience does not merely provide the opportunity to illustrate "timeless truths", it is an integral ingredient in the process of the church's current expression of its total—historical and geographical—consciousness. In the registering of this consciousness the whole church is destined to play an active part and one of the ambitions of the church should be to emancipate all those elements in the church which are still predominantly passive, still occupying the role of consumers of spiritual goods, so that they assume the role of active and creative responsibility in the church. We can begin to see, therefore, that faith, or *the* faith, is not something which is preserved by an institution throughout the ages so that any formulation of it or any element in it must be logically or linguistically compatible with past formulations. As Edward Schillebeeckx points out: "Now, however, the emphasis is rather that the faith remains identical with itself, dynamically, in its growth."[21]

This brings us to the second problem: how are the assertions of the church arrived at? In the past, the various kinds of official statements of the church were the result of a mixture of approaches. There were elements of the mechanical transmission of formulae sanctified by the passage of time. Thus many of the encyclicals of the popes, even today, contain large sections of quotations from previous popes. There were elements of the process of deductive reasoning and this was the basis of development in either dogmatic moral or social teaching. The function of a specific historical situation was to provide the occasion for or the stimulus to a further explication of what was claimed to be implicitly contained in previous teaching. There were elements of oracular insight in many of the pronouncements of the magisterium of the church, the claim to access to privileged knowledge which resulted from the mere investiture of papal or episcopal authority. The overall dynamic of this process of the formulation of ecclesiastical assertions was authoritarian and communication was almost exclusively downward. In the cultural context in which this took place, it is difficult to imagine how this could have been otherwise. It must be supposed, therefore, that the oracular style of arriving at the formulations and the predominantly downward communication of them to a mass of the members of the church which was largely uneducated, passive, and inarticulate, was an adaptation of the structure and function of the church to that cultural situation.

But these conditions have changed radically. There has been an educational revolution in which, in the developed countries at least, the mass of the members of the church are educated and articulate. The decline of metaphysics and the elimination of Latin as the language of theology have opened theological issues to the scrutiny and the appraisal of an increasing number of men. Theologians, when challenged, can now no longer scurry into the tortuous thickets of scholastic jargon to avoid embarrassing encounters. The revolution in world communication media makes it possible to transmit, analyse, and criticize ecclesiastical assertions, dispelling any aura of the sacred and leaving them with value and impact only to the extent that their intrinsic worth wins for them.

The magisterium of the church, the role of the pope and bishops in the church, need the scarifying effect of the process of secularization. They need to be rescued from the elements of the sacred and even the magical which remain even in the post-Vatican II era. The church needs to be rid of the claim to power which is still too closely associated with the magisterium, and to develop, especially in its doctrinal and moral formulations, the reality of communion. For the reality of communion to be made possible, there has to be an increase in the amount and the quality of communication or dialogue within the church.

No doubt there has been a startling increase in the amount of dialogue and communication within the Catholic church, and not only in actual practice but also as a result of structural modifications. The senate of bishops, the increased importance of episcopal conferences of bishops, the senates of priests in many dioceses, the councils of laymen and apostolic groups, right down to parish councils, all give testimony to the reality of horizontal and upward communication in the church. Yet these developments are not without ambiguities. There is still a prevalent, if not explicitly stated, view that all this is a concession to the modern mood; that the upward communication *helps* pope and bishops in their task; that the type of consultation available is restricted to certain areas of administration and practical policy. In spite of these developments an outmoded conception of the role of the pope and the bishops remains, and while it remains many of the official pronouncements "of the church" will remain personally and culturally limited and fail to be authentic statements of the church in the integral and comprehensive sense of the word.

The difficulty is that while the pope and bishops are thought of as exercising a power to teach in such a way that they can, in the last analysis impose, by divine right, doctrinal formulations or patterns of behaviour on the members of the church, or on the church generally, the debilitating tensions which are evident in the church today will continue.

One of the most important of these tensions is also the third of the questions asked above: what is the relationship between the assertions of the magisterium and the individual conscience? The tension between the official statements of the magisterium and the individual conscience has arisen in the church not simply because people have become irresponsible, disobedient, or materialistic, but because there is, first of all, a growing awareness in the church of personal responsibility for the self, for society, and for the church. It has arisen, secondly, because the prevailing authoritarian emphasis in the role of pope and bishops is structured on the assumption of the passive function of the individual conscience and cannot allow for or cope with, in crucial cases, the creative function of conscience.

Unfortunately, the difficulty is often posed in terms which presume that Catholics today want to be able to do what they like. This is not the problem. A correct statement of it is that Catholics want to be able to do what they think they ought to do without carrying an unnecessary burden of guilt by living in conflict with an injunction uncompromisingly imposed.

The crucial question is: does an assertion of the magisterium, even if appropriately arrived at, *dominate* the individual conscience or does it offer a *service* to it? Another way of asking the question is: does an assertion of the magisterium make all other moral considerations irrelevant, so that it alone must prevail, or does this assertion help rescue the individual from the limitations of his own personal and narrowly conditioned experience, but in such a way that it is considered, with due weight, among the other relevant and possibly conflicting moral factors?

Unless we assign a magical quality to assertions of the magisterium, we are constrained to settle for the latter alternative. Assertions of the magisterium cannot dominate the individual conscience in such a way as to render all other factors irrelevant, for three reasons. First of all, conscience has the creative function of applying the law of Christ to new historical situations and of working out its implications in conditions not previously experienced. Secondly, it would render the role of the pope and bishops quite incompatible with the notion of service Vatican II so often described. Thirdly, no general law or assertion can simply cater for all the moral exigencies of human persons each of whom is unique.

John L. McKenzie says that the "teaching office is not commissioned to tell people what to do, but to make it possible for people to decide what to do".[22] Personal faith is fundamentally commitment; dogmatic formulae mediate this commitment, its awareness and its expression; moral formulae mediate the fulfillment of the conditions under which commitment is effected. They cannot simply dominate commitment nor provide a univocally specific programme for commitment.

The reason for this long digression in analysing the three crucial problems is to illustrate that the role the pope and bishops continue to exercise in the church is not only becoming increasingly incredible, but appears incompatible with and even alien to the contemporary conception which the church has of itself as a dynamic community. The idea of the dominant role of the pope and bishops complements the notion of the members of the church as *belonging* to the church. But the members of the church do not belong to the church, they *are* the church. However, the emphasis in the Vatican Council on the church as a community does not demand the elimination of the role of pope and bishops. It demands that their role be reinterpreted in the light of the New Testament descriptions of their function and in the light of the present needs of the church. The task, therefore, is to suggest a role or function for pope and bishops which will satisfy these demands.

We saw earlier that it is essential in analysing this role to observe the correct methodological direction by beginning with the church and then assessing the function of the pope and bishops in relation to the church. A brief description of some of the important characteristics of the post-Vatican II church was offered, but it is necessary now to attempt to crystallize these in a functional definition of the church. In the light of what has been claimed so far, it is feasible to describe the church as the sacrament of reconciliation in the world. The word "sacrament" includes the two ideas of symbol and agent. The word "reconciliation" indicates the reconciliation of man with himself, of man with other men, and through this, of man with God. The church is the symbol and the agent of the community of men, celebrated in the liturgical meal of the Eucharist. But for the church to be, first of all, an effective and credible symbol, it must itself be an authentic and credible community of free human persons. The reality of community demands not only liturgical or ceremonial communion, but also communication. And here we have the clue to a contemporary appraisal of the role of the pope and bishops.

In the first place, it seems that there is no New Testament justification for making authority, or power, or jurisdiction, the central or most important features of the function of the apostles. As John L. McKenzie points out, "When the New Testament uses the word 'didaskein' (teach) and its cognates, it is safe to say that the words never mean the kind of 'authoritative teaching' which is treated in modern theology."[23] We have seen that Christ was most careful to distinguish the function of the apostles from that of men who exercise political power. But does this strip the successors of the apostles of any function? Perhaps we can learn a lesson from Paul's analogy in I Corinthians 12, where he insists that the variety of functions in the church is similar to the variety of functions of the organs of the human body. The various organs are structurally distinct, but often it is very difficult to state, specifically, what is the essential function of each. The hand can scratch, sign a declaration of war, grasp and feel, even "read" braille; it can also conduct a symphony or write a poem. The eye is the organ of seeing, but it can also speak a language. The papal and episcopal structures remain, but their function in a new context can be quite different.

Once we are free of the notion that authority is essential to their function, and when we realise fully the implications of the church conceived as a community, we can suggest that the pope and the bishops can best be described as *agents* of communion and communication in the church. In this capacity they serve and facilitate the inherent vitality of the church. Moreover, this twofold aspect corresponds to what was described as the power of orders and the power of jurisdiction. The former concerns the ceremonial life of the church, the latter its conscious life. Yet the substitution of the word "agent" for the idea of power eliminates the misgivings of contemporary experience and an idea which is basically incompatible with the spirit of the New Testament.

In their capacity as agents of communion the pope and bishops would provide links among the churches of the world in celebrating, liturgically, the death and resurrection of Christ and the promise and reality of the redemption of the world. They would symbolize the pan-racial, pan-national community of men. This kind of symbolism and celebration is immensely important, but its impact is vitiated if it takes on the appearance of a celebration of the glory and influence of Rome or a testimony to the world-wide power of the pope.

In their capacity as agents of communication in the church, the pope and the bishops, the latter at the local or national level, the former at the international level, provide the focal points at which is crystallized and articulated the total conscience of the church. Now it is possible to distinguish three elements in the total consciousness of the church. The first is what can be called the historical consciousness of the church, that is, the wealth of experience it has accumulated throughout the ages, the legacy of the "traditional" formulations and expressions of the awareness of the church, the scriptures, the decrees of the councils, and the writings of the great theologians. The second is what can be called the horizontal consciousness of the church, that is, the variety of the responses of the church in any age to local conditions and national and racial characteristics. The third is what can be called the existential consciousness of the church in contact with contemporary influence and values.

The bishops provide the links throughout the church for the fusion of these three elements which go to make up the present consciousness of the church. They should be the experts in the historical awareness of the church and make available to the members of the church its vast historical experience. Through episcopal conferences, through international meetings of bishops, and through the pope, individual churches should be rescued from capitulating to secularist influences, that is, to specifically local, temporal, and culturally conditioned influences. Thus horizontal communication amongst the various local churches saves each of them from the servitude of a limited local vision. But the bishops are especially the agents of the existential awareness of the church, of what we could call upward communication. This develops from the dialectic of creative Christian living in the world. Christians living everyday lives in politics, science, philosophy, business, labour, and industry, provide the watershed of the contemporary consciousness of the church, but so far, in the church, there have not been developed adequate channels for the communication of this.

Unfortunately the prevailing dynamic of communication in the Catholic church is still downward. There is not yet the free flow of communication at all levels which should be characteristic of the community of love. Fear and coercion, of the moral kind, still appear only too frequently and these result in constrictions of the vital spontaneity which should be a hallmark of the church. Part of the difficulty is that most of the bishops in the church were consecrated in pre-Vatican II days and continue to regard themselves and their priests as ecclesiastical civil servants for transmitting the directives of Rome, for imposing assent to timeless dogmatic truths, and demanding adherence to absolute moral injunctions. Another difficulty is structural. While the Vatican Council established the principle of the collegiality of the bishops, it did not, as Edward Schillebeeckx points out,[24] go far enough. It needed to establish the principle of the collegiality of the pope to insure the possibility of the full flow of three way communication in the church.

One of the unfortunate consequences of the persisting civil servant mentality of many of the bishops in the Catholic church is a startling proliferation of structures in the church. Consultative bodies, councils, committees, and senates multiply rapidly, and often this occurs to compensate for the failure of the agent of communication to be just this. The danger is that the church will become more organized and institutionalized than ever, that it will become more than ever before introvertedly preoccupied with its own concerns and in the multiplication of structures and functions, all the more oblivious to the needs of the world which the church is destined to serve. A multiplication of communication structures does not of itself guarantee increased communication. The fundamental need is for a change of heart and perspective on the part of the principal agents of communication, the pope and the bishops.

The problem reduces itself to one of leadership. This concept of the role of the pope and bishops in the church is free of the sacred, static, absolute, and dominative connotations associated with the feudal mode or style of bishops in the past. "Leadership appeals to motives which are beyond the reach of obedience as such."[25] The idea of the role of leadership, moreover, complements the dynamic notion of the church as the pilgrim of the future. If the pope and the bishops are to be of service to an eschatologically orientated pilgrim church, they must not be the solemn prophets of the dangers ahead, the pusillanimous advocates of the status quo, or even worse, of a return to the past. They must be, preeminently, what Harvey Cox colourfully calls "God's avant-garde". If the pope and the bishops were credibly leaders, many of the tensions in the church would be dispelled and the present proliferation of structures would be unnecessary. In their role as leaders the pope and the bishops would be rid of its preoccupations with ecclesiastical trivia.

A number of conditions are probably necessary before the role of pope and bishops is seen less as the exercise of authority and more as that of leadership. The leaders would have to be elected by the whole church. To insure that the best man is selected, candidature would have to be open to all members of the church, including laymen. Secondly, the prospective candidates would have to be rescued from the stifling subculture of seminary-Rome-chancery, which instils a set of specifically ecclesiastical values and almost incurably limits the personal and the Christian vision. Thirdly, the principle of planned obsolescence would have to apply so that the maximum of vitality can be brought to the role of leadership. This would probably demand a tenure of office limited to ten years. Fourthly, the style of life demanded of a Christian leader would require the repudiation of the continuing extravagance of episcopal dress and ceremonial; the elimination of the use of the royal or oracular plural unless it reflected, authentically, the view of the whole church; the eschewing of merely conventional gestures and rhetoric.

In this capacity the pope and the bishops would be the agents of the unity, of the holiness, of the catholicity, and of the apostolicity of the church. As the agents of the unity of the church they would not attempt to impose uniformity, but be the mediators of diverse views and attitudes. As the agents of the holiness of the church they would champion the transcendence of the church by insuring that it did not become identified with a particular age or a particular culture but remained at home only in the future. As the agents of the catholicity of the church they would ensure that the church espoused and enshrined all positive human values; that it became credibly the champion of the abundance, of the diversity, of the richness and the totality of human life. However, this abundance would not entail espousing the cause of an occult world or dimension by the use of esoteric techniques. It would entail the inventive, creative process of establishing a relationship with God in this world. As the agents of the apostolicity of the church they would insure that the church remained true to the spirit of the paradigm of the apostolic age.

Does this result in the elimination of the authority of the church? I have claimed that the exercise of authority is not the central function of the pope and the bishops. Christ certainly gave authority to his church. However, he gave it to the whole church and the authority which he gave it is that of love. He gave the love which has the power to bind and to loose, the complete power over the world, over life and death, which comes with love, the frightening power to create!

In a symposium entitled "The Cool Generation and the Church", the American magazine *Commonweal* investigated the attitudes of some young Catholic college students and graduates to the church today.[26] Among some of the more pungent comments were:

The fact that the church fails to inspire rage in us is indicative of the extent to which it has failed to touch our generation.
When Pope Paul says the church is not divided on birth control to the point where the issue is in doubt, we get turned off. His is a lie.
I have never gone to an institution—they've all been Catholic by the way—of which I can honestly say I'm proud . . . Catholic schools have a reputation of being provincial, of being one-minded, of being dogmatic.
And about the papal encyclicals: they're terrible; they stink; they don't say anything. What I'm waiting for, instead of a papal encyclical, is a new Bob Dylan album. Now there is somebody saying something that pertains to me. He inspires me.

These items illustrate the urgency of the task. The Vatican Council was a revolutionary event, but so far the Catholic church has not been sufficiently courageous to pursue the inexorable logic of this event. It has yet to acknowledge clearly and undertake decisively its secular task. We have seen that the two primary obstacles to this are an exaggerated view of the value of the liturgy, and the tendency on the part of the pope and the bishops to maintain, undiminished, their ecclesiastical power. And yet unless the church as a whole emancipates itself from concern with the minutiae of liturgical refinements, the futile ambition of preserving intact a whole rococo structure of dogmatic formulae which means little in today's world, and the appalling scramble to save ecclesiastical face at almost any cost, a whole generation will be lost to the church, and the church will fail to be true to itself and its destiny.

There is developing in many countries of the world, especially among the young, a moral sensitivity and perceptiveness which owes a great deal to the Christian tradition. The church is faced with the choice of being in the vanguard of this development, or seeing this moral evolution take place apart from and even, in some countries, in spite of the church. The issues of racial discrimination, of poverty, of under-development, of war and peace, of exploitation, of materialism, and the development of the human community of men are infinitely more important than most of the issues on the agenda of the meeting of the Senate of Bishops for 1967. Two-thirds of the world is on the verge or in the process of the greatest socio-economic revolution in the history of the human race, while a large percentage of the church, completely oblivious to it, carries on with its liturgical reforms and conventions and with official exclamations of dismay at the questioning of the existence of angels and the reality of the virgin birth.

But is socio-economic revolution the concern of the church? Is this not a demand that the church capitulate to merely secular issues and problems? It is necessary to return to the theme introduced at the beginning of this book. The church should be, as Christ was, concerned with the realities and the implications of love, not in its abstract and philosophical dimension, but in its concrete and practical application and realization. It must be concerned with love not in terms of the pious rhetoric of exhortation, but in the inventive dialectic of techniques for reconciling men and effecting their complete emancipation and salvation.

What we often fail to realize is that there is a variety of ways in which the church can capitulate to its secular milieu, and become, in effect, completely a child of its times. The obvious way is that taken by van Buren and Braithwaite in which Christianity is judged in terms of and adapted to comply with the reductionist criteria of a specific philosophical system. This danger is generally recognized in the church. A less obvious way is the one that has prevailed so often in the modern history of the church. Christians often give assent to a set of metaphysical or biblical theological assertions, observe a code of sexual ethics, perform the requirements of a sacred liturgy, and, feeling justified, allow themselves fecklessly to be overwhelmed by the pagan values and attitudes which prevail in their milieu. The insidious feature of a theology and a liturgy which are out of vital touch with the realities of life is that they can create the illusion of the Christian life while allowing anti-Christian and even pagan values to flourish unquestioned and unchallenged.

In his book *Capitulation*,[72] Carl Amery traces the development and the features of "milieu Catholicism" in West Germany since World War II. Other writers such as Gordon Zahn and Guenter Lewy have shown how German Catholics and German Christians generally found no fundamental incompatibility between their lives as Christians and their loyalty to Nazi Germany. Yet this phenomenon is not limited to Germany. In many of the Western countries the church is only too ready to champion nationalistic causes, bless wars that ensure the economic security of the wealthy, turn a blind eye to racial discrimination, and accept quite fecklessly the materialism and the consumer values of a capitalist ethos. A symptom of its acculturation to the consumer ethos in the Western world is that the concept of the church as the spiritual gravy-train to eternal salvation is only too prevalent. Ecclesiastical administrators see the maintenance of the schedule of this gravy-train as the all-important value and they are willing to compromise, usually unconsciously, with the secular powers to retain their own power and prestige which they regard as essential in carrying out the task they see for the church. For administrators of this kind, the twofold formula of internal discipline in faith and morals and freedom from interference if not actual support from the secular powers is all that is required for the health of the church. This only too often results in an unholy alliance between the Christian church and the secularist state. Beyond a number of issues like divorce, sexual morality, and abortion, which are among symbols of self-identity, the church can be relied on to give support to most policies of the state, no matter how pagan. In return the state ensures, within certain diplomatic limits, that the church maintains its prestige and privileges. But the function of the church as the leaven in society, as the salt in a culture, or as God's avant-garde, disappears. The church becomes effectively isolated and fundamentally secularist when in the interests of its institutional health it seeks political and social respectability.

The Secular Function of the Church

In each country this danger takes a different form. In the United States each of the churches and each of the religions tend to be regarded and in various latent and implicit ways to regard themselves as an integral part of American culture. Officially religion is regarded as a good thing because it tends to induce conformity, to act as a social and cultural integrator, and to further other major national values. As Will Herberg has pointed out in *Protestant, Catholic, Jew*:

> In so far as any reference is made to the God in whom all Americans "believe" and of whom "official" religions speak, it is primarily as sanction and underpinning for the supreme values of the faith embodied in the American Way of Life. Secularization of religion could hardly go further.[28]

Moltmann's concept of the role of the church in relation to the social and cultural milieu has already been referred to. He expresses the fear that the Christian church in the Western world is already deeply compromised by having accepted an essentially private role in life and by having surrendered the realms of justice and social order. "Our neighbour comes on the scene only in personal encounter, but not in his social reality." This religion Moltmann calls "the cult of the new subjectivity".

However, religion as the cult of subjectivity has its social and cultural implications. This very role that religion is expected to play is not just a retreat from the prevailing social order but a positive reinforcement of it. Moltmann goes on to claim that the church as the ideal of the human community, as distinct from and in contrast with the functional impersonal business community, acts as a kind of cultural and social sedative. Sociology has shown how often superorganizations and macro-structures in the political-economic complex allow for and even facilitate microstructures of various free associations; "the massive canyons of society allow complete freedom in the private sphere". This concession to "human" community and private freedom does nothing to alter the loss of the human in society, it provides only a "dialectical compensation and a disburdening of the soul" and while providing this "service" both to the individual and society remains radically impotent to disturb or alter that society.

Even as an institution among the other institutions of society, the church, Moltmann claims, tends to reinforce the culture in which it finds itself. It unconsciously connives at and makes possible the suspension of the question of meaning and purpose within the political-industrial complex and therefore quells a primary source of revolutionary ferment. In one sense the church is relegated to private life, but

> On the other hand, the ecclesiastical institution of religious modes of conduct acquires a new social significance. For indeed even the modern, institutionalized consciousness retains somewhere on the margin an inkling of the horrors of history . . . Yet this subliminal consciousness of crisis results in a general, if also non-committal, recognition of the religious institutions as the guarantors of life's security in general. The institution of the churches then has the effect of being an ultimate institution overshadowing the institutional security of life, and one from which security is expected against the ultimate fears of existence . . . This . . . is Christianity as prescribed by the social *milieu*.[29]

The really serious consequence of the church's preoccupation with its own institutional health is that the God, the consciousness of whom the church claims to develop and the awareness of whom it claims to bear, is not God at all but some spiritual Moloch. If it is the case that a relationship with and an awareness of God depends on the altruistic undertaking of creative responsibility for the destiny of man and the world, to the extent that the church nurtures a self-centred concern at the institutional or individual level, it becomes an obstacle to a vital relationship with the God of Abraham, of Isaac, of Jacob, and of Christ, and the god which it proclaims becomes a sophisticated metaphysical idol.

The issues which will count in the eschatological situation described by Christ in Matthew 25, when the nations are gathered together to be judged, will not be the abstract questions of dogmatic allegiance, liturgical discrimination, or the content of moral integrity. They will be the very real and concrete issues of food, clothing, life, and practical compassion. Those who feed the hungry, clothe the naked, welcome strangers and have compassion on prisoners will be saved. The rest will be repudiated.

The church bears, and will continue to bear, the name of God. It will continue to pose the challenge of Christ to find God, inductively, by living a life on the model of his own life, a life which is loving, creative, and reconciliatory, a life for others, a life open to and driving towards the infinite possibilities of the future. The church as a community is a living symbol of this. However, its very effectiveness as a symbol depends intrinsically on the extent to which the church is also an agent of creative love and reconciliation.

EPILOGUE

The philosophers have only interpreted the world in different ways; the point is to change it.

Karl Marx

One of the chronic faults with Christianity has been its propensity to speculate about the nature of God and in the course of this speculation to deduce norms of Christian behaviour which isolate, if not exactly alienate, the Christian from the urgent pressures of the ethic that Christ advocated and practised. The New Testament tells us clearly and unequivocally that God is love. The loving know God, the unloving know nothing of God. One of the specious advantages, however, of the speculative norms of Christian behaviour is that they can allow the Christian in unruffled conscience to transcend many difficult moral decisions raised by the exigencies of modern history.

Epilogue

The most intractable of Christian moral problems arises when there is question of choosing between two disparate groups of persons who, theoretically, should be the objects of that love. The problem arises when we are faced with the crucial choice between our obligations to love the affluent minority and our obligation to love the deprived majority. The Christian is then confronted with the alternatives of an assault on the political, social, and economic structures which perpetuate the imbalance—and this means, often, an assault on the people who constitute the minority—or a retreat into an abstract, formalized, spiritualized, and ceremonial love which leaves the concrete problems intact.

Ernst Troeltsch's monumental study *The Social Teaching of the Christian Churches*[1] has demonstrated how the Christian churches have never effectively established an intrinsic creative relation between the Christian ethic of love and the social realities of the world. The Christian response has always been to posit two worlds or two areas of Christian endeavour, the one in which religious needs (including the formal realization of the ethic of love) can be satisfied, the other in which compromise and acceptance of the world, as given, prevail. The religious world always provides an area of escape and release from the tension of the inexorable ethic of love while at the same time symbolizing its persistent demands. Even the so-called Christianization of the world amounted in the end to leaving everything, outwardly at least, exactly as it was before. The perennial difficulty has been that salvation or "deliverance from the world comes to be regarded as a completely sacramental miracle ... and the ethic of the Church becomes the ethic of the morality of grace". A consequence of this has been that the whole practice of charity tends constantly to be distorted. What was in the life of Christ a totally spontaneous gratuitous and altruistic concern for the welfare of others has again and again been made a means to the practice of ascetic self-denial, an instance of "good works", or a sign of the predestining favour of God.

This is not to say that Christianity has not had any influence on the social order or has not given rise to social change and revolution. As Troeltsch points out,[2] the Christian church has throughout its long history often exerted "a profound transforming influence" and "the most searching interference with the social order". Sometimes it has exerted this influence by its other-worldly indifference to existing social conditions and structures; at other times "by submitting existing conditions to the only valid test, the test of its own ideals and of its transcendent values". However, as a general rule, until the time of Calvin, Christianity neither sought nor found an intrinsic relationship, "an inward connection and historical continuity between the general political, economic, and social situation and the values of personal religion . . . social reform took the shape of philanthropy, which aided individuals and allowed conditions to remain as they were."[3]

With Calvinism a close integration of Christianity with modern economic and political forms was approved in the belief that they would lead to the development of a "holy community" and it was recognized, much more effectively, that spiritual values are conditioned by the material content in which they are placed. Yet even here the dualism persisted and was accentuated by the social ramifications of the Calvinist doctrine of predestination, and the fundamental individualism which was one of the sources of the modern capitalist culture.

Common to all the churches of the Christian tradition was the discomfort with and the uncertainty about that vast web of social relations and structures, the world. The churches have always seen the world in opposition to, as destined to be of service to, or by divine right subject to, the church. The radical Christian revolution of our day is precisely the exchange of these roles. Increasingly the church sees itself as of service to the world, and the Christian optimism implied in this is of profound significance at a time when the secularist seems to be declining into a pall of frustration and apprehension.

It is important to recapitulate and summarize some of the contextual features and causes of this change in the Christian church's conception of its role in relation to the world.

a) One of the most important is the dissolution of the magical-sacramental view of the church itself as a means for transmitting, in a rather mechanical and ontological way, Truth, Grace, or the Word.

b) Under the influence of the process of secularization the church has been forced to surrender the dualism which has become almost synonymous with Christianity. The consequence of this is that the only way to God is through the world.

c) The complementary influences of science and modern philosophical criticism have required a new Christian epistemological stance—that of an existential process of inductive verification.

Talk about God has meaning in relation to and must be verified in terms of fashioning the future.

d) Man's technological prowess has mediated the revelation of a hitherto obscured or unacknowledged aspect of the biblical message. Man is made in the image and likeness of God, the Creator. It is only by assuming responsibility for his world and by courageously undertaking the task of creative autonomy that man can be reconciled with himself, realize fully the image of God in himself, and hope to establish a relationship with and thus a verification of God.

e) Christian detachment from *this* world, and at the same time the basis for his optimistic and joyous immersion in it, is the biblical hope and promise of the future. An antithetical spiritual world or a monastic or scholastic remoteness can no longer provide a refuge from nor a substitute for the implementation of the Christian ethic of altruistic love in specific measures for personal and social change. The perspective and the Christian hope of the future provide an eminently *creative distance* from the world while providing at the same time that the Christian does not become submerged in the world, completely identified with the *now*, its structures, values and axioms.

f) Human history, or social change, becomes the primary and immediate focus of Christian endeavour, and the ambition which both inspires and defines the church. Creative involvement in social change becomes the fundamental Christian task, human reconciliation the ultimate objective and all of these indispensable conditions for verification of the Christian God hypothesis.

g) The Christian church, therefore, must be at one and the same time, the eschatological symbol of the ultimate trans-racial, trans-social, and trans-national unity of all men *and* the prime stimulus to the adopting of specific measures and even radical means to achieve this ambition. The eschaton will come, not because we dutifully await it on the top of some lonely hill, but because we create it in the midst of the complexities of contemporary society. Both the Christian lexicon and the Christian ceremonial have to be fundamentally reinterpreted so that the tremendous resources of dedication and commitment in the church are no longer dissipated in futile abstractions but are focussed and directed towards the realization of the community of men.

From the vortex of cultural change over the past two decades it is possible to discern, not without ambiguities, both the challenges and the possibilities of renewal for the Christian church. Essential to this process of renewal is a greater clarity and certitude about its basic goals. The Catholic church especially has been notoriously preoccupied with its own institutional health. In the Vatican Council it set out to concentrate more on the world, but basically once again in its own interests. Ironically, however, the inexorable logic of the movement of "aggiornamento" begun by John XXIII may well result, in the last analysis, in a primary and altruistic concern for the world, which is, after all, the appropriate outlook for the Christian individually or collectively. At the moment, however, the Christian and especially the Catholic has a double task: first, that of transforming the church to make it an effective symbol and instrument for what appears to be the Christian task today, and, secondly, that of transforming the world. He can neglect neither, for to despair of the church would be to jettison the magnet of the future and begin to subside into the present, while to concentrate exclusively on change in the church would be to exhaust energy on one means among others for responding to the problems of the world. Of the two tasks, however, the transformation of the world is the more important. There can be no comparison, from a human or Christian point of view, between the urgency of social and political action to redress the evils of racial prejudice and economic inequalities on the one hand and ecclesiastical action to influence a change in papal attitudes to birth control or the condemnation of Galileo on the other hand.

It is possible, therefore, that for the first time in the history of Christianity an intrinsic connection between the Christian ideal and Christian action in the whole range of the spectrum of social and cultural evolution is beginning to emerge. It is possible also that history will see the seeds of this movement, within the Catholic church at least, in the social encyclicals of the popes over the past hundred years. A close analysis of these documents reveals a progressive change in both ideals and orientation. Initially, Leo XIII and Pius XI could not suppress a yearning to revert to a past age in which the cultural content seemed more accommodating to the Catholic church. Gradually, however, especially in the encyclicals of John XXIII and Paul VI, the narrow horizons of the Christian past and the European scene are transcended and the future prospect of justice, equality, freedom, and peace among all men emerges as the dominant theme.

It would be possible to argue also that there are in Paul VI's *Progressio Populorum* intimations of a critical choice which will loom before the Christian church in the near future. In the growth of the theological problem of revolution, in the growing impetus of the new left movement both Christian and secular, in the new understanding of the humanism of Marx, in the obvious symptoms of decay in the individualist ethos of the Western world (perhaps John Updike's *Couples* best illustrates this), and in the desperate needs of the emerging nations, the urgency and the inescapability of the choice are taking form. Basically it is the choice as to which of the competing political, social, and economic systems meshes with the Christian ethic. Is an ethos which in the last analysis demands that individuals compete with each other or one in which individuals co-operate with each other more compatible with Christianity? This is, of course, a crude and totally inadequate distillation of the choice. An equally crude expression of the choice would be to say that the alternatives are capitalism or socialism, individualism or Marxism. Yet as the problems of world poverty and the threat of war increase, and as it becomes increasingly evident that the prevailing political, social, and economic forms of the West at best seem incapable of solving the problems and at worst seem destined to exacerbate them, Christianity seems destined to be forced to choose among existing theories. The only other course is to retreat once more into a realm transcending the sphere of specific ideologies, policies, and programmes and once more to make Christian charity innocuous by spiritualizing it and isolating it in the abstract realm of pious but impotent hope. In this century, the Christian churches have been almost fanatically averse to any association with the atheistic materialism of Marx. They have been, however, less than meticulously discriminating in their association with the gross materialism of Western capitalism, even though this ideology does pay lip-service to the Christian God. At this juncture all that can be done is to point out the inevitability of a conscious choice among ideologies if the dynamic of Christian love is to be released from its chrysalis of liturgical, spiritualized, and essentially private piety and spread into the concrete social dimension of life; all that can be done is to suggest, as has already been attempted, that the present socio-economic substructure of Christianity could be insidiously sapping its vitality while the apparently hostile socio-economic substructure suggested, especially in the early writings of Marx[4] could offer for the Christian churches a practical and immediate ideal which they could more appropriately adopt and creatively transform.

In *The Great Evasion,* William Appleman Williams claims that the United States has never really faced up to "any intellectual and moral confrontation with Karl Marx".[5] It has devised and resorted to a wide variety of techniques for avoiding this confrontation: it has consistently confused the theory of Marx with the reality of Russia; it has declared Marx's ideas illegal so as to define a dialogue with him as a crime under federal and state laws; it has re-defined Marx as someone or something else, for example, Lenin or Castro or Mao Tse Tung, that appeared easier to handle. America has

> never confronted his central insight that capitalism is predicated upon an overemphasis and exaltation of the individualistic, egoistic half of man functioning in a marketplace system that overrides and crushes the social, humanitarian half of man. We have never confronted his perception that capitalism is based upon a definition of man in the marketplace that defines the dialogue between man as a competitive struggle for riches and power.[6]

The same could be said of the Catholic church. A case could be made, argued, and defended that the social encyclicals of Leo XIII and Pius XI in dealing with "communism" do not deal with the praxis of Karl Marx. The target of the papal polemic and especially of that of Pius XI's *Divini Redemptoris* has little in common with a scholarly understanding and appreciation of the insights and views of Marx and a great deal in common with the vulgar image of communism precipitated by the confluence of practical political abuse of Marxist ideas in communist regimes and theoretical distortions cultivated by a capitalist culture with a vested interest in encouraging such distortions. The popes certainly understood the practical evils of "unbridled" capitalism and they, therefore, roundly condemned it. But what they settled for as the alternative or happy medium between communism and unbridled capitalism was, initially, a return to a no longer viable, greatly idealized "Christian order" of a bygone culture, and later on, a compromise with a modified capitalism. What the popes, and Christian literature generally, have not recognized and acknowledged is the spread of cultural exploitation, a deepening sense of alienation and the accelerating spiritual proletarianization of the mass of people in the Western world which has paralleled the rising material affluence of

Epilogue

these same masses and the increasing poverty and distress of the rest of the world. Certainly it is a commonplace in papal, episcopal, and Christian literature generally to bewail the growing materialism and the decline of the traditional values. But this malaise is invariably seen as the effect of abandoning a dualistic philosophical perspective, obsolete liturgical forms, primitive and static interpretations of the Bible and a respect for absolute "principles" and religious authority long since discredited. It is almost never seen as the result of a socio-economic culture in which the basic ground rules demand that human persons compete and where co-operation and community are defined, and therefore distorted, in terms of competition, a culture in which it is proclaimed that men are born equal, but which acknowledges that after that it is every man for himself.

Marx demanded the death of God as a condition for human co-operation. Nietzsche proclaimed the death of God as the consequence of human competition. The "death of God" has occurred, not in the citadel of communism, but in the jungle of human competition. In this jungle human depersonalization is both expressed and disguised in the multiplication of commodities and even God himself, or Grace, or the Word, or Salvation have become commodities among the thousands of others which so effectively occupy man in the process of consuming, and so distract him from his destiny to participate in creating the community symbolized at the Last Supper. The lords of this jungle will not allow the death of God. If necessary they will keep God embalmed and maintain, posthumously, his influence. The Bishop of Woolwich claimed that the church continues to live on its own fat, but the supply of this fat is now ensured by the monolithic enterprise of modern capitalism. The secular liberalism of nineteenth century Europe has lost its irreligious countenance and now finds it more profitable to encourage and sustain with a more pious mien the Christian church. As Jürgen Moltmann has shown, the church is an indispensable means of maintaining the illusion of community and a necessary safety valve against the pressure of the question of ultimate meaning. Don't expect community in socio-economic life; don't ask for meaning and creative participation in your work. The church, that other world, looks after these human needs, and this is a productive enterprise well worth subsidizing. A brief and somewhat trivial indicator is called for.

In the summer of 1968 the *New York Times* gave front-page

Epilogue

and generally sympathetic prominence to every event relating to the papacy extending from the possibility that the Pope might remove the 350-year-old condemnation of Galileo through the condemnation of birth control to the papal journey to Colombia. The fourth Assembly of the World Council of Churches, on the other hand, which dealt with the issues of the war in Vietnam, selective conscientious objection, the theology and morality of Christian revolutionary activity, and radical measures for the closing of the world poverty gap received much less prominence and sympathy. These issues cut too close to the bone of the American military-industrial complex and brought the question of meaning out of the hermetically sealed and innocuous isolation of the church. The papal activities, even the birth control issue, remained eminently ecclesiastical matters, and were therefore to be discussed and promoted. In the W.C.C. the Christian ethic of love showed disconcerting signs of emerging from the sphere of essentially private, ecclesiastical, and pious exhortation into the arena of concrete social structures and policies. This appeared as a dangerous trend, hence was spoken of disparagingly and mockingly as churchmen playing at games which were beyond their talent or competence.

Since the reign of John XXIII the Vatican has embarked upon a programme of easing tensions between the Catholic church and the Communist world. In 1937 Pius XI proclaimed: "Communism is intrinsically wrong and no one who would save Christian civilization may collaborate with it in any field whatsoever." After the Hungarian revolution in 1956 Pius XII asserted that for Christians "it is inconsistent to wish to sit at the table of God and at that of His enemies". But over the past five years Vatican diplomacy, following John's initiative, has pursued a less unqualified and intransigent policy towards Communist regimes. After tracing the contours of this policy, Peter Nichols in *The Politics of the Vatican* reaches this conclusion:

The various activities of the Papacy we have been examining have two sides to them. Either they are concerned with defending or improving the Church's position in a particular country or region so that it can carry out its work with more freedom; or they present the Pope as the "conscience of the world", calling on rulers to press forward with right-minded energy towards the solution of mankind's problems. Altogether, they constitute the Roman Church's claim to play a constructive part in temporal affairs, to be an influence on contemporary life and thought. This influence would, naturally, be regarded by the Church as of secondary consideration in comparison with the main purpose of ministering to souls. Its active pursuit of influence, nevertheless, forms a vast and varied corpus of "works".[7]

Nichols' analysis uncovers the dissipating dichotomy of purposes which continues to inspire Vatican policy and diplomacy. The primary intention remains "the salvation of souls", as if this were, though not unrelated to at least not intrinsically connected with, the material conditions of creation expressed in political, social, economic, and cultural structures and forms. Either of the two main trends of Vatican endeavour described by Nichols seems destined for futility or compromise and calculated ultimately to maintain the isolation of the Christian ethic of love from any far-reaching influence in anything but the narrowly private life of the individual. When it is thus restricted the private life and "the spiritual life" of the individual remain restricted and atrophied, for the Christian life, the life of the human relationship with God, tends to become that which is left over when all the vital connections have already been made.

Future opportunities for being "the conscience of the world" are severely limited and will lead to tedium and banality while the dictates of this conscience remain at the non-committal level of moralistic warning and pious exhortation. Conscience is an eminently practical faculty and its judgments essentially specific. It must hazard conclusions based on empirical evidence that this particular course of action is wrong and must be avoided, while that course is good and must be followed. To continue to exhort the combatants to peace in Vietnam, even to open diplomatic channels to bring the parties to the conference table, is not, really, to act as the voice of conscience. If the papacy brought together an internationally composed commission to attempt to reach a conclusion about responsibility for provoking and continuing the conflict, based on historical evidence, and declared its conclusions, in spite of possible consequences for the institutional health of the church in any country, then it would be functioning as the "conscience of the world". A genuine concern for the plight of the developing nations of the world and for the cultural proletariat and the alienated in the affluent nations of the world will demand, eventually, a criticism of the socio-economic structures and policies that lead to these evils and the advocacy of alternative structures and policies. Anything less would seem to compromise the claim of concern and lead to irrelevance and impotence.

The endemic malaise of modern Christianity reveals itself, however, in the claim that it is concerned with the salvation of souls, that its kingdom is not of this world. This allows the church to avoid a crucial and direct engagement with these peculiarly contemporary issues and evils. The claim is true, but what is demanded is a horizontal focus on these objectives, salvation and the kingdom, in, through, and on the other side of achieving salvation and creating the kingdom of reconciliation in this world. For as long as Christianity and the Vatican see peace among nations and the problems of poverty and hunger as issues only peripherally and rather disjunctively related to their "true" aim, they will always be able to retreat from a courageous and compelling confrontation of the problems. For as long as Christianity maintains this dual vision of reality it will continue to be mainly a refuge from, rather than a creative leaven in, reality.

This disjunctive vision can have more serious ramifications. It manifests itself in the diplomacy of the Vatican to achieve "religious freedom" especially in Communist countries. The Western world often looks with disfavour on this Vatican talent for accommodation and its rather avant-garde "liberalism" in relation to communism. A notable victory for the Vatican policy of encouraging Christian-Marxist dialogue and for its diplomacy in the Communist bloc occurred in Czechoslovakia. The dialogue contributed not insignificantly to a liberalization of the Czechoslovak regime. The diplomacy led to a religious-secular "rapprochement". But at what price? The Praesidium of the Communist Party's Central Committee pledged that the party "will strive to safeguard religious freedom" in return for an agreement by the churches "to respect the socialist character of society, to be loyal to the state and to refrain from influencing believers in their civic decisions".[8] The Communist regime thus violated its basic Marxist principles in allowing an area of human endeavour calculated to distract and divert energy from the creation of a better world and the church implicitly acknowledged the traditional Communist slander of other-worldly futility and ineffectiveness. The agreement to surrender any influence over believers "in their civic decisions" is not just an admirable retreat of the church from the politically privileged role it played in Eastern Europe in the past which allowed it to *dominate* believers in their civic decisions, but a capitulation.

At best, this kind of agreement postpones the day when the church must make clearer decisions about how it can espouse viable socio-economic theories to embody and extend the ethic of love into the concrete social dimension. At worst it can lead to the tolerance of social evils and even political atrocities in exchange for the freedom to retail "grace" through preaching and the sacraments. There are rather clear indicators in contemporary sensibility of a growing inability to accept this kind of grace as either authentically Christian or humanly relevant. Hence a pursuit of this kind of diplomatic policy by the Vatican or by Christianity in general to ensure the institutional survival of the church seems destined to effect either its extinction or its impotence.

If on the other hand the Christian church dedicates itself to the good of the world, to the salvation of the world, it will have to revive its capacity to assimilate, utilize, and at the same time Christianize available technical and ideological means. At the international level, however, as the world becomes polarized in a way predicted by Marx, this choice may be agonizing. It is no longer adequate for the church to adapt to and assimilate regional cultural forms and patterns as the Vatican Council advocates. The very international character of today's issues and crises seems calculated to precipitate a decision that transcends the easy pluralism of the church in a variety of regional cultures. Inexorably the fusing of the nations into a "global village" is crystallizing a unique crisis for the Christian church, and could lead to the greatest schism in the history of the church. The parties of this schism will not be the present progressive secularizers versus the conservative Christians, but on the one hand the Christians who will find their faith obliges them to advocate the economic, social, and political emancipation of the dispossessed and exploited areas of the world, even though this requires bloody revolution and insurrection, and on the other hand, those who will maintain a Christianity aloof from the movement in disapproval of means so alien to the Christian ideals. This reaction to a radical Christian commitment to a redress of the monstrous inequality in the world would arise from the twin sources of a church incurably enthralled by altruistic love as an eminently aseptic abstraction and of a church symbiotically related to a Western

Epilogue

world economically geared to the continuation of the inequality of wealth.

The choice facing the Christian church will not reduce itself to *Marx* or *Christ*. A Christian dedicated to an abolition of the injustice in the world which leads to poverty, malnutrition, and suffering will do what he has to do because of Christ. But to achieve his ambition the *kind of question* he will have to ask of himself and answer in an eminently decisive way is whether in attempting to correct these injustices he should resort to the socio-economic means suggested by Adam Smith or to those suggested by Karl Marx. The failure of the Christian church to ask and answer this kind of question, any evasive action through diplomatic and moralistic aloofness, or any dissipation of the basic issue by an effusion of pedantic scholastic refinements will simply ensure that, in a way prefigured by the French Revolution but with far greater and more devastating consequences, the church will be left in some tranquil but stagnant backwater of human history.

NOTES TO TEXT

INTRODUCTION

1 Eric Mascall, *The Secularization of Christianity* (London: Darton, Longman, and Todd, 1965), p. 109.
2 Harry Blamires, *The Christian Mind*, quoted by Mascall, *op. cit.*, p. 43.
3 Walter M. Abbot and J. Gallagher (eds.), *The Documents of Vatican II* (London: Chapman, 1966), p. 206.
4 Dom Sebastian Moore, *God Is a New Language* (London: Darton, Longman, and Todd, 1967), pp. 29-30.

1 Graham Greene, *A Burnt-Out Case* (London: Heinemann, 1961), p. 159.

PART I THE CULTURAL CONTEXT

1 The Post-secular Age

1 Harvey Cox, *The Secular City* (London: S.C.M., 1965), p. 2.
2 Ruel Tyson, "Urban Renewal in the Holy City", *The Secular City Debate*, ed. Daniel Callahan (New York: Macmillan, 1966), p. 48.
3 Cox, *op. cit.*, pp. 20-21.
4 *Ibid*, pp. 18-19. See also Colin Williams, *Faith in a Secular Age* (London: Collins, 1966), p. 34.

5 William Horosz, "Religion and Culture in Modern Perspective", *Religion in Philosophical and Cultural Perspective*, ed. J. Clayton Feaver and William Horosz (Princeton, N.J.: Van Nostrand, 1967), p. 309.
6 Bertrand Russell, *Why I Am Not a Christian* (London: Allen & Unwin, 1957), p. 63.
7 T. O'Dea, *The Sociology of Religion* (Englewood Cliffs, N. J.: Prentice-Hall, 1966), p. 81.
8 Bronislaw Malinowski, *Coral Gardens and Their Magic* (London: Allen & Unwin, 1935), p. 77.
9 J. Milton Yinger, *Religion, Society and the Individual* (New York: Macmillan, 1957), p. 47.
10 Emile Durkheim, *The Elementary Forms of the Religious Life* (London: Allen & Unwin, 1915), p. 44.
11 Joachim Wach, "Universals in Religion", *Religion, Culture and Society*, ed. Louis Schneider (New York: Wiley, 1964), p. 42.
12 Talcott Parsons, "Motivation of Religious Belief and Behaviour", *Essays in Sociological Theory* (Glencoe: Free Press, 1954), p. 165.
13 Claude Lévi-Strauss, *Structural Anthropology* (New York: Doubleday, 1967), p. 203.
14 *Ibid.*, p. 227.
15 *Ibid.*, p. 226.
16 See Marshall McLuhan, *Understanding Media* (New York: Signet, 1964), pp. 23 ff.
17 Richard Rubenstein, "Cox's Vision of the Secular City", Callahan, *op. cit.*, p. 133.
18 Callahan, *op. cit.*, pp. 97-98.
19 Cox, *op. cit.*, p. 254.
20 Claude Welch, Callahan, *op. cit.*, p. 157.
21 Brian Wicker, *Culture and Theology* (London: Sheed & Ward, 1966), p. 15.
22 *The Documents of Vatican II*, ed. Walter M. Abbot and J. Gallagher (London: Chapman, 1966), p. 206.
23 As to whether this was the case with Thomas Aquinas, see F. Copleton's *Aquinas* (Baltimore: Penguin, 1961), pp. 51 ff.
24 See Emile Rideau, *The Thought of Teilhard de Chardin* (New York: Harper & Row, 1965), p. 42.
25 Mircea Eliade, *Cosmos and History* (New York: Harper and Row, 1959), and *The Sacred and the Profane: The Nature of Religion* (New York: Harcourt, Brace, 1959).
26 Eliade, *Cosmos and History*, p. 152.
27 *Ibid.*, p. 160.
28 Robert Bellah, "Religious Evolution", *Reader in Comparative Religion*, ed. W. A. Lessa and E. Z. Vogt (New York: Harper & Row, 1965), p. 84.
29 Bronislaw Malinowski, *Sex, Culture and Myth* (London: Mayflower, 1967), p. 340.
30 For an analysis of the problems of defining "religion" see Schneider, *op. cit.*, pp. 24 ff., and Yinger, *op. cit.*, pp. 5-16, 49-72.
31 Talcott Parsons, "The Theoretical Development of the Sociology of Religion", *Essays in Sociological Theory*, p. 144.

32. *Ibid.*, p. 211.
33. Max Weber, *The Sociology of Religion* (Boston: Beacon Press, 1964), p. 1.
34. Joachim Wach, "Universals in Religion", Schneider, *op. cit.*, p. 39.
35. Durkheim, *op. cit.*, p. 41.
36. Yinger, *op. cit.*, pp. 54-55.
37. Durkheim, *op. cit.*, p. 44.
38. See Yinger, *op. cit.*, pp. 12 ff.
39. See especially Max Weber, *The Protestant Ethic and the Spirit of Capitalism* (New York: Scribner, 1958), and Ernst Troeltsch, *The Social Teaching of the Christian Churches* (New York: Harper & Row, 1960).
40. Clifford Geertz, "Religion as a Cultural System", Lessa and Vogt, *op. cit.*, pp. 204 ff.
41. See Yinger, *op. cit.*, p. 59.
42. W. Richard Comstock, "Theology after 'The Death of God'", *Cross Currents,* Summer 1966, pp. 273-74. See also Alan Richardson, *Religion in Contemporary Debate* (London: S.C.M., 1966), and Daniel Jenkins, *Beyond Religion* (London: S.C.M., 1962).
43. Schneider, *op. cit.*, p. 159.
44. See Robert Bellah, "Civil Religion in America", *Daedalus,* Winter 1967, pp. 1-19; Will Herberg, *Protestant, Catholic, Jew* (New York: Doubleday, 1960), especially pp. 72 ff.
45. James Bissett Pratt, "Objective and Subjective Worship", Schneider, *op. cit.*, pp. 155-56.
46. See *New Theology No. 5,* ed. Martin E. Marty and Dean G. Peerman (London: Macmillan, 1968), especially Michael Novak, "The Absolute Future", pp. 204 ff.
47. J. B. Metz, "The Church and the World", *The Word in History,* ed. T. Patrick Burke (New York: Sheed & Ward, 1966), p. 71.
48. Karl Rahner, "Christianity and Ideology", *Concilium,* VI, No. 1, 23 ff.
49. See Patrick Romanell, "Religion from a Naturalistic Standpoint", Feaver and Horosz, *op. cit.*, p. 73.
50. "A proposition is existential when I cannot apprehend or assent to it from the standpoint of a mere spectator but only on the ground of my total existence." Karl Heim, *Existentialist Thinkers and Thought,* ed. F. Patka (New York: Citadel, 1964), p. 64.
51. M. Weber, *op. cit.*; R. H. Tawney, *Religion and the Rise of Capitalism* (London: Penguin, 1938). See also Reinhard Bendix, *Max Weber: An Intellectual Portrait* (New York: Doubleday, 1962), especially pp. 50 ff.
52. A. N. Whitehead, *Science and the Modern World* (New York: Mentor, 1948; copyright, 1925, by The Macmillan Co., New York), pp. 18-19. See also E. L. Mascall, *Christian Theology and Natural Science* (London: S.C.M., 1956), p. 62.
53. Pitirim Sorokin, *Social and Cultural Dynamics* (New York: American Book Co., 1937), I, Pt. 1.
54. Robert Bellah, "Religious Revolution", Lessa and Vogt, *op. cit.*, p. 86.
55. Talcott Parsons, "Christianity and Modern Industrial Society", Schneider, *op. cit.*, pp. 295-96.

56 See Thomas F. O'Dea, "The Crisis of the Contemporary Religious Consciousness", *Daedalus,* Winter 1967, p. 131; J. Richard Shaull, *Containment and Change,* ed. C. Oglesby and J. R. Shaull (New York: Macmillan, 1967); *The Great Society Reader,* ed. M. E. Gettleman and D. Marmelstein (New York: Vintage, 1967).

57 H. Richard Neibuhr, "Religion and Socialism", Schneider, *op. cit.,* pp. 178-79.

58 Herbert Butterfield, *Origins of Modern Science* (London, 1949), p. 8.

59 W. C. Dampier, *A History of Science* (Cambridge: Cambridge University Press, 1966), pp. xiii-xiv.

60 Alan Richardson, *The Bible in the Age of Science* (London: S.C.M., 1961), p. 18.

61 Johan Huizinga, *The Waning of the Middle Ages* (London: Edward Arnold, 1924), p. 206.

62 *Ibid.,* pp. 195-96. See also Albert Mirgeler, *The Mutations of Western Christianity* (London: Burns & Oates, 1961), pp. 24 ff.

63 C. A. Coulson, *Science and Christian Belief* (London: Collins, 1958), pp. 46-47. See also A. N. Whitehead, *op. cit.,* pp. 106 ff. and 119 ff., and John Macquarrie, "The Changing Scientific Picture", *Twentieth Century Religious Thought* (London: S.C.M., 1963), pp. 240 ff.

64 F. C. Happold thus describes the significance of evolution: "Everything within the space-time continuum in which we are contained is governed by the law of evolution. Everything evolves, plants, animals, human beings, thought, religion, institutions, perhaps, in so far as he manifests himself within this continuum, God himself. That fact, with all its implications must be recognized and accepted." *Religious Faith and Twentieth Century Man* (Harmondsworth, Mddx.: Penguin, 1966), p. 55. In a lower key the Vatican Council acknowledged the same thing: "Thus the human race has passed from a rather static concept of reality to a more dynamic, evolutionary one. In consequence there has arisen a new series of problems, a series as numerous as can be, calling for new efforts and analysis and synthesis." *The Documents of Vatican II, op. cit.,* p. 203.

65 Werner Heisenberg, quoted in *Soundings,* ed. A. Vidler (Cambridge: Cambridge University Press, 1964), p. 35.

66 J. J. C. Smart, *Problems of Space and Time* (New York: Macmillan, 1964), p. 10.

67 J. Bronowski, *Science and Human Values* (Harmondsworth, Mddx.: Penguin, 1964), p. 21.

68 J. S. Habgood, "The Uneasy Truce Between Science and Theology", *Soundings,* ed. A. Vidler, *op. cit.,* p. 38.

69 Jacques Ellul, *The Technological Society* (New York: Random House, 1967), translator's introduction, p. xvi.

70 *Ibid.,* p. 132. Herbert Marcuse directs a similar indictment against modern technological society: "For 'totalitarian' is not only a non-terroristic economic-technical coordination which operates through the manipulation of needs vested by interests. It thus precludes the emergence of an effective opposition against the whole. Not only a specific form of government or party rule makes for totalitarianism,

but also a specific system of production and distribution which may well be compatible with a 'pluralism' of parties, newspapers, 'countervailing powers' etc." *One-Dimensional Man* (Boston: Beacon, 1967).
71 Herbert Kohl, *The Age of Complexity* (New York: Mentor, 1965), p. 15.
72 It is necessary to acknowledge the profound influence of Kant in the genesis of this outlook.
73 *The Revolution in Philosophy,* ed. G. Ryle (London: Macmillan, 1960), pp. 4-5.
74 Bertrand Russell, *Logic and Knowledge* (London: Allen & Unwin, 1956), p. 338.
75 Ryle, *op. cit.,* p. 46.
76 A. J. Ayer, *Language, Truth and Logic* (London: Gollancz, 1952), pp. 114-20.
77 J. O. Urmson, *Philosophical Analysis* (London: Oxford University Press, 1956), p. 128.
78 *The Revolution in Philosophy,* ed. G. Ryle, *op. cit.,* p. 67.
79 Ludwig Wittgenstein, *Tractatus Logico-Philosophicus* (London: Routledge & Kegan Paul, 1961), Conclusion.
80 Paul van Buren, *The Secular Meaning of the Gospel* (London: S.C.M., 1963); R. B. Braithwaite, *An Empiricist's View of the Nature of Religious Belief* (Cambridge: Cambridge University Press, 1955).
81 Kohl, *The Age of Complexity, op. cit.,* pp. 70-71.
82 See L. Wittgenstein, *Philosophical Investigations* (Oxford: Blackwell, 1953); *Logic and Language, First Series,* ed. A. Flew (Oxford: Blackwell, 1960); *Logic and Language, Second Series,* ed. A. Flew (Oxford: Blackwell, 1959).
83 Macquarrie, *op. cit.,* p. 305.
84 J. K. Galbraith, *The New Industrial State* (Boston: Houghton Mifflin, 1967); *Slant Manifesto* (London: Sheed & Ward, 1966).
85 Michael Harrington, *The Accidental Century* (Baltimore: Pelican, 1964).
86 *Slant Manifesto, op. cit.,* p. 35.
87 Galbraith, *op. cit.,* p. 60.
88 *Ibid.,* p. 319.
89 *Ibid.,* p. 320.
90 Ronald Gregor-Smith, *Secular Christianity* (London: Collins, 1966), p. 141.
91 Cox, *op. cit.,* pp. 17-37; A. van Leeuwen, *Christianity in World History* (London: Edinburgh House, 1964); Larry Shiner, *The Secularization of History* (New York: Abingdon Press, 1966).
92 Cox, *op. cit.,* p. 25.
93 Quoted by Cox, *op. cit.,* p. 32.
94 Shiner, *op. cit.,* p. 48.
95 P. 5 above.
96 Edmund R. Leach, "Two Essays Concerning the Symbolic Representation of Time", Lessa and Vogt, *op. cit.,* pp. 241-49.
97 Smart, *op. cit.,* p. 10.
98 O'Dea, *The Sociology of Religion, op. cit.,* p. 81.
99 Paul Tillich, *The Courage to Be* (London: Collins, 1962), pp. 124 ff. A similar distinction is made by Jacques Maritain between an existential existentialist and an academic existentialist, "a distinction between

the real movement of thought and what I shall call ideological discourse". *Moral Theology* (New York: Scribner, 1964), p. 359. ..
100 Sören Kierkegaard, one of the originators of the existential outlook, described the then prevalent Neo-Hegelian metaphysics as a "ballet of bloodless categories". See A. Vidler, *The Church in an Age of Revolution* (Harmondsworth, Mddx.: Penguin, 1961), p. 207.
101 Frederick Patka, *Existentialist Thinkers and Thought* (New York: Citadel, 1964), p. 21.
102 Macquarrie, *op. cit.*, p. 370.
103 Karl Heim, Frederick Patka, *op. cit.*, p. 64.
104 Cornelius van Peursen, *The Student World*, No. 1, 1963.
105 See *The Social and Political Philosophy of Jacques Maritain*, ed. J. Evans and L. Ward (New York: Scribner, 1955), p. 6.
106 *Ibid.*, p. 9.
107 See *The Documents of Vatican II*, p. 204; also pp. 224, 241-42, and 286. The term was first used in this social rather than the usual economic sense by John XXIII in *Mater et Magistra*, Nos. 59-67.
108 Samples from Marshall McLuhan and Quentin Fiore, *The Medium is the Massage* (Harmondsworth, Mddx.: Penguin, 1967), pp. 14, 16, 65, 24, 74-75.
109 *Ibid.*, p. 48.
110 For a criticism of the generalizations on which Marcuse's case rests see Allen Graubard, "Herbert Marcuse: One-Dimensional Pessimism", *Dissent*, May-June 1968.

2 Contemporary Conceptions of Church

1 Gustave Weigel, "Catholic Ecclesiology in Our Time", *Where Do We Differ?* (London: Burns & Oates, 1961), p. 11.
2 John Powell, *The Mystery of the Church* (Milwaukee: Bruce, 1967), p. 4. See also C. Journet, *L'Eglise du Verbe Incarné* (Paris: Desclée de Brouwer et Cie), p. 60.
3 This description by way of introduction deals only with the broad trends in Catholic ecclesiology.
4 Anna Morawska, "Secular Awareness and the Dark Night of the Church", *Cross Currents*, Winter 1968, p. 34.
5 Leslie Dewart, *The Future of Belief* (London: Burns & Oates, 1967), pp. 108-109.
6 Edward Schillebeeckx, *Vatican II: The Real Achievement* (London: Sheed & Ward, 1967), pp. 84 ff.
7 *Ibid.*, p. 35.
8 Dietrich Bonhoeffer, *Ethics* (London: S.C.M., 1955), p. 123.
9 Dietrich Bonhoeffer, *Letters and Papers from Prison* (London: S.C.M. Press, 1967), p. 211.
10 J. B. Metz, "Unbelief as a Theological Problem", *Concilium*, VI (New York: Paulist Press, 1965), pp. 59 ff.
11 W. Horosz, "Religion and Culture in Modern Perspective", *Religion in Philosophical and Cultural Perspective*, ed. J. C. Feaver and W. Horosz (Princeton, N.J.: Van Nostrand, 1967), p. 305.
12 Hans Küng, *The Church* (New York: Sheed & Ward, 1967), pp. 5-6.

13 *Ibid.*, p. 5.
14 *Ibid.*, p. 487.
15 See J. L. McKenzie, "World", *Dictionary of the Bible* (London: Chapman, 1965), pp. 942 ff.
16 Gerard Philips, "The Church in the Modern World", *Concilium*, VI, pp. 7 ff.
17 See Ernst Troeltsch, "Sect-Type and Church-Type Contrasted", *Religion, Culture and Society,* ed. Louis Schneider (New York: Wiley, 1964), pp. 457 ff.
18 Robert N. Bellah, "Religious Evolution", *Reader in Comparative Religion,* ed. W. A. Lessa and E. Z. Vogt (New York: Harper & Row, 1965), pp.73 ff.
19 "It is one of the most amazing facts of Western cultural history that the striking acceleration and intensification of technological development in post-Carolingian Europe emanated from contemplative monasticism." Ernest Benz, *Evolution and Christian Hope* (New York: Doubleday, 1968), p. 128. Benz notes also: "Late Pietism with its radical orientation toward the other world and the revivalist movement, with its partly chiliastic attitude, of the Rhineland, Westphalia, and Wurttemberg played a great role as an intellectual impulse for industrialization." (p. 129.)
20 Küng, *op. cit.,* p. 481.
21 Benz, *op. cit.,* p. 24.
22 See Albert Mirgeler, *The Mutations of Western Christianity* (London: Burns & Oates, 1964).
23 Benz, *op. cit.,* p. 22. See the precise theological significance of this change in B. C. Butler, *The Idea of the Church* (Baltimore: Helicon, 1962), pp. 217-18.
24 See Butler, *op. cit.,* pp. 105 ff.
25 Benz, *op. cit.,* p. 26.
26 See "Luther's Conception of the Church", Wilhelm Panck, *The Heritage of the Reformation* (New York: Glencoe, 1961), pp. 29 ff. See also Herbert Olsson's "The Church's Visibility and Invisibility According to Luther", Anders Nygren, *This Is the Church* (Philadelphia: Muhlenberg, 1952), pp. 226 ff.
27 See Carl Amery, *Capitulation* (New York: Herder, 1967); Jürgen Moltmann, *Theology of Hope,* tr. J. W. Leitch (London: S.C.M., 1967), especially pp. 314 ff.
28 *The Documents of Vatican II,* ed. Walter M. Abbot and J. Gallagher (London: Chapman, 1966), pp. 203 ff.
29 Benz, *op. cit.,* p. 64.
30 J. B. Metz, "The Church and the World", *The Word in History,* ed. T. Patrick Burke (New York: Sheed & Ward, 1966), p. 71.
31 Benz, *op. cit.,* p. 126.
32 *Ibid.,* p. 117.
33 J. B. Metz, "Unbelief as a Theological Problem", Burke, *op. cit.,* pp. 59-60.
34 See Colin Williams, *Faith in a Secular Age* (London: Fontana, 1966), p. 34.
35 Karl Rahner, "Christianity and Ideology ", *Concilium*, VI, No. 1, 23 ff.

36 See H. Kohl, *The Age of Complexity* (New York: Mentor, 1965), and Herbert Marcuse, *One-Dimensional Man* (Boston: Beacon, 1967).
37 *The Documents of Vatican II,* pp. 24 ff. and 78 ff.
38 C. Davis, *A Case of Conscience* (New York: Harper & Row, 1967).
39 See John Macquarrie, *Twentieth Century Religious Thought* (London: S.C.M., 1963), pp. 318 ff.
40 See "The Elementary Forms of the Religious Life", Lessa and Vogt, *op. cit.,* pp. 56 ff.
41 See D. Evans, *Communist Faith and Christian Faith* (London: S.C.M., 1965), pp. 20 ff.
42 See Sigmund Freud, *The Future of an Illusion* (London: 1928).
43 Paul van Buren, "An Empiricist's View of the Nature of Religious Belief", *The Existence of God,* ed. John Hick (London: Macmillan, 1964), pp. 229 ff.
44 Paul van Buren, *The Secular Meaning of the Gospel* (London: S.C.M., 1963), p. 183.
45 See F. Patka, *Existentialist Thinkers and Their Thought* (New York: Citadel, 1964), pp. 21 ff.
46 Paul Tillich, *The Courage to Be* (London: Collins, 1962), p. 124.
47 Macquarrie, *op. cit.,* p. 193.
48 *Ibid.,* p. 197.
49 Paul Tillich, *Systematic Theology* (Welwyn: Nisbet, 1953), Vol. I, p. 8.
50 Metz, *op. cit.,* pp. 79-83.
51 Benz, *op. cit.,* pp. vii-viii.
52 See J. Maritain on the distinction between "community" and "society", *Man and the State* (Chicago: University of Chicago, 1951), pp. 2 ff.
53 Report given at Boston College Institute on the Underground Church, 19 April 1968.
54 See H. Cox, *The Secular City* (London: S.C.M., 1965), pp. 40 ff.
55 See T. J. J. Altizer, *The Gospel of Christian Atheism* (London: Collins, 1967), pp. 108 ff.; T. J. J. Altizer and W. Hamilton, *Radical Theology and the Death of God* (Copyright (c) 1966, Indianapolis: The Bobbs-Merrill Company, Inc.), pp. 95 ff.
56 Thomas W. Ogletree, *The "Death of God" Controversy* (London: S.C.M., 1966), p. 65.
57 T. J. J. Altizer, *Cross Currents,* Summer 1967, pp. 274 and 278.
58 Bonhoeffer, *Letters and Papers from Prison,* p. 211.
59 John S. Godsey, *The Theology of Dietrich Bonhoeffer* (Philadelphia: Westminster, 1952), p. 281. See also Martin E. Marty, *The Place of Bonhoeffer* (London: S.C.M., 1963).
60 John Robinson, *Honest to God* (London: S.C.M., 1963), *The New Reformation* (London: S.C.M., 1965). For a critique of Robinson's ecclesiology see Richard P. McBrien's *The Church in the Thought of Bishop John Robinson* (London: S.C.M., 1966).
61 Robert Adolfs, *The Grave of God* (London: Burns & Oates, 1967); Ivan Illich, *America,* 27 April 1968, pp. 568 ff.
62 Robinson, *The New Reformation,* p. 46.
63 Cox, *op. cit.,* p. 105.

64 Bernard Murchland, *The Secular City Debate*, ed. D. Callahan (New York: Macmillan, 1966), pp. 17 ff.
65 *Ibid.*, p. 20.
66 Arend van Leeuwen, *Christianity in World History* (London: Edinburgh House, 1964), pp. 400-403.
67 Benz, *op. cit.*, p. 142.
68 Daniel Callahan, "Putting the Liturgy in Its Place", *National Catholic Reporter*, 9 August 1967.
69 A. R. Vidler, "Religion and the National Church", *Soundings* (Cambridge: Cambridge University Press, 1964), p. 262.
70 *Ibid.*, pp. 262-63.
71 See Robert N. Bellah, "Civil Religion in America", *Daedalus*, Winter 1967, pp. 1 ff.
72 *Slant Manifesto* (London: Sheed & Ward, 1966). See also T. Eagleton, *The New Left Church* (London: Sheed & Ward, 1966), and Brian Wicker, *Toward a Contemporary Christianity* (Notre Dame, Ind.: University of Notre Dame Press, 1967), pp. 222 ff.
73 *Slant Manifesto*, p. 5; Wicker, *op. cit.*, pp. 21 ff.
74 *Slant Manifesto*, pp. 6 and 12.
75 *Ibid.*, p. 93.
76 *Ibid.*, p. 63.
77 Harvey Cox in the introduction to Stephen Rose's *The Grass Roots Church* endorses Rose's attempt to outline an "organic-adaptive structure" to replace the ecclesiastical bureaucracies which have proved obstacles to the role of the church in the world. (New York: Holt, Rinehart & Winston, 1966), p. xiii.
78 See *The Documents of Vatican II*, p. 78, p. 206, p. 232, p. 237, etc. Also *Christians in a New World*, ed. David L. Edwards (London: S.C.M., 1966), especially "An Impatient World's Challenge to the Church", pp. 67 ff. In preparation for this conference four volumes of essays dealing with the church's involvement in the world were published in 1966 by Association Press in New York: *Christian Social Ethics in a Changing World*, ed. John C. Bennett; *Responsible Government in a Revolutionary Age*, ed. Z. K. Matthews; *Economic Growth in World Perspective*, ed. Denys Munby; *Man in Community*, ed. Egbert de Vries. *The Church Amid Revolution*, ed. Harvey Cox, is a selection of papers from this conference (New York: Association Press, 1967).
79 Benz, *op. cit.*, p. 117.
80 W. Pannenberg, J. B. Metz, J. Moltmann, and K. Rahner have all been active participants in Christian-Communist dialogue.
81 Thomas F. O'Dea, "The Crisis of Contemporary Religious Consciousness", *Daedalus*, Winter 1967, p. 130.
82 Robinson, *The New Reformation*, p. 40.
83 Karl Rahner, *New Theology No. 5*, ed. Martin E. Marty and Dean G. Peerman (New York: Macmillan, 1968), p. 205.
84 Daniel Callahan, "The Absolute Future", *ibid.*, p. 208.
85 K. Rahner, *Theological Investigations*, IV (Baltimore: Helicon, 1966), pp. 323 ff., and *Theological Investigations*, V (Baltimore: Helicon, 1966), pp. 135 ff. See also Harvey Cox, "Ernst Bloch and 'The Pull of the Future'", *New Theology No. 5*, pp. 191 ff.
86 Cox, *The Secular City Debate*, ed. Callahan, p. 203.

87 "Evolutionary Progress and Christian Promise", *Concilium,* June 1967, pp. 18 ff.
88 Richard Shaull, *Christians in a New World,* ed. Edwards, pp. 18-19; "Revolutionary Change in Theological Perspective", *The Church Amid Revolution,* ed. Cox.
89 Teilhard de Chardin, *The Phenomenon of Man* (London: Collins, 1959), pp. 222 ff.
90 For a theological appreciation and criticism of Teilhard see Benz, *op. cit.,* pp. 221 ff. (Cf. Richard Shaull, "The Christian World Mission in a Technological Era", *Cross Currents,* Fall 1965, pp. 461 ff.) Also see Emile Rideau, *The Thought of Teilhard de Chardin* (New York: Harper & Row, 1967), pp. 179 ff., pp. 202 ff.
91 Jürgen Moltmann, *Theology of Hope,* tr. J. W. Leitch (London: S.C.M., 1967), p. 85.
92 *Ibid.,* p. 86.
93 *Ibid.,* p. 225.
94 Wolfhart Pannenberg, "Appearance as the Arrival of the Future", *New Theology No. 5,* pp. 112 ff.
95 *Ibid.,* p. 119.
96 Moltmann, *op. cit.,* p. 304.
97 *Ibid.,* p. 305.
98 *Ibid.,* p. 323.
99 *Ibid.,* p. 324.
100 *Ibid.,* p. 327.
101 *Ibid.,* p. 330.
102 Carl E. Braatan, "Toward a Theology of Hope", *Theology Today,* XXIV, No. 2, 221.
103 Martin E. Marty, "Springs Eternal", *The Critic,* February-March 1968, p. 70.
104 Moltmann in an article, "The Theology of Hope Today", *The Critic,* April-May 1968, says, "beyond the theism which maintains that 'God is' and the atheism which asserts that 'God is not' they have found a new possibility of a theology of the God who 'is coming' ". (p. 22.)
105 Marty, *The Critic,* p. 72.
106 Moltmann, "The Theology of Hope Today", p. 21.
107 *Ibid.,* p. 22.
108 K. Rahner, *The Christian of the Future* (New York: Herder & Herder, 1967), p. 81.
109 J. B. Metz, "Creative Hope", *New Theology No. 5,* p. 136. See also "The Church and the World", *The Word in History,* ed. T. Patrick Burke (New York: Sheed & Ward, 1966), pp. 70 ff.
110 *Ibid.,* p. 139.
111 *Ibid.,* p. 139.
112 *Ibid.,* pp. 137 ff.
113 Benz, *op. cit.,* pp. 35 ff.
114 Maynard Kaufman, "Post-Christian Aspects of Radical Theology", *Toward a New Christianity: Readings in the Death of God Theology,* ed. T. J. J. Altizer (New York: Harcourt, Brace & World, 1967), pp. 343 ff.
115 *Ibid.,* p. 346.
116 *Ibid.,* p. 348.
117 *Ibid.,* p. 353.

118 Rosemary Ruether, *The Church Against Itself* (London: Sheed & Ward, 1967).
119 *Ibid.*, p. 3.
120 *Ibid.*, p. 4.
121 *Ibid.*, p. 10.
122 *Ibid.*, p. 29.
123 *Ibid.*, p. 62.
124 *Ibid.*, p. 139.
125 *Ibid.*, p. 13.
126 *Ibid.*, p. 138.
127 Irving Howe, "New Styles in 'Leftism' ", *The New Radicals*, ed. Paul Jacobs and Saul Landau (New York: Vintage, 1966), p. 289.
128 Daniel Callahan, "Pie-in-the-Sky Theology?" *Commonweal*, 29 March 1968, pp. 48 ff.
129 *Ibid.*, p. 43.
130 Ruether, *op. cit.*, p. 13.
131 Robert Bellah, Lessa and Vogt, *op. cit.*, p. 74.
132 See Donald P. Warwick, "Personal and Organizational Effectiveness in the Roman Catholic Church", *Cross Currents*, Fall 1967, pp. 401 ff.
133 Rose, *op. cit.*, pp. xiii-xiv.
134 *Christians in a New World*, ed. Edwards, pp. 67 ff.
135 *The Documents of Vatican II*, p. 288.
136 *Ibid.*, pp. 147, 163, 585.
137 *Ibid.*, p. 585.
138 *Ibid.*, p. 237.

PART II THEOLOGICAL PROBES

3 The Too Subtle God

1 *The Documents of Vatican II*, ed. Walter M. Abbot and J. Gallagher (London: Chapman, 1966), pp. 216 ff.
2 Werner Pelz, *Prism*, April 1963, p. 23.
3 Dietrich Bonhoeffer, *Letters and Papers from Prison* (London: S.C.M. Press, 1967), p. 196.
4 Anthony Flew, *God and Philosophy* (London: Hutchinson, 1966), p. 149.
5 See John L. McKenzie, "Flesh", pp. 280 ff., and "Spirit", pp. 842 ff., *Dictionary of the Bible* (London: Chapman, 1965).
6 David Hume, *Dialogues Concerning Natural Religion* (New York: Hafner Library of Classics, 1948).
7 Emmanuel Kant, *Critique of Pure Reason*, tr. M. Kemp Smith (London: Macmillan, 1933), "Transcendental Dialectic", Book II, chap. iii, sec. 4.
8 David Hume, *A Treatise of Human Nature*, Book I, Part III, sec. 7.
9 John Macquarrie, "How Is Theology Possible", *New Theology No. 1*, ed. M. E. Marty and D. G. Peerman (London: Macmillan, 1964), p. 28.
10 A. J. Ayer, *The Existence of God*, ed. John Hick (London: Macmillan, 1964), p. 219.
11 R. B. Braithwaite, "An Empiricist's View of the Nature of Religious Belief", Hick, *op. cit.*, pp. 229 ff.

12 Paul van Buren, *The Secular Meaning of the Gospel* (London: S.C.M., 1963).
13 For Flew's parable, see *New Essays in Philosophical Theology*, ed. A. Flew and A. MacIntyre (London: S.C.M., 1955), p. 96.
14 See Hick, *op. cit.*, pp. 25 ff.
15 *Ibid.*, p. 255.
16 *Loc. cit.*
17 *Ibid.*, pp. 256-57.
18 See Thomas Aquinas, *Summa Theologica* (New York: Benziger, 1946), I, Q. 46, 2, pp. 242 ff. Also see F. C. Copleston, *Aquinas* (London: Penguin, 1955), pp. 136 ff.
19 Brian Wicker, *Culture and Theology* (London: Sheed & Ward, 1966), pp. 47 ff.
20 Hume, *A Treatise of Human Nature*, p. 66.
21 G. E. Moore, "Is Existence a Predicate?" *Logic and Language, Second Series*, ed. A. Flew (Oxford: Blackwell, 1959).
22 H. S. Leonard, "The Logic of Existence", *Philosophical Studies*, VII (June 1956), No. 4.
23 C. B. Daly, "Metaphysics and the Limits of Language", *Prospect for Metaphysics*, ed. Ian Ramsey (London: Allen & Unwin, 1961), p. 191.
24 Etienne Gilson, *The Christian Philosophy of St. Thomas Aquinas* (London: Gollancz, 1957), p. 44.
25 C. A. Paul, "Wittgenstein", *The Revolution in Philosophy*, ed. Gilbert Ryle (London: Macmillan, 1960), p. 92.
26 Gilson, *op. cit.*, pp. 105-106.
27 John Hick, *Philosophy of Religion* (Englewood Cliffs, N.J.: Prentice-Hall, 1963), pp. 22-23. See also J. J. C. Smart, "The Existence of God", and J. M. Findlay, "Can God's Existence Be Disproved?" Flew and MacIntyre, *op. cit.*
28 Hick, *The Existence of God*, pp. 259 ff.
29 *Nietzsche: An Anthology*, ed. Otto Manthey-Zorn (New York: Washington Square Press, 1964), pp. 94-95.
30 W. Richard Comstock, "Theology after 'The Death of God' ", *Cross Currents*, Summer 1966, p. 267.
31 *Ibid.*, p. 269.
32 *Ibid.*, p. 270.
33 John A. Robinson, "Can a Truly Contemporary Person Not Be an Atheist", *The New Reformation* (London: S.C.M., 1965), Appendix I, pp. 106 ff.
34 Hick, *Philosophy of Religion*, p. 37.
35 Emile Durkheim, *The Elementary Forms of the Religious Life* (London: Allen & Unwin, 1915).
36 Sigmund Freud, *The Future of an Illusion* (New York: Doubleday, 1964).
37 Baastian van Iersel, *The Bible on the Living God* (London: Sheed & Ward, 1965).
38 *Ibid.*, p. 2.
39 *Ibid.*, p. 4.
40 J. B. Metz, *The Word in History*, ed. T. P. Burke (New York: Sheed & Ward, 1966), p. 75.
41 *Ibid.*, p. 76.

42 Comstock, *op. cit.*, p. 298.
43 Gabriel Vahanian, *The Death of God* (New York: Braziller, 1961), p. 182.
44 *Ibid.*, p. 190.
45 Thomas J. J. Altizer, *The Gospel of Christian Atheism* (London: Collins, 1967).
46 Thomas W. Ogletree, *The "Death of God" Controversy* (London: S.C.M., 1966), p. 26.
47 W. Hamilton, *The New Essence of Christianity* (London: Darton, Longman & Todd, 1966).
48 *Ibid.*, p. 40.
49 *Ibid.*, p. 61.
50 *Ibid.*, p. 63.
51 W. Hamilton, *National Catholic Reporter*, 15 February 1967.
52 Thomas J. J. Altizer and William Hamilton, *Radical Theology and the Death of God* (Copyright (c) 1966, Indianapolis: The Bobbs-Merrill Company, Inc.). (Hamilton's essay, "Thursday's Child".)
53 *Ibid.*, pp. 87-88. Reprinted by permission of the publishers.
54 *Ibid.*, p. 7.
55 Altizer, *The Gospel of Christian Atheism*, pp. 102 ff.
56 *Ibid.*, p. 103.
57 Ogletree, *op. cit.*, p. 65.
58 Altizer, *The Gospel of Christian Atheism*, p. 108.
59 *Ibid.*, pp. 108-109.
60 *Ibid.*, p. 110.
61 *Ibid.*, p. 111.
62 See the work of the Catholic New Left in England in this regard, especially *Slant Manifesto* (London: Sheed & Ward, 1966); Terence Eagleton, *The New Left Church* (London: Sheed & Ward, 1966); Brian Wicker, *Culture and Theology* (London: Sheed & Ward, 1966); Brian Wicker, *Culture and Liturgy* (London: Sheed & Ward, 1963).
63 Karl Barth, *The Epistle to the Romans*, tr. E. Hoskyns (London: O.U.P., 1933), p. 40.
64 Quoted by W. Richard Comstock, *Cross Currents*, Summer 1966, p. 289.

4 Christ the Man of the Future

1 Maynard Kaufman, "Post-Christian Aspects of Radical Theology", *Toward a New Christianity: Readings in the Death of God Theology*, ed. Thomas J. J. Altizer (New York: Harcourt, Brace and World, 1967), p. 346.
2 *Ibid.*, p. 351.
3 See Alan Richardson, *The Bible in the Age of Science* (London: S.C.M., 1961); R. H. Fuller, *The New Testament in Current Study* (London: S.C.M., 1963); J. Robinson, *A New Quest of the Historical Jesus* (London: S.C.M., 1959).
4 Fuller, *op. cit.*, p. 11.
5 John Macquarrie, *Twentieth Century Religious Thought* (London: S.C.M., 1963), p. 333.
6 *Ibid.*, p. 337.

7 J. B. Metz, *The Word in History*, ed. T. P. Burke (New York: Sheed & Ward, 1966), pp. 70-71.
8 Fuller, *op. cit.*, p. 65.
9 John A. Robinson, *The New Reformation* (London: S.C.M., 1965), pp. 40-41.
10 John A. Robinson, *Honest to God* (London: S.C.M., 1963), p. 67.
11 *Ibid.*, p. 65.
12 Cited in *Soundings*, ed. A. Vidler (Cambridge: Cambridge University Press, 1964), p. 151.
13 *Ibid.*, p. 154.
14 *Ibid.*, p. 160.
15 Helmut Thielicke, *Herder Correspondence*, October 1967, p. 283.
16 Richard L. Rubenstein, *The Secular City Debate*, ed. D. Callahan (London: Macmillan, 1966), p. 136.
17 Joseph Bourke, "The Historical Jesus and the Kerygmatic Christ", *Concilium*, I, No. 2, January 1966, 19.
18 *The Listener*, 10 November 1966.
19 Nicholas Berdyaev, *Truth and Revelation* (New York: Collier, 1962), p. 122.
20 Yves Congar, "Christ in the Economy of Salvation and in Our Dogmatic Tracts", *Concilium*, I, No. 2, 6.
21 Carl E. Braatan, "Towards a Theology of Hope", *Theology Today*, XXIV (July 1967), 214 ff.
22 Berdyaev, *op. cit.*, p. 149.
23 N. Berdyaev, *Dostoevsky* (New York: Meridian, 1957), p. 198.

5 The Morality of the Noosphere

1 Teilhard de Chardin, *The Phenomenon of Man* (London: Collins, 1959), p. 227.
2 *Ibid.*, p. 222.
3 *Ibid.*, p. 226.
4 *Ibid.*, p. 231.
5 Arend van Leeuwen, *Christianity in World History* (London: Edinburgh House, 1964), p. 400.
6 *Ibid.*, p. 432.
7 John A. Robinson, *Honest to God* (London: S.C.M., 1963), p. 107.
8 Joseph Arntz, "Natural Law and Its History", *Concilium*, V, No. 1, 23 ff.
9 *Ibid.*, p. 23.
10 *Catholic Weekly*, 2 February 1967.
11 Gustafson, "Consent Versus Principles: A Misplaced Debate in Christian Ethics", *New Theology No. 3*, ed. M. E. Marty and D. G. Peerman (London: Macmillan, 1966), pp. 69 ff.
12 James Tunstead Burtchaell, "The Conservatism of Situation Ethics", *New Blackfriars*, September 1966.
13 Joseph Fletcher, *Situation Ethics* (London: S.C.M., 1966).
14 Burtchaell, *op. cit.*, p. 11.
15 Fletcher, *op. cit.*, p. 125.

16 *Ibid.,* pp. 127 ff.
17 Burtchaell, *op. cit.,* p. 11.
18 Albert Mirgeler, *Mutations of Western Christianity* (London: Burns & Oates, 1964), pp. 70-80.
19 F. C. Happold, *Religious Faith and Twentieth Century Man* (London: Penguin, 1966), p. 29.
20 Burtchaell, *op. cit.,* p. 14.
21 Louis Monden, *Sin, Liberty and Law* (London: Chapman, 1966), p. 130.
22 *Ibid.,* pp. 5-6.
23 *The Documents of Vatican II,* ed. Walter M. Abbot and J. Gallagher (London: Chapman, 1966), p. 214.
24 For a discussion of the issues involved in abortion, see the symposium "Abortion" in *Commonweal,* Vol. LXXXVI, No. 15, 30 June 1967.
25 John Reed, "Natural Law Theology and the Church", *Theological Studies,* XXVI (1965), No. 1, 45.
26 *The Documents of Vatican II.*
27 F. Dostoevsky, *The Brothers Karamazov.*
28 Quoted by Fletcher, *op. cit.,* Introduction.

6 The Secular Function of the Church

1 *The Documents of Vatican II,* ed. Walter M. Abbot and J. Gallagher (London: Chapman, 1966), p. 288.
2 John Macquarrie, *New Theology No. 1,* ed. M. E. Marty and D. G. Peerman (London: Macmillan, 1964), p. 23.
3 "Gaudium et Spes", *The Documents of Vatican II,* par. 44, p. 246.
4 See J. L. McKenzie, *Dictionary of the Bible* (London: Chapman, 1965), pp. 760 ff.
5 J. B. Metz, quoted *Herder Correspondence,* August 1966, p. 245.
6 See *Objections to Roman Catholicism,* ed. M. de la Bedoyere (London: Constable, 1964), p. 26.
7 Daniel Callahan, "Putting the Liturgy in Its Place", *National Catholic Reporter,* 9 August 1967.
8 John A. Robinson, *Honest to God* (London: S.C.M., 1963), pp. 90 ff.
9 Yves Congar, *Power and Poverty in the Church* (London: Chapman, 1964), pp. 21 ff.
10 John L. McKenzie, *Authority in the Church* (New York: Sheed & Ward, 1966), p. 32.
11 *The Documents of Vatican II,* p. 200.
12 See Robert Adolfs, *The Grave of God* (London: Burns & Oates, 1967), pp. 96 ff.
13 See *Council Speeches of Vatican II,* ed. Y. Congar, H. Kung, and D. O'Hanlon (London: Sheed & Ward, 1964), pp. 36 ff.
14 McKenzie, *Authority in the Church,* p. 123.
15 *Ibid.,* p. 124.
16 Gregory Baum, *Concilium,* I, No. 3, 39.
17 *The Documents of Vatican II,* p. 113.

18 Karl Rahner, *Concilium,* I, No. 3, 55.
19 *The Documents of Vatican II,* p. 116.
20 Document on Church in the Modern World, "Gaudium et Spes", *ibid.,* par. 44, p. 246.
21 Edward Schillebeeckx, *Concilium,* I, No. 3.
22 McKenzie, *Authority in the Church,* p. 135.
23 *Ibid.,* p. 78.
24 Edward Schillebeeckx, *Vatican II: The Real Achievement* (London: Sheed & Ward, 1967), p. 17.
25 McKenzie, *Authority in the Church,* pp. 98-99.
26 "The Cool Generation and the Church", *Commonweal,* 6 October 1967, pp. 11 ff.
27 Carl Amery, *Capitulation* (New York: Herder, 1967).
28 Will Herberg, *Protestant, Catholic, Jew* (New York: Doubleday, 1960), p. 82.
29 J. Moltmann, *Theology of Hope,* tr. J. W. Leitch (London: S.C.M., 1967), p. 323.

EPILOGUE

1 Ernst Troeltsch, *The Social Teaching of the Christian Churches* (New York: Harper Torchbooks, 1960).
2 *Ibid.,* I, 86.
3 *Ibid.,* p. 88.
4 See Bernard Delfgaauw, *The Young Marx* (London: Sheed & Ward, 1967).
5 William Appleman Williams, *The Great Evasion* (Chicago: Quadrangle Books, 1964), p. 18.
6 *Ibid.,* p. 20.
7 Peter Nichols, *The Politics of the Vatican* (New York: Praeger, 1968), chap. 7.
8 Reported in *Commonweal,* 9 August 1968.